THE DICTIONARY OF HINDUSTANI CLASSICAL MUSIC

The Dictionary *of* Hindustani Classical Music

Bimalakanta Roychaudhuri

MOTILAL BANARSIDASS PUBLISHERS
PRIVATE LIMITED • DELHI

*Reprint: Delhi, **2007***
First Edition: Delhi, 2000

ISBN: 978-81-208-1708-1

MOTILAL BANARSIDASS
41 U.A. Bungalow Road, Jawahar Nagar, Delhi 110 007
8 Mahalaxmi Chamber, 22 Bhulabhai Desai Road, Mumbai 400 026
203 Royapettah High Road, Mylapore, Chennai 600 004
236, 9th Main III Block, Jayanagar, Bangalore 560 011
Sanas Plaza, 1302 Baji Rao Road, Pune 411 002
8 Camac Street, Kolkata 700 017
Ashok Rajpath, Patna 800 004
Chowk, Varanasi 221 001

Printed in India
BY JAINENDRA PRAKASH JAIN AT SHRI JAINENDRA PRESS,
A-45 NARAINA, PHASE-I, NEW DELHI 110 028
AND PUBLISHED BY NARENDRA PRAKASH JAIN FOR
MOTILAL BANARSIDASS PUBLISHERS PRIVATE LIMITED,
BUNGALOW ROAD, DELHI 110 007

Note

The author has given all rights of his published and unpublished works to Imdādkhāni School of Sitār, an institute founded by him in 1948. The first Bengali version of the present book was published in 1965 and received the Sangeet Natak Academy award in 1971 as the best book on music in Bengali language published during the period from 1960 to 1968. The book was later published in Hindi in 1975 by the Bhāratīya Jñānpīṭh of New Delhi. The Hindi translation was done by Śrī Madanlal Vyas of Bombay. The present English version of the book was made by the author himself in 1967 but could not be published earlier for want of a publisher. I express my gratitude to M/s Motilal Banarsidass for their kindly agreeing to publish the book. I am also grateful to Ms. Mitali Chatterji, Assistant Librarian, Asiatic Society and to Mr. Shabbīr Ahmad of Islamic Section, Asiatic Society, for the kind help rendered by them in the transliteration work.

S. CHANDA
President, Imdadkhani School of Sitar

Publishers' Note

We are pleased to bring out the English version of this works which has already been published both in Bengali and Hindi and had got Sangeet Natak Academy award in 1971.

In this English version 'Gharana-Table' has been left out because we plan to publish another book on *Gharana,* where the subject will be dealt with separately in detail.

Preface

The growing interest of the Western, especially the English-speaking nations towards the North Indian Classical Music is more evident now than ever before. It is no doubt a sign for us to be happy about; at the same time it causes us deep concern whenever we try to appreciate the great responsibility that has devolved upon us in presenting the correct interpretation of musical terms of the ancient Sanskrit Śāstras.

Aphoristic couplets of the ancient Sanskrit Texts, as they mostly are, even with their annotations, easily lend themselves to be misinterpreted today. Painfully bearing this in mind the author has attempted this dictionary with great trepidations. He has depended solely on his own inner resources in interpreting the musical terms rather than allowing himself to be influenced by any other publications in English or in any other languages, lest he should tread on the trap of terminological inexactitude. For the present author it has been a very difficult task indeed primarily for two reasons–

1. The technical terms that we have in Indian music are too difficult for a foreigner to comprehend fully unless these are presented in the right manner of interpretation.
2. However much the author may have tried to express himself in English, it is not his mother tongue and he is therefore, not infallible in expression.

The author has also tried, as far as possible, not to borrow terms used in the Western music to ease out the difficulty in explaining Indian terms; that would have been apparently easier and would have saved some amount of space but that short-cut would not have served the purpose intended.

A few words are necessary to explain certain features in the dictionary. It will be found that some of the Western musical instruments that have long come to be used in Indian music have also been described under the entry 'Vādya' (musical instruments) for the benefit of those Indians who are interested in them, with due apology to Western readers.

This dictionary, being the first comprehensive attempt of its kind, would naturally call for improvement and corrections. The author would feel gratified to have suggestions for improvement.

Calcutta, 1967 B.K. RĀYACAUDHURĪ

References

The following books and magazines have been consulted:

S = Sanskrit	B = Bengali
H = Hindi	M = Marathi
	E = English

Abhinava Rāgamañjarī (S)	–	Paṇḍit Viṣṇu Śarmā
Ānanda Saṁgīta Patrikā (B)	–	Magazine
Betāra Jagat (B)	–	Magazine
Catalogue of Indian Musical Instruments (E)	–	Col. P.T. French
Dictionary of Music (E)	–	R. Illing (Penguin)
Gītasūtrasāra (B)	–	Kṛṣṇadhana Bandyopādhyāya
Guide to the Musical Instruments exhibited in the Indian Museum Calcutta (E)	–	Dr. A.M. Meerwarth
Hindustānī Saṁgīta Paddhati	–	Paṇḍit Viṣṇunārāyaṇa
2nd Part (M)	–	Bhātakhaṇḍe
Hindustānī Saṁgīte Tānsener Sthān (B)	–	Bīrendrakiśor Rāyacaudhurī
Introduction to the Study of Indian Music (E)	–	E. Clements
Introduction to the Study of Musical Scales (E)	–	Alain Danielou
Lives of Great Musicians (E)	–	S.P. Banerjī
Music of Hindustān, The (E)	–	A.H. Fox-Strangways
Music of India, The (E)	–	Herbert A. Popley
Musical Instruments (E)	–	A.J. Hipkins
Musicians of India, The (E)	–	Harendrakiśor Rāyacaudhurī
On the Grāmas or Musical Scales of the Hindus (E)	–	J.D. Paterson

On the Musical Modes of the Hindus (E)	– Sir William Jones
Prakṛtivāda Abhidhāna (B)	– Rāmakamala Vidyālaṁkāra
Rāgas and Rāginīs (E)	– O.C. Gāṅgulī
Śabdakalpadruma (S)	– Rājā Sir Rādhākānta Deva Bahādur
Saṁgīta (H)	– Magazines
Saṁgīta Candrikā (B)	– Madanamohana Adhikārī
Saṁgīta Kalā Vihāra (H)	– Magazines
Saṁgīta Prakāśikā (B)	– Magazines
Saṁgīta Praveśikā (B)	– Murārimohana Gupta
Saṁgīta Sāra (B)	– Kṣetramohana Gosvāmī
Saṁgīta Sudarśana (H)	– Paṇḍit Sudarsanācārya Śāstrī
Saṁgīta Sudhākara (S)	– Paṇḍit Viṣṇu Śarmā
Saṁgīta Vijñāna Praveśikā (B)	– Magazines
Saṁgītaratnākara (S)	– Niḥśanka Śārṅgadeva (with Kallinātha and Siṁha-bhūpāla Ṭikā)
Saṁgīte Parivartana (B)	– Harinārāyaṇa Mukhopādhyāya
Science and Music (E)	– Sir James Jeans
Short Historical Survey of the Music of Upper India (E)	– A speech by Pt. V.N. Bhātakhaṇḍe
Smṛtira Atale (B)	– Dr. Amiyanāth Sānyāl
Souvenirs of Different Musical Soirees (E&B)	–
Sura – O – Saṁgati (B)	Dhurjatiprasāda Mukhopādhyāya
Surachandā (B)	– Magazines
Tablā-Prakāśa (H)	– Rāmasevaka Miśra
Tablā-Śikṣā (B)	– Durgādās Lālā
Tablā-Vādana (H)	– Gāndharva Mahāvidyālaya
Theory of Musical Evolution (E)	– Margaret H. Glyn
Treatise on the Music of Hindustān (E)	– Capt. Augustus Willard
Urdu – English Dictionary	– Rāmanārāyṇa Lāl
Yantrakoṣa (B)	– Rājā Sir Saurīndramohana Ṭhākura

Contents

The Symbols of Notations

For Articulation – (Phonetically written)

Sah, Ray, Gah, Mah, Pah, Dhah, Ni, Sah (ah = as 'a' in father). Tīvra Komala Gah and Tīvra Komala Ni are enharmonic notes, sharper than flat yet flatter than sharp Gah and Ni and may be called 'Augmented flat' and are symbolised by the sign b$^{\#}$ in the staff notations and by a dash – under tonic solfa notations.

Notations:-

Sah	Komala Ray	Śuddha Ray	Komala Gah	Tīvra Komala Gah
S	r	R	g	$\underline{g}$
C	^{b}D	D	^{b}E	b$^{\#}$E

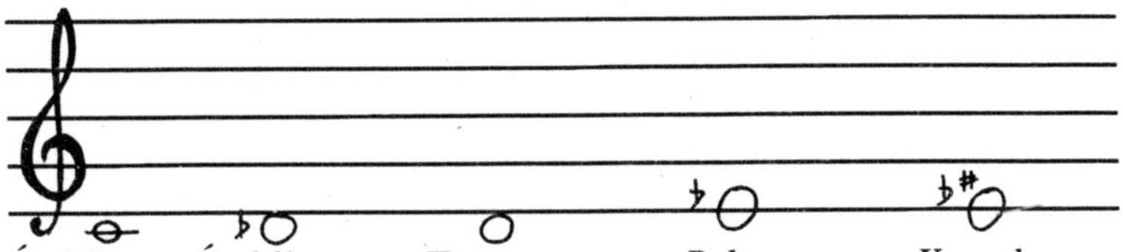

Śuddha Gah	Śuddha Mah	Tīvra or Kaḍi Mah	Pah	Komala Dhah
G	M	m	P	d
F	F	$^{\#}$F	G	^{b}A

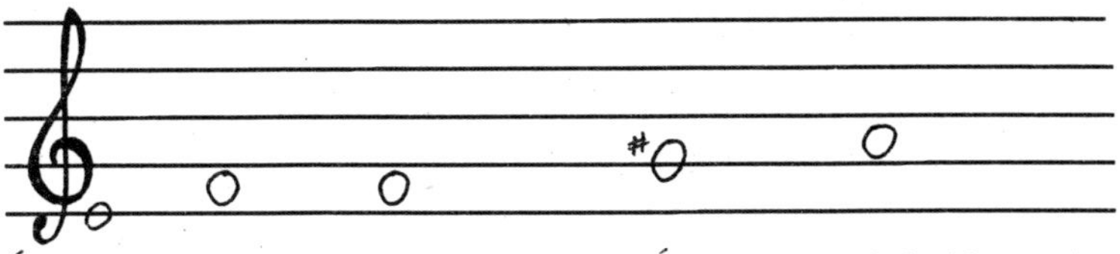

Śuddha Dhah	Komala Ni	Tīvra Komala Ni	Śuddha Ni	Sah (Octave)
D	n	$\underline{n}$	N	Ṡ
A	^{b}B	b$^{\#}$B	B	C

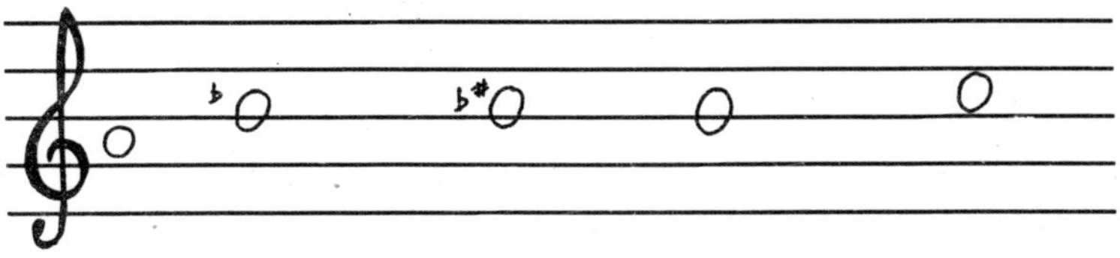

The Dictionary

1. Abhirudgatā

Vide 'Mūrcchanā'

2. Ābhoga

The fourth or the last stanza of a Dhrupada or Ālāpa. The melodic range of this stanza is between M and Ṗ or more. It invariably contains the name of the composer in case of songs. Its etymological meaning is 'The end'.

3. Acala Svara

Svara is a note. S and its major consonant P are regarded as fixed or immovable notes since they do not undergo any change into either sharp or flat; all other notes can be raised or lowered from their natural position. 'Acala' means that which does not move i.e., S and P.

4. Acala Ṭhāṭa or Acala Thāṭa

Here the Ṭhāṭa means the frets of a stringed instrument. Acala means immovable. The instruments which carry 22 or 23 frets i.e., for all the sharp and flat notes of two gamuts, so that the frets do not require to be moved for sharps or flats, are called instruments having Acala Ṭhāṭa. North Indian Vīṇā is an ideal instrument of Acala Ṭhāṭa since its frets are so firmly fixed with wax and other things that they cannot be moved easily. Such frets usually bear the following notes–

ṃ P̣ ḍ Ḍ ṇ Ṇ S r R g G M m P d D n N Ṡ ṙ Ṙ ġ Ġ
Some times Ġ is dropped to make 22 notes.

5. Ādhicakradāra

Cakra is cycle and Ādhi is half. Technically, that rhythmic composition which is once played in full cycle without break, followed by playing thrice the latter half portion of it to reach the Sama. The whole thing is considered to be a single piece (vide 'Cakradāra').

6. Ādhunika Saṁgīta

Those songs or melodic compositions which do not follow any Śāstrīya rules or even those melodies not found in the older Śāstras but are compositions of modern musicians are called Ādhunika Saṁgīta or modern music. The word Ādhunika is an adjective from Adhunā meaning the present time. The music of the 'Talkies' and of the stage etc. fall under this category. Modern music always serves the purpose of the present period and in course of time falls out of vogue and vanishes. If one of these modern melodies has the quality to outlast time, it, in course of years, may be considered to have reached the classical standard. It may be noted that Kīrtana and folk music are no less classical than Dhrupada etc. Only, their form is different. However, they are no less rigid and no less true to the tradition than the classical form.

7. Āḍi

It is a rhythmic variation. In Indian music a particular Tāla (vide) of 16 Mātrās or beats, divided into four equal parts is called Tritāla and has been accepted as the primary or fundamental Tāla with reference to which any other Tāla or rhythm appears different just as the diatonic major scale i.e., Indian Bilāvala Ṭhāṭa (vide) has been accepted as the fundamental scale, with reference to which other scales are considered (vide 'Ṭhāṭa'). This Tritāla has sixteen Mātrās or beats and when a composition (melodic or rhythmic) of twelve equal Mātrās can be exactly fitted into the time taken by 16 Mātrās, of course both the percussion instrument and melodic instrument must be played concurrently, and are brought to Sama simultaneously, then the instrument playing twelve Mātrās will have played the composition in Āḍi rhythm to the instrument playing 16 Mātrās. In other words, the equal division of 12 within the equal division of 16 Mātrās is called Āḍi rhythm on the part of 12 i.e., 12 is an Āḍi of 16. It can be said that in Āḍi the time of each Mātrā is increased to $1^1/_3$ of the Mātrā in the division of 16 i.e., Tritāla. Āḍi is a relative term and can only be expressed and understood with reference to another Tāla (here Tritāla) playing simultaneously. When a Tāla of 12 Mātrās is played independently of Tritāla, it makes a different variety called Ekatāla and not Āḍi of anything (vide 'Tāla', 'Mātrā' & 'Laya').

8. Āgantuka Svara

The note which is usually omitted in a Rāga but introduced into it for ornamentation. Accidental note.

9. Āhata

The Sound or Nāda that is produced physically is called Āhata i.e., struck. All of the mundane sounds are Āhata Nādas and from these, musical sounds are chosen (vide 'Anāhata').

10. Alaṁkāra

Literally means ornaments. In Indian music a precomposed melody i.e., a song or a Tarānā is a fixed thing and the musician, while singing that particular composition, decorates it with various extempore melodic and also rhythmic phrases within the Rāga and Tāla limits. Everything that a musician sings except the fixed composition mentioned above can be called Alaṁkāra since this decorates or enhances the beauty of that particular composed melody. Taken together the whole performance is called Indian Music. In Śāstras the term Alaṁkāra has been specified to mean:

(1) The technique of sound production either vocally or manually and is called Śabdālaṁkāra i.e., ornaments relating to sound production, for instance Gamaka, Āśa, Mīḍ, Kṛntana, Sparśa, and many others which indicate the way a note is to be produced. These are described under proper heads.

(2) Short melodic composition known as Kalās in a particular series to be used in the performance and is called Varṇālaṁkāra i.e., Alaṁkāras composed of Varṇa or notes. The Śāstra describes only 63 varieties of this Alaṁkāra but holds that they are infinite.

Alaṁkāra composed of Sthāyī (vide) Varṇa (vide):

(1) Prasannādi – S S Ṡ

(2) Prasannānta – Ṡ Ṡ S

(3) Prasannādyanta – S Ṡ S

(4) Prasannamadhya– Ṡ S Ṡ

(5) Kramarecita – SRS, SGMS, SPDNS (all taken together form the Alaṁkāra, the commas indicate slight break while rendering them vocally or instrumentally). Each of these small portions, separated by commas, is called a Kalā (vide)

(6) Prastāra – SRṠ, SGMṠ, SPDNṠ

(7) Prasāda – ṠRS, ṠGMS, ṠPDNS

Alaṁkāras composed of Ārohī (ascending) Varṇa:

(8) Vistīrṇa – S R G M P D N

(9) Niṣkarṣa (a) SS RR GG MM PP DD NN
Gātra Varṇa
(b) SSS RRR GGG MMM PPP DDD NNN

or (c) SSSS RRRR GGGG MMMM PPPP DDDD NNNN

(10) Bindu SSS R GGG M PPP D NNN

(11) Abhyuccaya S G P N

(12) Hasita – S RR GGG MMMM PPPPP DDDDDD NNNNNNN

(13) Preṅkhita – SR RG GM MP PD DN

(14) Ākṣipta – SG GP PN

(15) Sandhipracchādana – SRG GMP PDN

(16) Udgīta – SSS RG MMM PD

(17) Udvāhita or Udvādita – S RRR G M PPP D

(18) Trivarṇa – SR GGG MP DDD

(19) Veṇī – SSS RRR GGG MMM PPP DDD
It is called Gātra Varṇa if NNN is added as in 9 (a) and(b).

Alaṁkāras composed of Avarohī (descending) Varṇa:

(20) to (31) is the repetition of the above (8) to (19) in the descending order e.g., Bindu - NNN D PPP M GGG R SSS

Alaṁkāras composed of Sañcārī Varṇa:

(32) Mandrādi – SGR RMG GPM MDP PND

(33) Mandra Madhya – GSR MRG PGM DMP NPD
(34) Mandrānta – RGS GMR MPG PDM DNP
(35) Prastāra – SG RM GP MD PN
(36) Prasāda – SRS RGR GMG MPM PDP DND
(37) Vyavṛtta – SGRMS RMGPR GPMDG MDPNM
(38) Skhalita – MDPN NPDM
(39) Parivartta – SGM RMP GPD MDN
(40) Ākṣepa – SRG RGM GMP MPD PDN
(41) Bindu – SSSRS RRRGR GGGMG MMMPM PPPDP DDDND
(42) Udvāhita – SRGR RGMG GMPM MPDP PDND
(43) Ūrmi – SMMMSM RPPPRP GDDDGD MNNNMN
(44) Sama – SRGM MGRS, RGMP PMGR, GMPD DPMG, MPDN NDPM
(45) Preṅkha – SRRS RGGR GMMG MPPM PDDP DNND
(46) Niṣkujita – SRSGS RGRMR GMGPG MPMDM PDPNP
(47) Śyena – SP RD GN MṠ
(48) Krama – SR SRG SRGM, RG RGM RGMP, GM GMP GMPD, MP MPD MPDN
(49) Udghāṭita – SRPMGR, RGDPMG, GMNDPM
(50) Rañjita – SGRSGRS, RMGRMGR, GPMGPMG, MDPMDPM, PNDPNDP
(51) Sannivṛtta-pravṛtta – SPMGR RDPMG GNDPM
(52) Veṇu – SSRMG, RRGPM, GGMDP, MMPND
(53) Lalita Svara – SRMRS, RGPGR, GMDMG, MPNPM
(54) Huṁkāra – SRS, SRGRS, SRGMGRS, SRGMPMGRS, SRGMPDPMGRS, SRGMPDNDPMGRS
(55) Hlādamāna – SGRS, RMGR, GPMG, MDPM, PNDP
(56) Avalokita – SGMMRS, RMPPGR, GPDDMG, MDNNPM

Seven extra Alaṁkāras:

(57) Tāramandra Prasanna – SRGMPDNṠṠ
(58) Mandratāra Prasanna – ṠṠNDPMGRS

(59) Āvartaka	–	SS RR SS RS, RR GG RR GR, GG MM GG MG, MM PP MM PM, PP DD PP DP, DD NN DD ND
(60) Sampradāna	–	SS RR SS, RR GG RR, GG MM GG, MM PP MM, PP DD PP, DD NN DD
(61) Vidhūta	–	SGSG RMRM GPGP MDMD PNPN
(62) Upalola	–	SRSRGRGR, RGRGMGMG, GMGMPMPM, MPMPDPDP, PDPDNDND
(63) Ullāsita	–	SSGSG, RRMRM, GGPGP, MMDMD, PPNPN.

11. Ālaṁkārika Pada

When a small combination of notes decorates either a single note or another combination of notes in a composition, this combination of notes is called Ālaṁkārika Pada or grace phrase. In notation, this Ālaṁkārika Pada is written on the upper left corner of the note or combination of notes to which the decoration is needed.

12. Ālaṁkārika Svara

A note that decorates another note is called an Ālaṁkārika Svara or a 'Grace-note'. This grace-note can never come into more prominence than the note it is decorating. In notations, the grace-notes appear in a smaller type on the upper left corner of the main note thus decorated.

13. Ālāpa

A free-lance composition, obviously extempore, to delineate a Rāga by gradual exposition and at the earlier stage free from rhythmic bounds. Indian music can very well be compared with literature. In language we use alphabets, in music we use the Varṇas SRGM etc. as symbols of musical notes. As in literature we use words to denote a concept, so in music we use short phrases of notes arranged in a particular manner to denote the concept of a particular Rāga. As in literature we arrange the words to form a sentence, so in music we arrange the phrases to form an idea of a Rāga. As in literature we have two types of 'Compositions' - one is poem bound by metre and the other is prose unbound by metre, so also in music we have songs or Tarānās (vide) bound by metre and Ālāpa unbound by or free from rhythm. As in prose we write an essay on any subject so in Ālāpa we musically compose an 'Essay' on a particular Rāga. The difference is, the former is read and the latter is heard.

So far so good. But in Ālāpa there are two portions, the first one is unbound by rhythm and the second portion is bound by rhythm. The second portion is composed of Jhālā (vide) and Tāraparaṇa (vide). The unbound portion has four stanzas which may be called a sort of movement and will be fully described later. The readers must have understood in a very general manner what Ālāpa is. Now let us examine in details the character and the sequences of Ālāpa.

Ālāpa can be classified in two ways, firstly from the point of view of scope or extent which is like a canvas, small or large, to a painting. Secondly, from the point of view of character or the nature of Ālāpa. As there are various schools of painting, each different from the other, so there are mainly four different methods of rendering Ālāpa. We now come to the details of classification:

(1) Divisions depending on the extent

(a) Aucār Ālāpa
(b) Bandhān Ālāpa
(c) Qaid Ālāpa
(d) Vistāra Ālāpa

(a) *Aucār Ālāpa* – Aucār literally means custom. In musical terminology it may mean perfunctoriness. Aucār Ālāpa is not a conventional Ālāpa but is a mere introductory delineation of a Rāga used as a prelude to a more serious musical performance dealing with that particular Rāga. This type lacks the vastness of a serious and complete Ālāpa.

(b) *Bandhān Ālāpa* – This Ālāpa contains in the first portion or 'Movement' a specific composition well known as representing a particular school or Gharānā of music. For some time the musician employs these particular melodic compositions to impress upon the listners the speciality of his particular Gharānā or school. Bandhān here means precomposed. After the musician is satisfied about the recognition of his school or Gharānā by the listners, he goes on with extempore Ālāpa compositions.

(c) *Qaid Ālāpa* – Each important note is taken as the central note round which short compositions are spun to expose the Rāga gradually. At first shorter and gradually longer melodic phrases are used. Generally the Aṁśa (vide) note is selected first but the fundamental note or S is also used at the beginning. Literally Qaid means 'Kept under regulations'.

(d) *Vistāra Ālāpa* – In this Ālāpa there are no such conditions as above i.e., neither particular melodic composition of a school nor any particular note is stuck to. From the beginning the musician unfolds the Rāga by extempore melodic compositions. Vistāra Ālāpa resembles Aucār Ālāpa to some extent but is vaster and so to say, spread on a larger canvas.

The above are the four main classes from the point of view of extension, but one can combine the classes to make further six varieties viz.,

(a) Aucār-Bandhān
(b) Aucār-Qaid
(c) Aucār-Vistāra
(d) Bandhān-Qaid
(e) Bandhān-Vistāra
(f) Qaid-Vistāra.

Now we shall classify Ālāpa character-wise. The character here means (primarily indicates) one of the different methods according to particular schools or Gharānās of musicians. As in Western classical compositions different conductors differ in their treatment of a particular symphony so also in Indian music a particular song or composed music may be treated in four different technical ways (or characteristics). We name these ways as 'Vāṇīs' meaning here technical styles of exposition.

(a) Gauḍa, Gauḍahāra or Gobarahāra Vāṇī
(b) Ḍāgara Vāṇī
(c) Nauhāra Vāṇī
(d) Khaṇḍāra Vāṇī

Vāṇī literally means words articulated.

(a) *Gauḍa, Gauḍahāra* or *Gobarahāra Vāṇī* – Perhaps this style evolved in the region of Gauḍa, the ancient name of Bengal. This is known as Śuddha or Pure Vāṇī also. There is no unnecessary ornamentation of the notes which are used in a single and undecorated method. Only Mīḍ (vide) and Āśa (vide) are the technical Alaṁkāras used in this Vāṇī. Gauḍa Vāṇī is used in the stringed instrument Rabāb (vide) mostly. This Vāṇī is mostly employed in Śānta or peaceful and Bhakti or devotional emotions.

(b) *Ḍāgara Vāṇī* – Probably this Vāṇī evolved in a place used to be known as Ḍāgara in India. This is more poetic and florid decorated than (the foregoing) Gauḍa Vāṇī. More technical Alaṁkāras are used such as Mīḍ, Āśa, Zamzamā (vide) etc. Śānta or peaceful, Karuṇa or pathos and Madhura or sweet or charming emotions find expression in this Vāṇī.

(c) *Nauhāra Vāṇī* – Some musicians hold that this name has been adopted from the strides of a lion, but others take it to be a regional Vāṇī. Almost all types of technical Alaṁkāras are used copiously in this Vāṇī which is suitable for all types of melodic instruments. The presiding emotion is Adbhuta or wonder.

(d) *Khaṇḍāra Vāṇī* – Perhaps this Vāṇī took its name from Kāndāhāra in India. This Vāṇī is made conspicuous by the dominance of Gamaka (vide) Alaṁkāra and is necessarily used in medium or fast tempo. Vīra or gallant and Adbhuta or wonder emotions are inspired through this Vāṇī.

It should be noted that in Vilambita Laya (vide) or slow tempo, Gauḍa or Ḍāgara Vāṇīs are invariably used and the performance takes the characters of either of the above mentioned Vāṇīs from the medium tempo. It is needless to mention that Indian Music generally starts in slow tempo and gradually grows faster becoming fastest towards culmination.

The above four Vāṇīs or styles of expression are equally used in Songs, Tarānās or Ālāpa.

These Vāṇīs have their counterparts in Gītis mentioned in Saṁgītaratnākara (vide 'Gīti').

In this connection it should better be observed that emotions or Rasas (vide) can be connected not so much with Rāgas as have been done in ancient Śāstras but more with the way a Rāga is played or sung. Let us take an example - "Come Here" can be used as an order, or as an entreatment and so the emotion expressed by the user is clearly manifested by the way he or she utters the words. Thus the emotion does not depend merely on the combination of words themselves but on the way of its expression. After this we come to the proper sequential technicalities of Ālāpa.

Originally there were thirteen stages in a complete Ālāpa but one of those stages had long fallen into disuse. As such at present there are twelve, arranged in a strictly proper sequence. Rarely does one find nowadays a musician who can demonstrate an Ālāpa in a complete sequence articulating every stage. The purpose of following the sequences in strict manner is to make the whole performance smooth, gathering gradual speed and blending the transition from one stage to the other in such a way as to make it one unbroken whole from the beginning upto its culmination. Thus an Ālāpa by itself will have served its purpose of leaving the listeners in quintessence of artistic and aesthetic ecstasy. Vocal Ālāpa invariably uses articulated syllables having no meaning, so are the types of songs known as Tarānās (vide). It is not at all because of the incapability of the musicians who thus use syllables without meaning [to compose a song of a poetic nature or otherwise having some meaning], as has been erroneously supposed by some musicologists, but it is for the purpose of making the listeners concentrate upon only the melody of the Ālāpa so that their attention may not be divided between the melody and the meaning of the song. In instrumental music this question does not arise and the listeners do have the purest form of melodic or Rāga music. The following are the thirteen stages of a complete Ālāpa:

(a) Vilambita, (b) Madh or Madhya, (c) Druta, (d) Jhālā, (e) Ṭhoka, (f) Laḍī, (g) Laḍaguthāo, (h) Laḍalapeṭa, (i) Paraṇa, (j) Sāth, (k) Dhuyā, (l) Māṭhā, (m) Paramāṭhā - (this has become obsolete). These are also known as Aṁgas i.e., parts of Ālāpa. Stages numbered b and c are called Joḍ (vide).

(a) *Vilambita* – The meaning is 'Slow' (vide 'Laya'). The Sthāyī, Antarā, Sañcārī and Ābhoga stanzas of an Ālāpa are rendered in slow tempo. It should never be forgotten that at every step the tempo should be slightly faster. Nonetheless the overall tempo of these four stanzas is slow. To make the gradual rising of the tempo smoother, this Vilambita stage has been further subdivided into three steps viz., - (i) Vilambita-Vilambita, (ii) Vilambita-Madhya, and (iii) Vilambita-Druta. We hope that the intention of this subdivision is by now quite clear. Let us now examine each of the foregoing stages in detail.

(i) *Vilambita-Vilambita* – One may begin the Ālāpa either from (x) the Graha (vide) Svara and soon come to the Aṁśa

Svara, should this be other than the Graha; then the Saṁvādī of this Aṁśa should be dwelt upon, ending the Tāna on the Nyāsa (vide) Svara. Secondly, one may begin from (y) Ṣaḍja and then, coming to Aṁśa and its Saṁvādī, should finish it on the Nyāsa Svara. Lastly, one may begin from (z) the Aṁśa Svara and end on the Saṁvādī. It should be noted that in Ālāpa everything that is played or sung in the first three stages is called Tāna and the ending of Tāna is marked by a compositional phrase called Moharā (vide). If we once more draw literary comparison we can call the Tāna a sentence and the Moharā a stop. Allowing a melodic composition to continue for some length of time without a Moharā would certainly be extremely boring to both the performing musician and his listeners, so a Moharā has long been introduced. Moharā has another important function; it helps the musician to change the pattern of Tāna composition with ease, which would have been difficult otherwise.

(ii) *Vilambita-Madhya* – It is almost like the foregoing step i.e., Vilambita-Vilambita but small Tānas of comparatively faster tempo should be inserted in between the slower Tānas. Viḍāra Tānas (vide) are also used in this step. The use of Cikārī (vide) is also oftener in Vilambita- Madhya. Antarā stanza is to be used here.

(iii) *Vilambita-Druta* – It should be comparatively faster. Sañcārī and Ābhoga stanzas are employed. Also small Tānas of faster tempo are inserted.

In all of the foregoing three steps Moharās of a slow tempo should be used so as to assure the listeners that Vilambita tempo is still continuing. Moharās differ with the tempo (vide 'Moharā').

(b) *Madh* or *Madhya* – or the stage having medium tempo - glimpses of rhythm appear from this stage. This stage has also been subdivided into three steps: (i) Madhya-Vilambita, (ii) Madhya-Madhya, (iii) Madhya-Druta. These words Vilambita, Madhya or Druta are relative terms and no particular or definite measurement of tempo can be fixed for them. The tempo depends entirely on the musician and his listeners. But it should be remembered that certain instruments allow very slow tempo and others do not; it will be fully dealt with in the description of instruments and under Śvāsa.

(i) *Madhya-Vilambita* – Worthwhile musicians call this stage 'Ḍagar Kī Baḍhat.' Ḍa, Ga, and Ra are the three strokes used in playing Vīṇā and 'Baḍhat' means 'Increase'. When the tempo or speed of these strokes Ḍa, Ga and Ra is increased, it is called 'Ḍagar Kī Baḍhat'. This means that the Madh stage should be played faster than the foregoing Vilambita stage, Cikārīs, Mīḍ and Syṁut (Āśa) are more frequently used than in the previous stage. Sixty three Alaṁkāras mentioned elsewhere can be selectively used in this stage (vide 'Alaṁkāra').

(ii) *Madhya-Madhya* – Musicians call this 'Madh-Joḍ' and sometimes 'Barābar Kī Joḍ', (vide 'Joḍ'). Among the various meanings of the Hindi word 'Barābar', the primary meaning is 'Equal'. But here we should rather select another meaning 'Smooth'; from the nature of the Joḍ employed, this meaning suits the best. In this stage Gamaka-Joḍ is also used. Mīḍ or Āśa become less frequent and the notes are rendered independently, Cikārī (vide) is used the least. Since Gamaka Alaṁkāra is used, its nature sometimes becomes that of using Khaṇḍāra Vāṇī (vide); Viḍāra (vide) style of compositions are also sometimes introduced.

(iii) *Madhya-Druta* – Some musicians call it 'Laḍī-Joḍ'. It is almost like 'Madhya-Madhya' but a little faster in tempo and use of Cikārī is still lesser.

(c) *Druta* – This stage resembles the whole of Madhya stage but is in faster tempo and the Cikāri is entirely omitted. This stage has also been subdivided into three steps (a) Druta-Vilambita, (b) Druta-Madhya, and (c) Druta-Druta.

The reason for these subdivisions has been fully explained previously. It is needless to go into details of these subdivisions in this Druta stage.

(d) *Jhālā* – Although the foregoing stages are both in vocal and instrumental music, Jhāla and subsequent stages are purely for instrumental music. From this stage the rhythmic nature of Ālāpa fully manifests itself. Sometimes musicians introduce Jhālā from 'Druta-Madhya' step mentioned above. Jhālā is an onomatopoeic word, resembling the sound produced by drone strings or Cikārī (vide). These drones – the combined sounds of Lower P, middle and upper S – produced by striking all the drone strings at a time by the plectrum worn on the forefinger or held, serve the purpose of a harmonic background against which Rāga melody has its smooth exposition effected by the same plectrum that produces the drones. The strokes are played in such quick and alternate successions of one stroke to the main string producing melody followed by three strokes on the drone strings called Cikārī producing the harmonic background, as to make the whole performance a homogeneous whole which is called Jhālā. Pakhāvaj – a type of drum – can be played as rhythmic accompaniment from this stage, although usually this accompaniment does not begin before the stage numbered six i.e., Laḍī.

(e) *Ṭhoka* – This is a variety of Jhālā. In Jhālā we have a drone background against which a melody is played. Whatever rhythmic sense filters through the ears is produced by the variation and alternation of strokes on the drone strings and the main string or strings which can be called melody strings i.e., melody is produced on these strings and the rest are either drones or sympathetic strings. At this stage i.e., Ṭhoka, rhythmic variation is produced mostly by varieties of strokes that invite more than cursory attention; sometimes the beauty of these stroke-varieties completely overshadows the melodic portion. The strokes on the main string produce complex rhythmic sounds. Although the Rāga composition is always there, yet it is kept subdominant to the rhythm produced by stroke varieties and alternate strokes played on Cikārīs as in Jhālā. From this stage the importance of rhythm slowly replaces that of melody. The word 'Ṭhoka' is derived from a Hindi word the meaning of which is 'To strike'.

(f) *Laḍī* – Literal meaning of this Hindi word is 'Garland'. From this stage onwards everything falls under the category broadly known as Tāraparaṇa (vide). Usually it is from this stage that the accompanying percussion instrument is introduced. In Ālāpa, as in Dhrupada, Pakhāvaj is used invariably. It is needless to say that from this stage rhythm becomes dominant, Rāga or melodic portion becomes just perfunctory. Laḍī is a garland composed of Bolas (vide) used in a percussion instrument. A short Bola-phrase is taken into consideration and only the particular alphabets used in this small phrase are played with varieties of rearrangement or combinations for sometime both in the percussion instrument and in the melodic string instrument. The Bolas of melodic instruments though greatly differ from those of the percussion instru-

ments, yet the sound of the percussion Bolas is copied in the string instrument with its own Bolas (vide). In Laḍī the Bolas that are used should be simple and not complex (vide 'Bolas'). An example may be helpful: Take for instance, a short Bola phrase used in Pakhāvaj, 'Dhumakiṭa Tāka Tāka'. This phrase is composed of simple Bolas and not complex such as 'Kre' or 'Ghran' etc. If we spread this Bola phrase in different arrangements we get: Dhumakiṭa Tākatāka, Dhumakiṭa Tākatāka, Dhumakiṭa Dhumakiṭa, Tākatāka Dhumakiṭa, Tākadhuma Kiṭadhuma, Kiṭakiṭa Tākadhuma and so on. If we play this Bola in string instrument with its own Bola we get: Ḍārāḍāḍā Rāḍāḍārā, Ḍārāḍāḍā Rāḍāḍārā, Ḍārāḍāḍā Ḍārāḍāḍā, Rāḍāḍārā Ḍārāḍāḍā, Rāḍāḍārā Ḍārāḍāḍā, Rāḍārāḍā Rāḍāḍārā etc. It should be borne in mind that there is no fixed instrumental counterpart of percussion Bolas; the musician is primarily concerned to reproduce the percussion rhythm with whatever Bolas he considers suitable for himself and these Bolas usually vary with individuals.
In the end of a particular variety of Laḍī, a Tihāī (vide) is played instead of a Moharā and this Tihāī marks the end of that Laḍī. One can play as many different varieties of Laḍī as suit the mood of the occasion without becoming boring.

(g) *Laḍaguthāo* – This is a portamento word combining 'Laḍī' meaning 'Garland' and 'Gutthī' meaning 'Pierce', or 'Sew' or 'Poke'. Laḍaguthāo is nothing but Laḍī as previously described, only it uses complex Bolas. This complexity of Bolas is indicated by the word 'Gutthī' meaning 'Poking' or 'Piercing' (vide 'Bola'). As in Laḍī, we can use a Bola-phrase-'Kredhāāney Dheṭedheṭe' and its string equivalent 'Ḍreḍā ārā Ḍereḍere'.

(h) *Laḍalapeṭa* – It is also like Laḍī and Laḍaguthāo. In this stage some Alaṁkāras such as Āśa or Syuṁt and Chūṭ (vide) are copiously used in melodic exposition.

(i) *Paraṇa* – (vide 'Paraṇa'). The musician plays the rhythm of a Tāla in Cikārī strings and then on the main string reproduces a 'Paraṇa' which he ends in 'Sama'; the accompanying percussionist also reaches his 'Sama' simultaneously with the principal musician. This stage is also called 'Tāraparaṇa' (vide). Here, at this stage, after the string instrumentalist has played a particular Paraṇa and has reached his Sama, the accompanying percussionist reproduces the same Paraṇa on his instrument in reply to that of the chief instrumentalist who has reverted to the playing of a Tāla in Cikārī strings as in the beginning. This type of play is called 'Javāb (reply) Saṁgat' (accompaniment) on the part of the percussionist.

(j) *Sāth* – Literal meaning 'Together'. This is exactly like Paraṇa, the difference being that the Paraṇa should be played simultaneously by both the chief instrumentalist and the accompanying percussionist, and both should reach the Sama at the same time to the satisfaction and relief of the listeners.

(k) *Dhuyā* – When Laḍī and Laḍaguthāo are played on the Cikārī strings, i.e., entirely without melody— since one cannot play a melody on Cikārī as they are drone strings , it is called Dhuyā.

(l) *Māṭhā* – When Laḍī and Laḍaguthāo are played on the melody string and the drone strings.one after the other i.e., at first a Bola phrase is played on the main string and the same is repeated on the Cikārī strings, it is called Māṭhā.

(m) *Paramāṭhā* – When Laḍī or Laḍaguthāo or Paraṇas are played partly on the main string and partly on the drone strings, it is called Paramāṭhā. This stage has long since been obsolete.

The last three names Dhuyā, Māthā and Paramāṭhā are perhaps slang derivation from Śāstrīya names Dhruva, Maṇṭha and Pratimaṇṭha respectively, although their meanings greatly differ from those of their modern rendering.

14. Alpatva

Meagreness. This word is used with reference to the use of notes, that is, a note is sustained longer than a grace note yet not emphasised or dwelt on; used in passing, a transitional note.

15. Aṁga

The literal meaning is limb or part. In Hindustāni music the gamut of 8 notes has been divided into two parts viz., lower and upper tetrachords which are called 'Pūrvāṁga' and 'Uttarāṁga' respectively. 'Uttara' here means the upper and 'Purva' means the lower. It can be seen that each of the notes in the Pūrvāṁga (i.e., SRGM) has its corresponding consonant note in the Uttarāṁga (i.e., PDNṠ). Here the consonant of S is P, that of R is D, that of G is N and that of M is Ṡ. It is evident that a note and its consonant both cannot exist in any one Aṁga or tetrachord. The exception is in case where M is considered a consonant of S in the Aṁga SRGM (vide 'Vādī').

16. Aṁga Prādhānya

Prādhānya means dominance. A Rāga (vide) is said to have a particular Aṁga Prādhānya i.e., the dominance of one tetrachord when the Aṁśa (vide) note of that Rāga lies in that particular Aṁga. For example, the Aṁśa note of Rāga Yamana is G and it lies in the lower tetrachord i.e., Pūrvāṁga. As such Yamana is called a Rāga of Pūrvāṁga Prādhānya or, in other words, Pūrvāṁga Pradhāna Rāga. Prādhānya is an abstract noun from Pradhāna.

17. Aṁśa

The literal meaning of this is 'Part', yet when used with reference to music it is the most important note in a Rāga. The almost central note around which other notes are composed to express the spirit and idea of a Rāga. It is this note with which the relations of other notes used in a Rāga are determined according to their importance in mutual relationship viz., consonance, dissonance or assonance. In order to determine such relationship this principal note or Aṁśa Svara is called Vādī only when its Saṁvādī, Anuvādī and Vivādī notes are taken cognizance of and then these notes are used in the Rāga according to certain rules. Vādī and Saṁvādī etc. are relative terms indicating the relationship between any two notes of the scale and have nothing to do with reference to any Rāga. Vādī of a Rāga is a misnomer but has come into currency through misunderstanding spreading over more than a century. The present practice has been to call the principal note Vādī instead of Aṁśa of a Rāga (vide 'Vādī').

18. Anāgata

Literally 'Which is not come'. In music when the real 'Sama' or main rhythmic accent of a particular composition of the accompanying percussion instrument falls after that of the vocalist or instrumentalist, the apparent main accent of the latter is called 'Anāgata Sama'. In other words, the apparent 'Sama' or main accent of the musician appears before that of the accompanyist i.e., whose real 'Sama' has not yet come. This is a rhythmic variation and is an accomplishment of the musician rather than his rhythmic weakness as may appear to some of the listening public. Vide 'Tāla'. In the Śāstras the explanations of these terms are simple; when the musician (vocal, instrumental) or a dancer synchronises the starting of his or her music or dance with that of the accompanying percussionist, it is called 'Sama Graha' (starting together). The meaning of 'Sama' here is 'At a time'. When the starting of the musician or the dancer follows that of the accompanyist it is called 'Atīta (past) Graha' and when the starting of the accompanyist follows that of the musician or the dancer it is called 'Anāgata Graha'.

19. Anāghāta

The literal meaning is 'Without beating', (Āghāta is 'Beating', Anāghāta is 'Not beating'). This is a rhythmic variation resembling syncopation. When the rhythmic accents of music fall in between the rhythmic accents of the percussion accompaniment, it is called Anāghāta variation of rhythm. The unaccented place between two beats is called the Anāghāta place, and utilization of such places by the beats of the music is one of the rhythmic variations a musician can do.

20. Anāhata

The Śāstras admit two varieties of sound— one is produced by striking on something and the other is self-emanating or Anāhata i.e., not-struck. This latter is unnecessary in mundane affairs. Anāhata sound is self-emanating, spontaneous, infinite and metaphysical.

21. Anibaddha

The music which is not bound by Tāla, Chanda or Mātrā, non-rhythmic, i.e., Ālāpa.

22. Antarā

In Dhrupada and Ālāpa we have four stanzas or Tukas, similar to movements in Western music. Antarā is the second stanza. The scale limit for this second stanza is between middle G and upper G. For Khayāl and other varieties of songs, there being usually two stanzas of Sthāyī and Anatarā, the limit for Antarā has been fixed between middle G and upper P. The literal meaning of Antarā is 'Near', or 'Proximate' since this stanza is proximate to the principal stanza or Sthāyī, it is called 'Antarā' (vide 'Dhātu').

23. Antara Gāndhāra

G having 4 Śrutis i.e., G of the diatonic major scale, or the natural G of the present day (vide 'Śruti').

24. Anudātta

Low sound.

25. Anuloma

The simile has been drawn from the body hair or the Loma or the wool. 'Anu' is 'Towards', so 'Anuloma' is 'Towards the pile of the wool'. In music it means the natural sequence of going up, i.e., S R G M P D N Ṡ. It is also called Āroha.

26. Anuvādī

The note that follows the Vādī or the principal note. The meaning here appears to be somewhat vague. We know that the fourth or the fifth note from the principal note is called Saṁvādī or consonant. Likewise we call the third from the principal note Anuvādī or assonant, viz., G is an Anuvādī of S, M is of R, P is of G, D is of M, N is of P and S is of D. In the Śāstras mention has been made of consonant i.e., Saṁvādī and dissonant i.e., Vivādī and the rest are called Anuvādī or assonant. In Western music due importance has been given to the third, fourth and the fifth notes as it is in Indian music and this kind of relationship between different notes of a gamut seems to be universal (vide 'Vādī').

27. Apanyāsa

Rarely now is this word used. The ending note of a small phrase of the composition of a Rāga is called Apanyāsa note. For example, ṆRGmP is a small compositional phrase expressing the Rāga Yamana and the ending note P is Apanyāsa Svara or note (vide 'Bidārī').

28. Ārcika

Vide 'Tāna'.

29. Āroha

Vide 'Anuloma' and 'Avaroha'.

30. Ārohī Varṇa

Notes arranged in ascending order (vide 'Varṇa').

31. Āśa or Syuṁt

When in a stringed fret instrument a note is played and while the sound persists, another note is produced by sliding the fingers to a different fret, it is called Āśa and is a Śabdālaṁkāra (vide 'Alaṁkāra'). The same act on a non-fret instrument is called Syuṁt.

32. Āśraya Rāga

Vide 'Ṭhāṭa'.

33. Āsthāyī

Hindustānī rendering of the word Sthāyī. The Principal or the first stanza or Tuka of a song or an Ālāpa is called Sthāyī because part of this portion is repeated in a musical performance over and over again after every other thing such as Tāna or Bāṁta (vide). In Ālāpa, although the scope of repetition is nil, yet the first stanza is called Sthāyī and the scale limit of this stanza is from middle S to middle N. It is in this stanza that the concept of a Rāga is fully established. The meaning of Sthāyī is 'Basic' or 'Fundamental' at best with reference to songs (vide 'Dhātu').

34. Aśvakrāntā

Vide 'Mūrcchanā'.

35. Ātāī

Musicians bereft of theoretical knowledge and ignorant of the correct sequences of a musical exposition.

36. Ati Komala

'Ati' is 'Very', 'Komala' is 'Flat'. When a note is lowered more than its usual flat position, it is called 'Ati Komala'; viz., R has been placed on Raktikā Śruti, the Komala R is on the previous Śruti Rañjanī and the Ati Komala R is placed on Dayāvatī which is still prior to Rañjanī. Similarly D is on Ramyā Śruti, Komala D is on Rohiṇī Śruti and Ati Komala D is on Madantī Śruti. R and D are the only notes that can have Ati Komala flattening. In Rāga 'Śrī' for instance, the Ati Komala R and D are used.

37. Atīta

Literally means 'Which is past or gone'. In music when the real

Sama or main rhythmic accent of a particular composition of the accompanying percussion instrument falls before that of the vocalist or instrumentalist, then the main accent of the latter is called Atīta Sama i.e., the apparent Sama. In other words, the main accent of the musician appears after the actual Sama of the accompanyist which is already past. This is a rhythmic variation and is an accomplishment of the musician rather than his rhythmic weakness as may appear to some of the listening public. The Tāla following Sama is also called 'Atīta Tāla'. Here the 'Tāla' means beating.

38. Auḍuva or Auḍava

Having five. Uḍu is a star which lies in the sky. According to Indian philosophy the ether sky is the fifth of the five elements viz., Earth, Water, Fire, Air and Ether (or Pṛthvī, Jala, Agni, Vāyu and Ākāśa). Hence Auḍuva has been fixed to mean 'Having five', although it seems far fetched. Whenever any two notes excepting S of a scale of seven notes are dropped, the scale formed by the remaining five is called Auḍuva scale. In no case can S be dropped. There are many Rāgas having scales of five notes and they are known as Auḍuva Rāgas.

39. Āvardā

The popular form of the word Āvarta or cycle. The entire cycle of a melodic or rhythmic composition is called Āvarta or Āvardā.

40. Avaroha

Descending. The opposite of Āroha or ascending; is also called Viloma (vide) viz., NDPMGRS.

41. Avarohī

Composing the notes in descending order is called Avarohī (vide 'Varṇa').

42. Bāḍhat (or Baḍhat)

(a) The process of progressing from slow to fast tempo.
(b) The gradual extempore exposition of a Rāga. This is the most common interpretation of Bāḍhat.
(c) The portion of Ālāpa having medium tempo is called Ḍagar Kī Baḍhat (vide 'Ālāpa').

43. Bahutva

In a particular Rāga, some note or notes are used more frequently than others; these notes are known to have Bahutva or predominance in that particular Rāga. Usually in any Rāga the Aṁśa Svara takes predominance. Aṁśa Svara means the most important note of a Rāga, which in common parlance is called Vādī. It does not necessarily mean numerical predominance. In other words, it would not do to scan Rāga Yamana for instance, and find out which of the notes appears more in number in a particular composition; it is also to be determined if that particular note has been used in such a way as to make it more important than other notes. So Bahutva has another import which is 'Importance'. For instance if we scan this Saragam in Rāga Yamana - 'ṆRG, RG, ṆR, ṆG, RS'– we find 'S' appears once, 'R' four times, 'G' thrice and 'Ṇ' also thrice. Numerically 'R' takes up the character of Bahutva and 'S' being used only once, becomes most insignificant, which can be called the Vivādī note. However, that is not the case because mere numerical importance cannot confer Bahutva to a note. 'G', although used thrice in this particular Saragam, becomes the most prominent note as it has become the central note around which the whole composition has been woven. That shows the importance of this note although, numerically its uses are fewer than those of 'R'. So in the Sanskrit Śloka 'Prayoga Bahula Svara' – 'The note that is numerous in application' the common meaning of 'Bahula' is numerous but in this context it should also be interpreted as 'Important'.

44. Bāī

Vide 'Tayafā'.

45. Bāj

The style and technique of playing instrumental music is called Bāj – or style e.g., Dhrupadī style, K̲h̲ayāliyā style, Ṭhumrī style, Masīdk̲h̲ānī Bāj, Rezāk̲h̲ānī Bāj, Pūrvī Bāj, Imdāk̲h̲ānī Bāj etc.

Technique is a word which includes a number of things, one of which is the sequence of playing a Rāga through the medium of an instrument. For this sequence there are conventional rules. Whenever these rules are absent, such playing cannot be properly known to have any style or Bāj and should rather be called a freelance playing, pleasant or unpleasant depending upon the artiste's personal talent. This type of instrumental playing does not represent any Gharānā or tradition and cannot be strictly called 'Classical'. Sometimes the style or Bāj is called Cāla or Calana. The present author recommends the word 'Vādakī' for instrumental music similar to the word 'Gāyakī' for vocal music (q.v. 'Imdādkhānī', 'Masidkhānī' and 'Rezākhānī').

46. Bāṁṭa

This word is derived from the word 'Banṭana' meaning distribution. The words of a song or Bolas of a Tarānā or Gat can be distributed in such a manner that the original rhythm of the composition undergoes various changes - something like extemporization. This is done mainly to extemporize rhythmic composition. In case of the words of a song, sometimes it happens that they lose their character and are rendered to rhythmic sounds without conveying any meaning. It may be mentioned here that in classical music the literary quality of a song is of the least importance excepting in Ṭhumrī songs. The words of a song merely serve to express the rhythmic beauty of a composition as different from the melodic beauty. In Dhrupada only Bāṁṭas are permissible and not Tānas; in Khayāl songs both Bāṁṭa and Tāna are used.

47. Bandiś or Bandeja

This Hindustānī word literally means well-composed music etc. Usually the best compositions enjoy the dignity of being called Bandejī (adjective from Bandeja). The compositions of old masters, such as Tānsen, Sadāraṅg, Bahādur Sen, are called Bandejī. Even the present day masters can have Bandejī compositions – Rabīndra-Saṁgītas are certainly the examples of best compositions in Bengali songs. In usual parlance the Bandejī compositions are those that are equally charming both in melodic and rhythmic aspects.

48. Barābara

A variety of Laya. If each beat of time cycle contains a single Bola or musical note, such musical time is known as Barābara Laya; it is also called Madhya Laya or intermediate time. Here Barābara means 'Equal' i.e., music and time are equal in Laya.

49. Bemaṁcā

In percussion instruments such as Mṛdaṅga or Pakhāvaj, when, during playing Paraṇa (q.v.), the Sama (q.v.) does not seem to appear as expected, a Tihāī is added immediately after the Sama passes away unnoticed, to come to Sama in the next cycle.

50. Bemāñjā

Vide 'Tihāī'.

51. Bhajana

Doxological songs used for worship purposes. Lately, it has entered the field of classical music soirees.

52. Bhāo

The Hindi rendering of the Sanskrit word Bhāva. The emotional contents of a song, when expressed through gestures are called Bhāo. Ṭhumrī songsters, dancers, actors and actresses often express emotions through 'Bhāo'.

53. Bhāva

A Sanskrit word. The mental change brought about by the perception of sentiment or emotion known as Rasa is called Bhāva. To understand the process of this mental change from emotion or sentiment one has to consider four elements:

(1) Sthāyī Bhāva
(2) Sañcārī Bhāva, in other words Vyabhicārī Bhāva
(3) Vibhāva
(4) Anubhāva

(1) *Sthāyī Bhāva* – The primary change brought about in the mind by an emotion or sentiment is called Sthāyī Bhāva. It is believed that a particular sentiment brings about a particular Bhāva in the mind and as soon as that sentiment or emotion disappears, the change brought about in the mind also vanishes leaving the mind in the normal condition. That is the reason why it has been called Sthāyī Bhāva — its existence depending upon the presence of the emotion. 'Sthāyī' means 'Lasting'.

(2) *Sañcārī or Vyabhicārī Bhāva* – Other mental conditions, though secondary yet complementary to the primary mental condition i.e., Sthāyī Bhāva or emanating therefrom, are known as Sañcārī Bhāva of the Sthāyī Bhāva.

(3) *Vibhāva* – The ingredients of a Bhāva are known as Vibhāvas, viz., a garden , music, spring-season, war, fire, arms etc.
(4) *Anubhāva* – Actions expressing Bhāvas are called Anubhāva - viz., puckering of brows, jumping, winking, smiling etc.
Every Rasa or emotion has its different Sthāyī Bhāva, Sañcārī Bhāva, Vibhāva and Anubhāva (vide 'Rasa').

54. Bheruā or Bhaḍvā

The father or brother of a professional dancing woman or Bāī is known as Bheruā.

55. Bhinnā Gīti

Vide 'Gīti'.

56. Bidārī

Whatever divides or disintegrates is called Bidārī. There are two kinds of Bidārī as mentioned in the Śāstras:
a) Gīta Bidārī – When a song or a poem is divided in feet or metric units, it is called Gīta Bidārī (Gīta is song, Bidārī - one which divides) e.g., let us divide our national song:
Janaganamana / adhināyaka / jaya he / Bhārata / bhāgya bidhātā.
This is natural division and each division is called a Gīta Bidārī.
It would have been a faulty division if it were done thus-
Janaga / namana / adhinā / yakaja / etc.
b) Pada Bidārī – This refers to division of melodic phrases.
When a Bidārī or a division is done so as to end such a division in one of the following notes, it is called Pada Bidārī:

Aṁśa (q.v.) Svara i.e., the Vādī note, or its Saṁvādī (q.v.) i.e., either the fourth or the fifth (q.v.) of the Aṁśa Svara, or Anuvādī (q.v.) i.e., major third or the major sixth, and also the Nyāsa Svara or the ending note. Now, the Nyāsa Svara can well be one of the foregoing notes.

When a division has thus been made, the ending note of such a division is called Apanyāsa Svara; it can thus, also be noted that an Apanyāsa Svara can either be an Aṁśa Svara, or its Saṁvādī or its Anuvādī. Nyāsa Svara can likewise be either Aṁśa, Saṁvādī or Anuvādī Svara.

Any note, which is not a Vivādī or dissonant note of the Aṁśa Svara can complete a division and in this case that particular note is called a Sanyāsa Svara. When the phrases are divided into still smaller divisions, the ending note, not being a Vivādī note to the Aṁśa Svara, is called Vinyāsa Svara. This last one definitely establishes that the phrases can be divided into smaller sections and the ending notes of these sections are called Vinyāsa Svaras. In this case there remains some doubt as to the difference between an Apanyāsa and a Sanyāsa Svara. Let us explain the above by citing examples:

Examples of Pada Bidārī by the phrases in Yamana Rāga. Aṁśa note or Vādī Svara of Yamana is G and Nyāsa Svara i.e., the ending note of Yamana generally speaking is 'S'.

(a)	Pada Bidārī using Aṁśa note	–	ṆRG
(b)	" " " Saṁvādī of Aṁśa note	–	mDN
(c)	" " " Anuvādī of Aṁśa note	–	mGP
(d)	" " " Nyāsa Svara of Yamana	–	ṆRS

In (a) the Aṁśa Svara becomes the Apanyāsa Svara, in (b) the Saṁvādī of the Aṁśa Svara becomes Apanyāsa, in (c) the Anuvādī and in (d) the Nyāsa Svara becomes Apanyāsa.

The examples of Sanyāsa Svara would follow later. The note, not being a Vivādī note of the Aṁśa Svara i.e., G in Yamana, is called Sanyāsa Svara if it is an ending note. In the present major diatonic scale D is not a Vivādī note of G, so D can be used as an ending note, thus:

(e) *Pada Bidārī using a note not Vivādī of Aṁśa note* – mND. It is to be particularly noted here that the Saṁvādī notes of G (here Vādī note in Yamana) are both N and D, but as N has been particularly mentioned as the Saṁvādī note in Yamana Rāga, D is to be ignored as a Saṁvādī note in Yamana.

Now let us deal with Vinyāsa Svara. A note which is not a Vivādī note to the Aṁśa Svara, can be an ending note to smaller divisions of a Pada or phrase. In this case we are considering phrases containing six notes instead of three since it would not be convenient to break such phrases into smaller divisions.

(f) *Divisions of Pada Bidārī using notes not Vivādī to Aṁśa note* – the entire Pada is mNDmDP and when broken into two mND, mDP both D and P are the Vinyāsa Svaras.

The foregoing descriptions of Nyāsa etc. lead us to conclude that

(A) Vocal or instrumental music ends in a Nyāsa Svara.

(B) A Pada Bidārī ends in an Apanyāsa Svara.

(C) A note which is neither a Vivādī Svara of Aṁśa note nor

itself an Apanyāsa Svara, can be an ending note and then it is called a Sanyāsa Svara.

(D) Vinyāsa Svara ends the smaller divisions of a Pada or Phrase.

57. Bola or Vāṇī

In instrumental music different ways of producing a sound, by striking, plucking or thumping etc., have been called Bolas in musical terminology to symbolise the actions. Different instruments have different Bolas. In most of the Indian string instruments only two Bola–alphabets are used:—

(1) *Inward* – It has been called Saṁlekha in Saṁgītaratnākara and is represented by Ḍā.

(2) *Outward* – Saṁgītaratnākara calls it Avalekha and is represented by Rā.

There is an exception to this rule. In Sarod, Ḍā is an outward and Rā is an inward stroke by a plectrum. Some follow this rule in bowing an Esrāra also.

In Vīṇā, the Bolas are struck inwards and in Mahatī Vīṇā, mostly found in Upper India, the Bolas are struck in vertical movements, in other words by 'down from up' movements. Only the Cikārī is struck by up movement and the Bola used is obviously Rā (or Ra). The Vīṇā is played with three fingers of the right hand. On the main strings the Bola struck by the middle finger in downward movement is called Ḍa, the Bola struck by the forefinger downwards is called Ga, but when both the fingers use upward Bolas –which is seldom done, both movements are called Ra. The Cikārīs are struck by the little finger in upward movement only and such Bola is called Ra as mentioned above. Thus the Bola alphabets employed in North Indian Vīṇā are Ḍa, Ga, Ra. Besides these Tā, Nā, Ghā, Ghighi, Gheghe, Gheghāya, Drār, Ḍagara, Ghanā, etc. Bolas are used by combining the Bola alphabets Ḍa, Ga, and Ra in different combinations.

In Rabāb, Suraśṛṅgāra, Sitār, Sarod, Esrāra etc. the only Bola alphabets are Ḍā and Rā and by combining these two alphabets in different ways, innumerable Bola phrases have been created e.g., (1) Ḍā, (2) Rā, (3) ḌāRā, (Ḍā and Rā both having one Mātrā (q.v.) or beat each) (4) Ḍere or Ḍiri (having one Mātrā or beat, i.e., Ḍā half a beat and Rā half a beat) (5) Drā, (6) Raḍā,

(7) Dredā, (8) Dredār (9) Ḍāḍār, (10) Rāḍār, (11) Ḍārār, (12) Rāḍrā, (13) Ḍāḍrā etc.
In pursuance of percussion Bola phrases various Bola phrases have been composed for use in instrumental music by two Bola alphabets Ḍā and Rā, e.g.,:

	|	|	|	|
Percussion Bola phrase	– Dhādhā	Tereketẹ	Dhāgeddhi	Ghenenāg
	|	|	|	|
Instrumental Bola phrase	– ḌāRā	Ḍereḍere	Ḍārāḍḍā	Rāḍāḍār etc.

Bola alphabets and phrases as used in percussion instruments:

(1) Ta, (2) Da, (3) Na, (4) Tā, (5) Ti, (6) Nā, (7) Nān, (8) Tet, (9) Te, (10) Ṭe, (11) Ḍe, (12) Ten, (13) Den, (14) Dhen, (15) Ga, (16) Gha, (17) Gā, (18) Ghā, (19) Ge, (20) Ghe, (21) Kat, (22) Ka, (23) Ke, (24) Thu, (25) Tun, (26) Dhiṁgar, (27) Dhāṁgar, (28) Dhāgeddhi, (29) Terkeṭ, (30) Takiṭ, (31) Krān, (32) Kredhāne, (33) Dhumākeṭe, (34) Jhāṁ, (35) Gur, (36) Thai, (37) Tāṁu, (38) Khur, (39) Tittā etc.

Percussion Bolas have been named 'Pāṭa' in Saṁgītaratnākara and reference has been made of 'Hasta Pāṭa' i.e., Bolas for manual use. The instrument 'Paṭaha' being the symbolic source of all percussion instruments, the word 'Pāṭa' has been derived from that instrument.

Generally speaking, what are called Bolas in instrumental music are known as Vāṇī for vocal music. Some examples of Vāṇīs are as follows:

(1) Tā, (2) Nā, (3) Dim, (4) Tum, (5) Nātā, (6) Dāni, (7) Dere, (8) Dṛm, (9) Num, (10) Ālālum, (11) Āli, (12) Tele, (13) Odāni, (14) Oder, (15) Dernā, (16) Neri etc.

These Vāṇīs or vocal Bolas are used in Ālāpa and Tarānās (q.v.); besides these the Bolas for percussion instruments are also sung sometimes. These Bolas or Vāṇīs carry no meaning, their only utility lies in their rhythmic implications. When used vocally, they help appreciate pure melodic compositions apart from the literary merit of a song which often diverts attention of the listening public from the melody. The theory that these meaningless Bolas have come down from the original doxological phrase 'Ananta Hari Nārāyaṇa' appears to be wrong. Saṁgītaratnākara uses 'Tena, Tena' which, of course, refers to God (vide 'Khuli', 'Mudi' and 'Naṣṭa Bolas').

58. Cakradāra

Any 'Ṭukḍā', 'Toḍā', 'Tāna' or 'Tihāī' that is repeated once or more to reach the 'Sama' is called Cakradāra Ṭukḍā or Toḍā etc. Usually these Ṭukḍās or Toḍās are played thrice to reach the 'Sama', but can be played more than three times. When played thrice it may appear to resemble an ordinary Tihāī (vide), and often it becomes difficult to know one from the other. Cakradāra Tihāī is often heard. Tihāī itself is a small melodic or rhythmic phrase played thrice to reach the Sama. In Cakradāra Tihāī this complete Tihāī is played thrice to reach the Sama, to the listeners that small melodic or rhythmic phrase appears to have been played three times three i.e., in nine cycles.

59. Cāla

Generally it means the 'Way' and also the 'Style' with reference to various things such as the style of Dhrupada or Ṭhumrī; simple Cāla (way) or complex Cāla, fast or slow Cāla, with reference to time or Laya, when Cāla means a style e.g., the Seniyā style or Masīdk͟hānī style etc. Both Calana and Cāla have been derived from the same root meaning 'To move', yet their musical applications are different, although a little vague (vide 'Bāj').

60. Calana

Literally it means 'Movement' or 'The way of moving'. Musically it means (1) convention in using notes in a particular Rāga (2) convention in the development of a Rāga. In percussion instruments, it means Kāyadā (Q̄āedā) (vide) although some musicians do not consider Kāyadā (Q̄āedā) and Calana analogous.

61. Capaka

Those percussion Bolas that are played with the flat of the left palm are known as Capaka Bolas. In stringed instruments those Bolas are produced in a like manner i.e., by applying the flat of the right or left palm sharply over all the strings together. During this the normal production of sound with plectrum is temporarily suspended. The sound produced in Capaka action is anything but melodic. Capaka is evidently a variety of Śabdālaṁkāra.

62. Caturaṅga

From amongst various meanings of 'Raṅga' the one meaning

'Variegated' can well be applied in this connection. 'Catuḥ' means four, hence Caturaṅga is a type of song in the category of K͟hayāl having four variegated elements viz., (1) Song, (2) Meaningless articulated sounds called Tarānā, (3) Articulated notes S R G M etc. and (4) Articulated rhythmic compositional phrases to be normally used in percussion instruments. Rarely can these be heard today.

63. Chanda

Rhythm. When a line, either of a song or of any other composition of articulated but meaningless sounds, with or without melody, is composed in such a way as to have a definite and regular pattern of accented and unaccented beats and also of a pleasing timbre, then that line acquires a characteristic of a rhythm or Chanda. Chanda is the basis for all Tālas, Mātras and Layas, as we call the music composed within the bounds of Tāla, rhythmic, as different from Ālāpa.

64. Chāyālaga

'Chāyā', is 'Shadow' and 'Laga' is 'Attached with'. A Rāga, composed with a shadow or touch of another Rāga, falls under the category of Chāyālaga. Evidently it is a mixed Rāga. There are three categories of Rāgas (1) Śudh (Śuddha) or pure (2) Chāyālaga and (3) Saṁkīrṇa (vide).

65. Cheḍ

Derived from the Hindi word 'Cheḍnā' meaning 'To sound by plucking or by striking'. Strings can either be played upon with a melody or merely be sounded by plucking, as in harpsichord or striking as in piano. Those strings in pluck instruments that are merely sounded and not played upon with melody are called Cheḍ strings generally. In particular, those strings that are struck to produce drones or Jhālā are called so.

66. Chūṭ

Derived from 'Chuṭnā' meaning to run, but in music it means to jump. When a note is produced by jumping from the same but in other gamut, the action is called 'Chūṭ' and is treated as a Śabdālaṁkāra. At present the jump from any note to another even in the same gamut is also called Chūṭ, the only condition being that one or more notes used in the Rāga will have to be scaled e.g., in the scale SRMPNṠ, SM or RP or MN are the instances of Chūṭ. Originally, SṠ would have been the only case of Chūṭ.

67. Cikārī

Onomatopoeic word to denote the strings sounded in Jhālā (vide 'Cheḍ').

68. Cillā (Chillāh)

A period of forty days is called Cillā – a Hindī word. During the stage of practice, the intending professional musicians take the vow of observing a Cillā, a mental resolve that during those forty days, barring meagre hours for sleep and food etc. they would practise the lessons on music for hours on end. Often they carry on a Cillā with or without a short break, for five, ten or twelve years, before they are permitted by their teachers to come out in public for demonstrations.

69. Classical Saṁgīta

What is classical Saṁgīta? Is it a particular Rāga creation or a particular Rāga composition by an old master? If we take only the creation of old masters as classical music then the next question may be asked – how old? Is there any limit? Besides, what would then be the fate of innumerable Rāga creations and musical compositions by contemporary masters?

It is not a Rāga out of so many mentioned in the Śāstras, nor a song, Saragam, or a Gat composition by old masters of the sixteenth century or earlier; it is the form of presentation that has evolved over so many centuries since Amīr Khusro, that is called classical and this form is in the constant process of evolution. The form of presentation of a Khayāl song prevalent fifty years ago is certainly not the same today, it has undergone gradual changes since then and it is the natural process of any living art.

A Rāga creation by a maestro yesterday is as much classical as Darbārīkānhaḍā of the sixteenth century. The only condition is that the new Rāga is presented in the conventional manner suitable for any of the form of Ālāpa, Dhrupada, Khayāl, Ṭhumrī, Ṭappā or Gat etc. There are conventional sequences of presentation of each of the foregoing forms, and that is classical presentation of a Rāga melody, generally known as classical music (Saṁgīta).

70. Ḍāgara Vāṇī

Vide 'Gīti' or 'Ālāpa'.

71. Dakśiṇa Bhāratīya

South Indian, also known as Carnatic with reference to music.

72. Damkham

This is a compound Hindi word. Kham means clapping of hands and Dam means restraint. With reference to rhythm this compound word means 'Restraint and claps', i.e., a rhythmic composition having unaccented and accented beats is said to have 'Damkham' variety of rhythm. e.g., Dhere Keṭe Tāg Dhā.

3|	|	|	|	|+
—	Dhere	keṭe	Tāg	Dhā

The Mātrā marked 3 is left unaccented and is called Dam while others are accented and are called Kham.

73. Deśī Saṁgīta

Regional music, i.e., all varieties of music other than the classical ones are called Deśī or regional music. Under this we have folk music, light music, etc. Kīrtana has often been reckoned as Deśī Saṁgīta although the present author prefers it to be called classical because of its nature and its tradition of nearly four centuries. In the Śāstras, the music employed for the worship of God was called Mārga Saṁgīta and all other varieties then prevalent were called Deśī Saṁgīta (vide 'Classical Saṁgīta' and 'Mārga Saṁgīta').

74. Dhā

It is a technical term to indicate the most important of the beats in a Tāla, in other words 'Sama', on which beat both the main musician and the accompanist meet together.

75. Dhāḍi

The father or the brother of a Dumnī is called Dhāḍi (vide 'Dumnī').

76. Dhaivata

The sixth of the Indian gamut of seven notes. Dhaivata or Dhā contains three Śrutis viz, Madantī, Rohiṇī and Ramyā; it itself is on this last Śruti Ramyā. Modern theorists have placed Dhā quite erroneously on its initial Śruti Madantī (vide 'Śruti').

77. Dhamāra

A variety of Tāla. When a Dhrupada is composed in the Dhamāra Tāla, it is usually known as Dhamāra. Such Dhrupadas are generally lighter in nature and are mostly love-songs. Whenever the songs depict the episodes of Holi festival, they are known as Horīs. Dhamāras mostly use Nauhāra Vāṇī and various Alaṁkāras forbidden in other Dhrupadas. In the days when Khayāl was unknown, Dhamāras used to lighten the effect of the sober grandeur of Dhrupadas on the audience who eagerly awaited its appearance and felt relieved on hearing it. This form of Dhrupada became so popular in those days that the name Dhamāra – a Tāla name - permanently stayed on to be applied to it (vide 'Ālāpa').

78. Dhātu

The body of a musical composition is called Dhātu. There are four and sometimes five Dhātus or paragraphs in a composition; often there are only two such in a lighter composition.

(a) *Udgrāha* – The opening paragraph or stanza of a composition is known as Udgrāha Dhātu.

(b) *Melāpaka* – The paragraph joining the opening paragraph and the 'Dhruva' paragraph, following it, is called Melāpaka Dhātu.

(c) *Dhruva* – The particular paragraph which is repeated from time to time, is called Dhruva Dhātu. At present, in all musical performances, a paragraph or a certain portion of the composition is often repeated after every improvisation done by the musician. The Śāstras hold that Melāpaka and Ābhoga Dhātus can be omitted but never the Dhruva Dhātu. From those compositions having three Dhātus or paragraphs only, the Melāpaka can be dropped, not the Dhruva.

(d) *Ābhoga* – The last paragraph or stanza of a composition and, in case of songs, the paragraph containing the name of the writer is called the Ābhoga Dhātu.

(e) *Antara or Antarā* – If a paragraph is introduced between the Dhruva and Ābhoga, then it is known as Antara or Antarā Dhātu, according to Śāstras. Dhātus, as explained, resemble the Tukas Aṁśa, Kali or Caraṇa used in the modern times. Dhruva is similar to the Sthāyī Tuka, Antarā and Ābhoga are also the same as found at present. We can however, find some similarity between Melāpaka Dhātu and Sañcārī Tuka. Melāpaka combines the Udgrāha and the Dhruva, so also Sañcārī, it pervades through Sthāyī and Antarā Tuka, in a way combining both. Udgrāha, as mentioned and explained in the Śāstras, is obsolescent today but we can draw a similarity between this and the sort of a prelude or overture which invariably appears to introduce a Rāga at the beginning of a musical performance at present, and which is commonly known as 'Āucar' (vide Ālāpa). At present another paragraph is being used in instrumental Gat—composition. This paragraph is called Māṁjā or Māṁjhā which is placed between Sthāyī and Antarā. Formerly it was a part of Sthāyī (vide 'Tuka').

79. Ḍhīmā Laya

Vide 'Laya'.

80. Dhrupada

Literally 'Dhruva' means immovable, unalterable or permanent. In this sense God is the only 'Dhruva' and any literary composition dealing with the various attributes and praises of God is known as 'Dhruva Pada'. The contraction of 'Dhruva Pada' has come to be known as 'Dhrupada'. It has not yet been definitely known as to when the present day 'Dhrupada' came into being. It is said that both Nāyaka Gopāla and Baijū Bāvrā were responsible for the inception of Dhrupada as found today. Some hold that Rājā Mānsingh of Gwālior (1486 -1526) introduced the Dhrupada. At present the Dhrupadas composed by Miyān Tānsen seem to have been recognised as the ideal prototype. Ustāds belonging to some of the Gharānās sing Dhrupadas composed by Baijū Bāvrā or Nāyaka Gopāla, but such Gharānās are rare; besides their history is mostly based on hearsay. As such no dependable information can be had in this respect. Most of the Dhrupadas prevalent in Northern India today were either composed and sung by Miyān Tānsen or by other renowned composers after him.

Miyān Tānsen's lineage has been divided into three sections. His direct line, also known as Rabābī Gharānā, used to compose Dhrupada in Gauḍahāra Vāṇī. His daughter's line known as Binkār Gharānā used Ḍāgara, Nauhāra and Khaṇḍāra Vāṇīs in Dhrupada. These are the two main lines of Miyān Tānsen.

However, one of his sons, Sūrat Sen, who went to Jaipur, founded the Seniyā Gharānā of Jaipur. This Gharānā is still recognised as Jaipur—Seniyā Gharānā (vide 'Gharānā').

A Dhrupada has four or five stanzas, usually four viz., Sthāyī, Antarā, Sañcārī and Ābhoga. Some name Sañcārī as Bhoga but descendants of Tānsen consider 'Bhoga' to be a separate stanza (vide 'Sthāyī etc.). Of all the songs the Dhrupadas are known to be the most sober and mostly contain elements of abstention, piety and wisdom. Also, Dhrupadas use only the sober i.e., slow Tālas. Light Tālas i.e., quick Tālas, are not to be used with Dhrupada. Dhrupada compositions are either doxological or contain praises to the kings. Some contain philosophical preachings also. Some contain emotional activities of Srī Kṛṣṇa. Dhrupadas composed in Dhamāra Tāla are known as Dhamāras, those composed in Jhāṁptāla are known as Sādarās and those composed in Dhamāra Tāla and containing the activities of Lord Kṛṣṇa on the occasion of the spring festival are known as Horīs. Sometimes even Ṭappās containing the same descriptions are known as Horīs but Horī usually indicates Dhrupadas in Dhamāra Tāla.

81. Dhuna

Any melody composition that is not bound by the Rāga rules but depends on freelance artistic promptings is called a Dhuna. There are many melodies known by Rāga names which the experts still call Dhuna, such as Kāphī, Dhānī and many others. Although the scale with Komala G and Komala N is called Kāphī Ṭhāṭa and is the basic scale in our Śāstras, the melody known as Kāphī is considered by many experts as a Dhuna. A Dhuna may sometimes contain shades of many Rāgas.

82. Dhuyā

Common name for Dhruva. That stanza or line of a song which is repeated often is called Dhuyā. The Sthāyī portion of a song can be called a Dhuyā also. The portion "Jaya he, Jaya he, Jaya Jaya Jaya Jaya he" of Indian National Anthem is the Dhuyā.

83. Dhvani

Sanskrit name for sound. Although every note is a sound, every sound is not a note (vide 'Svara').

84. Druta Laya

Fast tempo – the word is relative since it is twice as fast as Madhya laya or medium tempo (vide 'Laya').

85. Dumnī or Domnī

Women who earn their living by musical profession only in front of the ladies in Pardā and never come out before the males, are known as Dumnīs.

86. Gamaka

It is an important variety of Śabdālaṁkāra (vide Alaṁkāra). A very wide scope is given to it in the Śāstras. Though various Alaṁkāras fall under this category, the present practice has been to limit it to a particular variety of Alaṁkāra viz., a particular way to produce and often repeat a particular note or a series of notes taking the grace of either the previous note or the following note. For example:

(1) *Ascending Gamaka* – S^R R^G G^M M^P. Here after S has been articulated the grace of R is added; next when R is articulated the grace of G is added to it and so on till the series is completed, the whole thing being an unbroken continuity. The principal notes i.e., the notes on top right corners of which the graces have been added, should each appear independent and unconnected to the next principal note. This may appear contradictory since already this has been used as grace note, but the notes with their graces should be kept independent by putting a gap, ordinarily imperceptible, before going to the next note, that is by making the graces terminate abruptly.

(2) *Descending Gamaka* – ${}^{R}S$ ${}^{G}R$ ${}^{M}G$ ${}^{P}M$ – This is just like the above excepting that the graces come before the principal note as they appear on the top left corner of the principal notes. Here the trace of the grace note, first articulated, sways to the principal note which dwells a little longer than the grace note before going to the next grace note. These Gamakas are many times less difficult in practice than they appear in theory demonstrations. Sometimes musicians call a certain Alaṁkāra like – Āśa (vide) as Gamaka and use it in Dhrupada. Most of the varieties of Gamaka are used in Khaṇḍāra Vāṇī style of music. We may now deal with the varieties and descriptions of Gamaka as found in the Śāstras.

Fifteen varieties of Gamaka in Saṁgītaratnākara:

(1) *Tiripa* – Pleasing vibration of sound resembling that of Ḍamarū (vide) i.e., a small double-headed drum, shaped like an hour-glass. At present the speed of this vibration of sound is four times in a beat, e.g., SSSS, RRRR etc.

(2) *Sphurita* – Same as above but three times in a beat e.g., SSS, RRR etc.

(3) *Kampita* – Same as above but twice in a beat e.g., SS, RR, GG etc.

(4) *Līna* – Same as above but once in a beat e.g., S, R, G, M etc.

(5) *Āndolita* – Same as above but the speed is once in half a beat. This should not be confused with Kampita where the speed is twice in a beat. In other words, two sounds should be actually produced in a beat. In Āndolita, on the other hand, only one sound should take up half the beat and the other half should remain unsounded. For example, S -, R -, G -, etc. One note and the dash constitute one beat.

(6) *Bali* – A mixture of quick, asymmetrical and heterogeneous vibration of sounds e.g., SSS, GGG, PP, RR, GGG, RS.

(7) *Tribhinna* – A quick vibration of sounds spread over the three i.e., lower, middle and upper gamuts e.g., P̣ P̣ P̣, SSS, NNN, DDD, GGG, RRR, DDD, NN, ṠṠ.

(8) *Kurula* – It is almost like Bali (above) but with some knot of notes inserted in between and to be produced very softly e.g., SSS, GGG, RGRGR, GGG, MMM, DPDPM, GGG, RGRGRS. Here we prefer to call RGRGR, DPDPM, RGRGRS, knots since the Śāstras name them as Granthis. As a matter of fact any small and irregular cluster of notes can be called a 'Knot'.

(9) *Āhata* – This is the one we have already discussed under Descending Gamaka.

(10) *Ullāsita* – Vide Ascending Gamaka.

(11) *Plāvita* – A vibration where each note is elongated to three beats e.g., S - -, R - - etc.

(12) *Gumphita* – A vibration which is pleasing and at the same time sombre and deep – e.g., GS__PmG; the Mīḍ connecting S and P is elongated and deep.

(13) *Mudrita* – A vibration produced by humming with lips unparted.

(14) *Nāmita* – When the sequence of notes follows in the descending order e.g., Ṡ N, ND, DP, etc.

(15) *Miśrita* – A mixture of all or some varieties mentioned above, e.g., SSS, GGG, RRR, MMM, DD, PP, RR, GG, N D P M G R S etc.

The following are the names of the Gamakas mentioned in Saṁgīta-Pārijāta. Descriptions are unnecessary.

(1) Cyavita, (2) Kaṁpita, (3) Pratyāhata, (4) Dvirāhata, (5) Sphurita, (6) Anāhata, (7) Śānta, (8) Tiripa, (9) Gharṣaṇa (10) Avagharṣaṇa, (11) Vikarṣaṇa (12) Svasthāna, (13) Agrāvasthāna, (14) Kartarī, (15) Punaḥsvasthāna, (16) Sphuṭa, (17) Naimnya, (18) Suḍhālu, (19) Gumphita, (20) Mudrā.

The names of the twentytwo Gamakas in circulation in the Seniyā Gharānā:

(1) Humpita, (2) Khādat, (3) Gaṇapat, (4) Āhata, (5) Andāhata, (6) Āndolita, (7) Prahata, (8) Bruvāhata, (9) Durāhata, (10) Atharat, (11) Śānta, (12) Tiripa, (13) Khareśana, (14) Okhareśana, (15) Nisuthāna, (16) Okharsuthāna, (17) Kartarī, (18) Syuṁt, (19) Nimni, (20) Dhāla, (21) Suhāna, (22) Madarā.

87. Gāna

Generally a song but specifically the literary composition of a song without music; in the Śāstras this is known as 'Mātu'.

88. Gāndhāra

The third note of the Indian gamut of seven notes. The root meaning of this note is not clearly given and opinions about it vary considerably. In the Śāstras the Gāndhāra is allotted two Śrutis viz., Raudrī and Krodhā and is placed on the latter. Whenever Gāndhāra takes two Śrutis from the following note Madhyama and thus becomes a note of four Śrutis, it is called Antara-Gāndhāra. This is our present day natural Gāndhāra. As a result, the following note Madhyama is left with two Śrutis only. The Antara Gāndhāra, after taking two Śrutis from Madhyama, acquires four Śrutis viz., Raudrī, Krodhā, Vajrikā and Prasāriṇī and is itself placed on the last. But if Gāndhāra takes only one of the four Śrutis of Madhyama i.e., if it stays on the Vajrikā Śruti, it is known as Sādhāraṇa Gāndhāra having three Śrutis. This Sādhāraṇa Gāndhāra is known as Tīvra Komala Gāndhāra i.e., sharpened flat Gāndhāra and it lies in between the flat and the natural (vide 'Śruti').

89. Gāndhāra Grāma

Mention has been made of three Grāmas in the Śāstras, viz, Ṣaḍja Grāma, Madhyama Grāma and Gāndhāra Grāma. Ṣaḍja and Madhyama Grāmas were used in the ancient days for mundane music and the use of Gāndhāra Grāma, being reserved for the higher world, was forbidden. The inter-relation of the notes in three Grāmas differs in the number of Śruti intervals between the notes thus: The allotment of Śrutis in Ṣaḍja Grāma:
S, M, P four Śrutis each, R, D three Śrutis each and G, N two Śrutis each; in tabular form:-

IIII	III	II	IIII	IIII	III	II	IIII
S	R	G	M	P	D	N	(Ṡ)

The allotment of Śrutis in Madhyama Grāma:
S, M, D four Śrutis each, R, P three Śrutis each and G, N two Śrutis each; in tabular form:-

IIII	III	II	IIII	III	IIII	II	IIII
S	R	G	M	P	D	N	(Ṡ)

The allotment of Śrutis in Gāndhāra Grāma:
G, N four Śrutis each, S, M, P, D three Śrutis each and R two Śrutis.
In tabular form:-

III	II	IIII	III	III	III	IIII	III
S	R	G	M	P	D	N	(Ṡ)

90. Gat

Derived from Gati or motion. However, it is not precisely known how a particular composition for instrumental music has come to be known as Gat. Many say that the Gat has motion, but so have other musical compositions such as Dhrupada, K͟hayāl etc. It appears likely that there could not be found any other name for such compositions for instrumental music and so the name Gat has been used as in case of Śruti. Gat is a melodic composition bound by rhythm using Varṇas (notes) and Bolas (strokes) to be used in instrumental music. Originally such Gats were composed in pursuance of K͟hayāls and Tarānās (vide). There are mainly two types of Gats (1) Masīdk͟hānī (2) Rezāk͟hānī. (Vide Masīdk͟hānī and Rezākhānī). Masīdkhānī Gats follow the style of slow and medium Khayāls and Rezākhānī Gats the style of Tarānās which are usually fast in tempo. In Gat composition the presence of the stanzas viz., Sthāyī and Antarā can be found as in Khayāls. In modern times another stanza named Mānjhā i.e., 'Middle' has been added between Sthāyī and Antarā which takes the form and scope of Sañcārī Tuk or Stanza. Compositions for percussion instruments commonly known as Ṭhekās (vide) are also called Gats. Some hold that Kāyadā (Qāedā) (vide) of a Ṭhekā is also known as Gat and some again consider long compositional phrases for percussion instruments without Tihāī as Gats e.g., –

+| | | | 2| | | |
Ghenā Katā Gheghe Nāk Tāg Gheghe Nāke Dhin
0| | | | 3| | | |
Dhage Trikit Tunā Katā Gheghe Nāk Gheghe Nāk
+| | | | 2| | | |
Tāg Gheghe Nāk Dhene Dhāge Trikit Tunā Gheghe
0| | | | 3| | | |
Nāke Trikit Tunā Gheghe Nāke Trikit Tunā Katā.

91. Gāthika

Vide 'Tāna'.

92. Gati

Another name for the popular meaning of Laya (vide). Literally it means 'Motion' or 'Movement'. Gat as played in instrumental music has taken its name from Gati but it is not clear how.

93. Gauḍī Gīti

Vide 'Gīti'.

94. Gāyaka

Singer. The Śāstras mention five classes of singers:

(1) *Śikṣākāra* (teacher) – one who is expert in imparting lessons in singing.
(2) *Anukāra* (copyist) – one who copies the singing of others.
(3) *Rasika* (sentimental) – one who sings being absorbed in sentiment.
(4) *Raṁjaka* – one who sings readily to please the listeners.

(5) *Bhāvuka* (imaginative) – the singer who is capable of effecting new developments in musical culture.

95. Gāyaka Doṣas

Defects of a singer:

(1) To sing with locked jaw,
(2) Loud and unattractive voice,
(3) The sound of inhaling by mouth,
(4) Fright,
(5) Attempt of finishing the song with needless haste,
(6) Uncontrollable tremor in voice and absence of steadiness,
(7) Opening the mouth vary widely while singing,
(8) The deviation of notes from their proper places,
(9) Harsh voice resembling a 'Caw',
(10) Faltering and missing the beats of a Tāla,
(11) Singing with the throat stretched up and forward,
(12) Singing with voice resembling the bleat of a goat,
(13) Singing with the veins of forehead, face and throat perceptibly swollen,
(14) The throat taking the shape of a gourd while singing,
(15) Singing with the throat unusually bent,
(16) Stretching the body while singing,
(17) Singing with eyes closed,
(18) Singing without sentiment,
(19) Using unusable notes,
(20) Indistinct articulation,
(21) The voice that does not reach either the depth of heart, or the throat or the cerebral region i.e., a muffled voice,
(22) Unsettled mind,
(23) To mix pure and Chāyālaga Rāgas without knowing the rules,
(24) Inattention,
(25) To sing in a nasal voice.

96. Gāyaka Guṇas

Virtues or good qualities of a singer:

(1) Charming voice,
(2) Dear to the sight,

(3) Expert ability in Graha and Nyāsa; at present the quality of starting and ending the music well,
(4) Expert knowledge of Rāgas and Rāginīs,
(5) Expert knowledge both in rhythmic and in a-rhythmic music,
(6) Expert in the knowledge of all the varieties of Alaṁkāras,
(7) Voice independent of instruments,
(8) Knowledge of Tāla, tirelessness, experience in pure and mixed Rāgas, knowledge of unusable notes in a Rāga,
(9) Capability of demonstrating Sthāyī, Sañcārī etc. Varṇas easily,
(10) Shunning of all defects,
(11) Knowledge of Laya,
(12) The capability of performing a musical demonstration in a well-orderly manner,
(13) Power of comprehension,
(14) Unrestricted flow of the voice,
(15) The charming quality of songs even if sung in desolation,
(16) Wise in the worship of God,
(17) The capability of maintaining the purity of tradition or Gharānā of one's Guru (teacher),
(18) Expert ability in the culture of music.

97. Gazal (G͟hazal)

Originally love songs composed in Persian were known as G͟hazals. At present, love songs or any other songs composed in different languages and sung in the G͟hazal—style also pass as G͟hazals.

98. Gharānā

Literally means lineage. In Hindustāni music there are different Gharānās each differing from the other in marked diversity in the exposition of Rāgas, in the use of Alaṁkāras, in the use of Vāṇīs or ways etc. Each of these diverse Gharānās impresses the listeners with variety of aesthetic pleasure, each enjoyable in a distinct way. Whenever any worthy innovation is brought about by a creative musician and if that innovation has a lasting quality then that becomes a distinct characteristic of all the generations of pupils belonging to that lineage thus establishing a Gharānā. Gharānā also means 'Style' in a loose sense, and in the field of Hindustāni music, there have evolved various styles in the presentation of music. A particular Rāga can be presented in diverse styles in different Gharānās; even the same composition can be presented differently with equal charm. Some theoreticians had tried to underestimate and undermine the importance of Gharānās by imputing mean and selfish motives to the traditional musicians but their attempts had failed hoplessly. The result is that today the listening public has become more conscious to appreciate different musical expositions according to different Gharānās.

99. Ghaṣiṭ

A Hindi name for Āśa. In the Śāstras this has been named 'Khaśita' (vide 'Āśa').

100. Gīta

The general name for all varieties of songs. Specifically it indicates the folk songs.

101. Gīta Bidārī

According to the Śāstras, it is analogous to Gīta Khaṇḍa. Bidārī literally means 'That which pierces', hence here the thing that pierces a song into portions (vide 'Bidārī').

102. Gīta Khaṇḍa

Khaṇḍa is a part. A small part of a song is called Gīta Khaṇḍa. Each of the four stanzas of a song can be called Gīta Khaṇḍa in a general way, but a portion of a line is also known as Gīta Khaṇḍa viz., the portion of the Sthāyī usually known as Mukha of Sthāyī. Mukha literally means the mouth but here the meaning should be the fore or principal part since it is this portion that is repeated throughout the performance after demonstrating each Tāna or Bāṁta or whatever extempore Vistāra is done so that the performer can revert to the main composition of a song. Usually this part ends in the principal 'Sama'.

103. Gīti

Generally it means 'Gīta'. In a special sense, it means the way of singing. There are five ways of singing mentioned in the Śāstras and it is also mentioned that these Gītis are the pillars of Rāgas and to each Gīti has been allotted several particular Rāgas.

(1) *Śuddhā Gīti* – This uses straight and soft notes.
(2) *Bhinnā Gīti* – This uses the notes articulated fast and charming Gamaka Alaṁkāras.
(3) *Gauḍī Gīti* – Sober, unbroken and using suitable Gamaka Alaṁkāras in all the three Gamuts, Mandra (lower), Madhya (middle) and Tāra (upper).
(4) *Vesarā* or *Vegasvarā* – (Vega is speed, Svara is having notes, i.e., in which notes are used in speed). Speed marks this Gīti.
(5) *Sādhāraṇī* or *Sādhāraṇa Gīti* – Means common Gīti i.e., in this all the other Gītis have been blended. Some correspondence is evident between these Gītis and Vāṇīs as commonly used at present in Ālāpa and Dhrupada. Śuddhā Gīti corresponds with Ḍāgara Vāṇī. Bhinnā Gīti corresponds with Khaṇḍāra Vāṇī. Gauḍī Gīti corresponds with Gauḍahāra or Gobarahāra Vāṇī. Sādhāraṇī Gīti corresponds with Nauhāra Vāṇī. Now we are left with Vesarā or Vegasvarā Gīti and it can be held that this Gīti corresponds with any song that is marked for speed, generally speaking (vide 'Vāṇīs' under 'Ālāpa').

104. Giṭkārī

Perhaps derived coloquially from Gīta-Kriyā i.e., performing a Gīta or Song. In present musical parlance it is a Śabdālaṁkāra and is another name for Khaṭkā. In vocal music what is known as Giṭkārī is called Khaṭkā in instrumental music (vide 'Khaṭkā').

105. Gobarahāra Vāṇī

A name for Gauḍahāra Vāṇī (vide 'Ālāpa' and 'Gīti').

106. Graha

Literal meaning is 'To grasp'. Musically, it indicates the note formerly used to begin a Rāga with. Although not given its former importance at present, many Rāgas use a particular note as the Graha Svara, e.g., Yamaṇa often takes Ṇ as its Graha Svara, Bhairavī and Bhīmapalāśrī take ṇ as their Graha Svara. The use of this Graha Svara is regulated by mainly three rules – (1) Aṁśa Svara or the principal note may be used as the Graha Svara, (2) Saṁvādī Svara i.e., consonant note or Anuvādī i.e., assonant note of the Aṁśa Svara may be thus used, and (3) The tonic i.e., Ṣaḍja can be used as the Graha Svara.

107. Grāma

Literally means a village. In music it carries the same meaning, but only in a figurative sense. The gamut in which can be found the assemblage of Murchanā, Krama, Tāna, Varṇas, Alaṁkāras and Jātis is called a Grāma. The Śāstras mention three types of Grāmas viz., Ṣaḍja Grāma, Madhyama Grāma and Gāndhāra Grāma and are differentiated by the different distribution of Śrutis in each (vide 'Gāndhāra Grāma').

Mention has been made of Grāma-Rāgas in the Śāstras but no reference has been made here for their obsolescence. In modern use the regions of scale are also known as Grāmas viz., Mandra (Lower), Madhya (Middle) and Tāra (Upper) Grāmas.

108. Halak Tāna

Vide 'Tāna'.

109. Halkā

A Svara composition or Vistāra in which the Svarapadas or phrases gradually diminish in size e.g.,

GGRS RGRG | MMGR GMGM | PPMG MP | DDPM PD | NNDP | MMGR | GG | RR | S |

The phrases are separated by vertical lines.

110. Harmony

Originally, the Western music was based on melody, a sort of freelance compositions according to the mood and creative power of the composer, similar to Indian Dhunas (q.v.). However, it was not so much bound by laws as our Rāga System is. The Western musicians and composers were thoroughly conversant with the notes, scales, octaves, thirds, fourths and fifths – that is, about the fundamentals of notes and their inter-relation. These fundamentals are the same as according to our Śāstras— Svara, Grāma, Vādī, Saṁvādī, Anuvādī etc. We also know the importance of the double, fourth, fifth and the third, which are, in our terms, bound to the fundamental note S by Vādī—Saṁvādī or Vādī—Anuvādī (third) relationship. According to the Śāstras, the doubles, the fourths and the fifths are Saṁvādī and the thirds Anuvādī.

In Western countries 'Plain Song' was sung in the churches in a congregation by women, men and children. Naturally it was not possible for all to stick to one scale, so it was sung in different Mūrchanās suiting the range of voice of the participants and the effect of Mūrchanās was pleasing. Because of its pleasing effect, some musicians were prompted to do some research work along this line and decided that the Mūrchanās used should be of the fundamental note, its double or its fourth or its fifth. As a result each note of the song expressed itself not singly but conjointly with its double, fourths and fifths. This in a nutshell, is the origin of harmony.

Since the notes were not expressed alone but together with their Saṁvādīs, so these two notes, thus punched, were known not as notes but as chords, and this system of singing was known as 'Organum'. Later, another system, known as 'Pedal' was invented in which the fundamental and its fifth used to be sounded continuously throughout singing.

From the 10th century to the 14th century A.D., various researches were done by different musical scholars and the use of third and the sixth note came into being, and what was hitherto a chord of two notes became a triad of three notes. From the 14th century A.D., various experiments were done with harmony and by the 15th century the Western music completely shifted from melody to harmony. With the development of harmony, the concept of counterpoint also emerged.

Indian Rāga music is based on the juxtaposition of individual notes while Western music is based on the succession or juxtaposition of triads i.e., three notes sounded simultaneously. This is known as music based on harmony, since the triads were then mostly composed of Vādī, Saṁvādī and Anuvādī Svaras e.g., SGP, MDṠ, RMD etc. If the individual notes of a triad are arranged in a uniform order i.e., the first notes, the second notes, and the third notes of all the triads of a composition are arranged in succession so that the successions of all the first notes, the second notes and the third notes produce three individual melodies pleasing to hear, then the original composition based on the succession of triads is called a counterpoint. Pure harmonic music does not lay as much stress on the underlying melody as on the triads themselves, but in the counterpoint both the triads and the melodies produced by their succession are equally appreciated.

Western connoisseurs and intellectuals consider harmony as vertical and melody as horizontal music, so a counterpoint is to be appreciated in both the ways simultaneously. The power for such appreciation is to be developed. After counterpoint, other forms of music such as canon, fugue etc. have been devised but their description is irrelevant for the present purpose. If the science of harmony is applied to Indian Rāga music, it will certainly come under the category of counterpoint and by the use of triads the Rāga laws will be violated at every step. As such, it can be said without the least hesitation that harmony or counterpoint is contrary to Rāga music.

111. Hindustāni Paddhati

The system of the Upper Indian Classical Music.

112. Imdādkhānī

Imdād Khān was born in Etāvā in Uttar Pradesh in India. His father Sahabdād Husayn Khān was a son of the brother-in-law of Haddu Khān, the famous Khayāl singer and was brought up under his roof. Sahabdād learnt Khayāl and also played on the Sitār. Imdād Khān also learnt songs and Sitār from his father. After the death of Sahabdād, Imdād Khān learnt Sitār from different Sitār players and evolved his own style of Sitār playing greatly improving on the then Sitār and Surabahār playing techniques. Since about 1920 it is his style of Sitār playing that has been holding the musical field firmly and predominantly. Sitār players of different Gharānās and styles have since been greatly influenced by this style. After Imdād Khān's death, his sons the late Ināyat Khān and the late Wahid Khān became famous by following their father's style. Ināyat Khān remained the foremost Sitār player of India for a quarter of a century till his death in 1938. His sons Vilāyet Khān and Imārat Khān are very well-known instrumentalists and Vilāyet is undoubtedly one of the best Sitār players of India today. Vilāyet has also evolved a style of his own, suiting the demands of the lay public and obviously with modern trend and less classical in character. Four generations of Sitār players have certainly established a classical style which we call Imdādkhānī style of Sitār playing.

Here is a comparison of the Imdādkhānī style with that of the previous style.

Style of Sitār & Surabahār playing followed by original Seniyās belonging to the Gharānā of Tānsen	**Imdādkhānī style of Sitār & Surabahār playing evolved by Imdād Khān**
(1) Surabahār played Ālāpa in Dhrupada style imitating the style of Vīṇā in which Mīḍ was limited to four notes only.	(1) Surabahār combined both the Dhrupada and the Khayāl style with various Alaṁkāras prohibited in Dhrupada style. Miḍ limit extended to seven notes.
(2) As in Vīṇā, two or three right-hand fingers were put into use in producing sound in Surabahār. Cikārī was to be played with the right little finger.	(2) Only the right fore finger produced everything required in Surabahār including the Cikārī.
(3) Limited scope for Alaṁkāras	(3) Alaṁkāra-scope made unlimited.
(4) Cikārī or Jhālā was rarely played and on Sitār Jhālā was never played.	(4) Cikārī or Jhālā became one of the most important sections of instrumental music.
(5) Gamaka Tāna, Halak Tāna and Tihāī etc. were very rarely played. The Sitār players mostly used the Vistāra style.	(5) All vocal Tānas, percussion Bolas and Paraṇas and innumerable varieties of Tāna and Tihāī were introduced.
(6) There was no cut and dried sequence in the playing of Gat-Toḍā; it had no speciality nor diversity in exposition. The Gat and Vistāra were the only things played on the Sitār.	(6) Gat-Toḍā was enriched by the introduction of the sequence of Ālāpa in 12 stages (vide Ālāpa). Masīdkhānī Gat underwent complete renovation with scope greatly increased. The modern practice has been to call it modern Masīdkhānī but the present writer prefers to call it Imdādkhānī.

A Sitār belonging to Jaipur Seniyā Gharānā was sent for repairs to Messrs Kānāilāl Brothers, the foremost Sitār makers of India. The proprietor, the late Kānāilāl Dās, pointing to the Sitār, remarked to the present author "Is it a fact that Jaipur Gharānā does not use Jhālā?" Actually no strings were provided for Cikārī in that Sitār. The late Prof. Barkat U'l-lāh Khān, the famous Sitār player of Seniyā Gharānā had only one gramophone record of his Sitār recital. The record is still with the present writer. Not as much as a drone besides the melody played on the main string could be heard in that record, let alone a Cikārī. Obviously, Prof. Barkat U'l-lāh belonged to the Seniyā Gharānā of pre-Imdādkhānī period and style.

In this connection, an eminent thinker and music critic, the late D.P. Mukherjee, wrote to the present writer:

"In support of history you can use the word 'Imdādkhānī Style'. It was in this way that 'Gharānā', 'Style', 'Cāl' 'Convention' were brought into existence in Literature, in Art, in Music, in Architecture." (vide 'Vādya' and 'Masīdkhānī').

113. Jābaḍā

It is a variety of Tānas articulated especially with the movement of jaw. Some hold that the Tānas articulated indistinctly are also known as Jābaḍā Tānas (vide 'Tāna').

114. Janaka Rāga

Vide 'Ṭhāṭa'.

115. Janya Rāga

Vide 'Ṭhāṭa'.

116. Jāti

According to the Śāstras, Jāti is so called owing to its being born of two Grāmas viz., 'Ṣaḍja Grāma' and 'Madhyama Grāma'.

Compositions using Varṇas (notes) and Alaṁkāras have been classified under Jātis. There are seven types of Śuddha or pure Jātis, each taking the name of a note viz., (1) Ṣāḍjī, (2) Ārṣabhī (from Ṛsabha) (3) Gāndhārī, (4) Madhyamā, (5) Pañcamī, (6) Dhaivatī, and (7) Naiṣādī or Niṣādī. There are various rules for pure and mixed Jātis mentioned in details in the Śāstras but it is needless to discuss them here as Jātis are no longer in use. Barring the pure Jātis mentioned above, there are about 129 mixed Jātis. Indian modes were known as Jātis until Rāga names replaced them. In modern use Jāti means class in music, and is used to denote:

(1) Quantitative class of scales, e.g.,

(a) Auḍuva Jāti or Pentatonic class i.e., scales using five notes.
(b) Ṣāḍava Jāti or Hexatonic class i.e., scales using six notes, and
(c) Sampūrṇa Jāti or Heptatonic class using all the seven notes. There are mixed classes under this classification taking into consideration the ascent and the descent. The following table explains all the varieties of Jātis with the name of an example Rāga for each;

	Ascent	Descent	Name of Jāti	Example Rāga
(1)	Sampūrṇa	Sampūrṇa	Sampūrṇa	Yamana
(2)	Ṣāḍava	Ṣāḍava	Ṣāḍava	Puriyā
(3)	Auḍuva	Auḍuva	Auḍuva	Bhūpālī
(4)	Sampūrṇa	Ṣāḍava	Sampūrṇa-Ṣāḍava	Zilaf
(5)	Sampūrṇa	Auḍuva	Sampūrṇa-Auḍuva	Cittamohinī
(6)	Ṣāḍava	Sampūrṇa	Ṣāḍava-Sampūrṇa	Khamāj
(7)	Ṣāḍava	Auḍuva	Ṣāḍava-Auḍuva	Chāyālī Toḍī
(8)	Auḍuva	Sampūrṇa	Auḍuva-Sampūrṇa	Deśa
(9)	Auḍuva	Ṣāḍava	Auḍuva-Ṣāḍava	Sohinī

Even in the above classification, mention has been made of Vakra i.e., notes used not in proper or natural order either in ascent or in descent or in both e.g., SMGPNDNṠ (ascent) – NDPMGMRS (descent). This is called Vakra Jāti having both ascent and descent order (vide Kūṭa Tāna).

(2) Qualitative class of Rāgas e.g.,

(a) Śuddha Jāti or pure class
(b) Chāyālaga Jāti or Rāga having a shadow of another Rāga
(c) Saṁkīrṇa Jāti or Rāga having several Rāgas mixed together (vide 'Śuddha', 'Chāyālaga' and 'Saṁkīrṇa').

117. Javāb Saṁgat

'Saṁgat' is accompaniment and 'Javāb' means 'In reply'. When the principal musician demonstrates various melodic and rhythmic phrases and after finishing those comes back to the original composition, the percussionist in the meantime reproduces rhythmic phrases of the same variety in reply to the former.

118. Jhālā

A Śabdālaṁkāra. Continuous playing of the drone strings of a pluck stringed instrument is called Jhālā. It is an onomatopoeic word. Although it appears continuous, actually Jhālā is not so, and is played by strokes alternately with the melody on the main string. Because of its speed it appears continuous and serves as a harmonic background for a gradual and slow unfolding of a melodic motif. Jhālā, with its innumerable rhythmic variations, is one of the most important and necessary constituents of instrumental music. The fundamental Bolas of a Jhālā are Ḍā in melodic string followed by Rā Rā Rā in the drones - four making a unit. Vocalists often copy this instrumental Śabdālaṁkāra by uttering Tā Nā Nā Nā in melody.

119. Jhaṁkāra

Onomatopoeic word for Jhālā (vide). In a general sense: twang produced by several strings tuned in consonance or in a pleasing manner.

120. Jhārā

A Śabdālaṁkāra. Loosely another name for Jhālā (vide). In the Imdādkhānī Gharānā (vide) the extremely quick and alternate succession of Bolas Ḍā and Rā on the main melody string is called Jhārā (vide 'Bolas').

121. Jhaṭkā

A Śabdālaṁkāra to indicate a note or a small phrase of notes produced in an unexpected and sudden jerk (vide 'Alaṁkāra').

122. Joḍ

The meaning of this Hindi word is 'Connection' or 'By which things are connected'. Why the middle portion of an Ālāpa is called Joḍ has never been logically explained by any one anywhere. The author is explaining the word according to his own lights. Ālāpa has two portions (1) A-rhythmic and (2) Rhythmic, which are commonly known as (1) Ālāpa and (2) Tāra-paraṇa including Jhālā. Joḍ serves the purpose of a connecting link between the two so that the transition may be smooth enough not to cause any break or jar in the whole ensemble. Having just a glimpse of coming rhythmic portion supplies this smooth transition (vide 'Ālāpa').

123. Joyārī or Javārī

A piece of bone, wood or metal which is placed on the Tablī or the drum of an instrument and carries the strings in such a way that they form an angle with it. It is this angle that prolongs the vibration which produces notes and it is on this angle that the timbre or the quality of the notes depends. The angle is often adjusted by filing the Savārī or the bridge whenever the strings, after being played upon for some time, cut into it. This filing and adjusting is called 'Javārī Sāph Karṇā' or 'Cleaning the Javārī'. The voice of an artist which is marked by a rich sound resembling that produced by two consonants played together, is often loosely known to have Javāri in it, although such use is arbitrary.

124. Juḍi Tār

In Sitār, Surabahār, Esrāra etc. a pair of strings lying side by side and tuned in lower S, is called Juḍi Tār. The meaning of Juḍi is 'A pair' and Tār is 'String'.

125. Kaḍi Madhyama

Augmented M. When M leaves its own Śruti and occupies Raktā, the second Śruti of P, it is called Kaḍi Madhyama (vide 'Śruti').

126. Kaiśikī Niṣāda

N of three Śrutis. It is also known as Tīvra-Komala N, an augmented-flat N and is used in such Rāgas as Bhīmapalāśrī etc. (vide 'Śruti').

127. Kākalī Niṣāda

When N leaves its own Śruti and occupies Kumudvatī, the second Śruti of S, it is called Kākalī N. This is the natural N of the present Bilāvala Ṭhāṭa or diatonic major scale.

128. Kalā

(1) Generally speaking it means 'Art', but in popular sense it indicates only three of the sixtyfour Kalās mentioned in the Śāstras viz., Gīta or vocal music, Vādya or instrumental music and Nṛtya or dance.
(2) A part, specially a small phrase, several of which together form an Alaṁkāra (vide) e.g., Veṇī Alaṁkāra - 'SSS, RRR, GGG MMM, PPP, DDD'. This entire series is Veṇī Alaṁkāra and each of the small phrases SSS or RRR etc. is Kalā.

129. Kalavānā (Qalawānā)

A type of K͟hayāl songs composed in Arabic. It is not to be found in India; only Qawwāls used to sing them.

130. Kampana

Meaning tremour, hence tremolo. When a note is made to quiver between two Śrutis, it is said to have 'Kampana'.

131. Kaṇa

This is a Śabdālaṁkāra (vide Alaṁkāra). Any note that enhances the beauty of another is called a grace note, and the slight touch of the latter is called Kaṇa.

132. Karnāṭaka Paddhati (Carnatic System)

This system of Indian Classical music is only prevalent in the South and the rest of India follows the Hindustānī system. Although some reference has been made to Carnatic system, it is not the intention to deal with it fully in this book.

133. Kattara

Those Bolas of percussion instruments viz., Pakhāvaj or Tablā that contain the particular Bola 'Kat' are known as 'Kattara' Bolas.

134. Kattara Jhālā

Those Jhālās (usually Ṭhoka Jhālās) that contain Kattara Bolas are known as Kattara Jhālā.

135. Kavvāl (Qawwāl)

The song composed in Arabic and sung by Kavvāls. Generally

'Kavvāl – Kalavānā' or 'Qawwāl-Qalawānā' are mentioned together. The songs in both cases are composed glorifying God.

136. Kāyadā (Qāedā)

Literally means 'Regulation', 'Established order'. In music it means: (1) A particular type of Vistāra (vide) with the pre-composed Bolas of percussion instruments, i.e., to re-arrange the pre-composed Bolas (which may be Ṭhekās also) according to one's artistic talent for the sake of variety. (2) A rhythmic composition for percussion instruments consisting of Khuli (vide) and Mudi (vide) Bolas and capable of undergoing Vistāra.

137. Khaṇḍāra Vāṇī

Vide Ālāpa. It is one of four technical styles or ways of exposition of a musical piece and resembles the Bhinnā Gīti mentioned in the Śāstras (vide 'Gīti').

138. Kharaja

Colloquial name for Ṣaḍja, the initial note of the Indian musical scale. Root meaning of 'Ṣaḍja' is 'Begetter of six' (Ṣaḍa = six, Ja = begetter or begotten). Begetter in the figurative sense here means the one in relation to which other six notes have been brought into existence. In Indian scales, a single note, unconnected to the fundamental one i.e., the tonic, cannot be considered independently, whereas in Western music each note has an independent existence fixed by the number of vibrations per second (vide 'Vajan'). Different writers have put different interpretation to the root meaning of Ṣaḍja. Some hold that Ṣaḍja was born out of six notes but this theory is obviously untenable since it admits pre-existence of other six notes while Ṣaḍja was waiting to be born. Some hold that Ṣaḍja is called so because it is produced by the combined effort of six organs viz., nose, throat, palate, heart, tongue and teeth. This is equally unjustifiable because all other notes can equally be produced by those six organs. Ṣaḍja has four Śrutis allotted to it viz., Tīvrā, Kumudvatī, Mandā and Chandovatī and is precisely placed on this last one. Considered as it is as the fundamental note, Ṣaḍja and its major consonant Pañcama do not undergo any alteration – either sharp or flat (vide 'Pañcama').

139. Kharaja Parivartana

Changing of the Kharaja or the tonic. In shifting the tonic from S to any other note, the Indian practice is to consider the new tonic a S and the following notes according to natural sequence. In Mūrcchanā it is different (vide 'Mūrcchanā'). For example SRGMPDNṠ is the natural scale. In shifting the tonic to say R, we get RGMPDNṠṘ, which is called a Mūrcchanā of R. But if R is considered S then the scale would become SRgMPDnṠ i.e., with G and N flattened, this becomes an instance of Kharaja Parivartana. Usually, the musicians play a Rāga, say, Gārā or Pīlū and mention them as Gārā from Pañcama or Pīlū from Pañcama when they consider Pañcama the tonic or S instead of the original S either for playing facility or for novelty. In this case it is only the drone strings that remind the listeners of the original tonic S. Were it not for these drones, the Rāgas thus played would not have been mentioned as Gārā or Pīlū from Pañcama and the question of Kharaja Parivartana would not have arisen, since the Indian S is not a note fixed by a particular number of vibrations attached to it.

140. Khaṭkā

Literally means 'Fear', 'Suspicion' etc. Musically it is a variety of Śabdālaṁkāra in the form of a knot, so to say to decorate another note e.g., ^{SṆRSṆ}S, the 'knot' of notes 'SṆRSṆ' written on the top left corner of S to decorate it and is produced so quickly as to appear almost a single note, although it is a phrase of notes.

141. K͟hayāl

One of the four major forms of classical music, viz., Dhrupada, K͟hayāl, Ṭhumrī and Ṭappā. The literal meaning of this Hindi word is frolicsome imagination. It is believed that fanciful deviation from the rigorous rules of Dhrupada (vide) was responsible for the evolution of a style of exposition of a song which became known as K͟hayāl. It is said that initially, the Qawwāls used to sing K͟hayāls as a form of folk songs. Later, in the fourteenth century A.D., Amir K͟husro introduced K͟hayāl as a form of chamber music in the court of Emperor Alāuddīn and in the fifteenth century A.D., Nawāb Sultān Husayn Shirqui of Jaunpur bestowed dignity of a form of chamber music to K͟hayāl in his own court. Various ornamentations, that were prohibited in Dhrupadas, were introduced in this form and thus enriched it. In the beginning, K͟hayāls resembled in many respects the Dhrupada form but in course of evolution have taken a distinct form of music. Later, K͟hayāls were further enriched by Shāh Sadāraṅg, a representative of the generation of Sarasvatī Devī, daughter of Tānsen. K͟hayāls as propagated by Amīr K͟husro and later by Sultān Husayn Shirqui were pursued in Delhi and those who cultivated them were known as belonging to Qawwāl Gharānā (vide). G͟holām Rasūl of Lucknow who was in the generation of the daughter of a Qawwāl, mixed the style of Sadāraṅg to the original style of Qawwāls. His two grand sons Shakkar and Mak͟khan became famous as K͟hayāl singers.

Nathhan Pīr Buk͟hsh, a member of the Dhrupada Gharānā, used to sing K͟hayāls as improved by Sadāraṅg. Although in his K͟hayāls a touch of Qawwāl style could be traced, the Sadāraṅg-style predominated. His grand sons Haddū, Hashshyū and Nathhū K͟hān became very famous in K͟hayāl singing. We can thus find principally three styles of K͟hayāls propounded by (1) Qawwāls which we call Qawwālī style, (2) their daughter's generations known as K͟hayāl style and (3) Nathhan Pīr Buk͟hsh known as Dhrupadī style. It may be mentioned in passing that propounders of Qawwāl style mostly sang Persian Rāgas and the ancestors of Bāqar 'Alī K͟hān of Rāmapur used to follow this style. The Masīdk͟hānī Gats (vide) for instrumental music had been originally composed on the basis of K͟hayāls.

142. Khuli

Literally 'Open'. In Tabla, the 'Bolas' (vide) are of two kinds, one is Khuli or open, the other is Mudi or closed. In producing Khuli Bolas the hands are withdrawn from the instrument to allow the sounds to persist. These are the Khuli Bolas in Tablā – Tā, Ḍā, Taḍān, Ten, Dhen, Tāgin, Nagin, Tin, Din, Dhān, Tān, Gin, Kin, Tuṁ, Tī, Diṁ, Da, Ra, Ṇa. In Bāyāṁ: Ghe, Ghī Ghiṁ, Gī, Giṁ, Ge, Ga (vide 'Mudi').

143. Kīrtana

This word has been derived from the root Kīrti meaning 'Achievement'. A song containing enumeration of such achievements is called Kīrtana. This word is specifically applied to describe even the day to day incidents of Śrīkṛṣṇa, Goddess Kālī and other deities. Kīrtana, which is so very popular in Bengal today, was given the present form and was widely popularised by Śrīgaurāṅga, as the chief medium of worship, towards the beginning of the sixteenth century.

144. Komala Svara

Flat notes. Excepting S, M and P all other notes can be flattened or made Komala. Literally Komala means 'Soft'. When Svaras are shifted from their natural Śrutis to preceding ones they are called Komala (vide 'Śruti').

145. Krama

The ascending and natural sequence of notes is known as Krama e.g., SRGMPDN; likewise the descending natural sequence is called Vyutkrama, in other words anti-Krama e.g., NDPMGRS. 'Ṭhāṭa' can be considered another name of Krama.

146. Kṛntana

It is a variety of Śabdālaṁkāra (vide 'Alaṁkāra') as a manual technique to produce a particular sound in a stringed instrument. Left fore-finger is placed say, on the fret of S and the middle finger on R, the plectrum strikes the string to produce the note R, while the sound persists the middle finger which has been placed on R is withdrawn in a lateral motion away from the instrument so as to produce a thrumming sound and this will produce the note S automatically. It appears rather a complicated Alaṁkāra in theory than it is actually in practice.

147. Kuāḍī and Barāḍī

(Vide 'Āḍi'). This is a rhythmic variation. There are two different interpretations of this word. (1) According to some, when the Ādi rhythm is doubled it is called Kuāḍī. In other words, when twelve equal beats are introduced in the time for sixteen beats it is called Āḍi (vide) and when twentyfour such beats are introduced within sixteen, it is called Kuāḍī. In this case each beat will have a time value of 2/3 of the original one in the division of sixteen. (2) The author, together with some others, holds that Āḍi of an Āḍi is Kuāḍī. To explain: Āḍi is a rhythmic variation based on twelve equal divisions of beats being fitted into sixteen equal divisions. In Kuāḍī we have to find out the Āḍi of this twelve divisions which mathematically comes to 16 : 12 :: 12 : ? (vide 'Āḍi') = 9. When these nine equal divisions are fitted into the original sixteen, then the former becomes Kuāḍī to the latter or, in other words, 9 is a Kuāḍī of 16, and the time for each beat will be $1\frac{7}{9}$ of the original beat. Some hold, however, that the division of 16 beats into twenty is called Kuāḍī. Some, again, hold that 9 in 16 is Barāḍī. The present writer considers 7 in 16 as Barāḍī.

148. Kūṭa Tāna

The sequence of notes in any other than the natural order is called Kuṭa Tāna. For example, 'SRGMP' is a sequence of notes in the natural order but 'SGRM̄P' is in an order where R and G have changed places. As such, it is not natural, but a Kuṭa Tāna (vide 'Tāna').

149. Lacāva Ṭhumrī

Vide 'Ṭhumrī'.

150. Laḍaguthāo

Vide 'Ālāpa.'

151. Laḍalapeṭa

Vide 'Ālāpa.'

152. Laḍī

Vide 'Ālāpa.'

153. Lāgdāṁṭ

It is a quality of the performance of a musical programme as a whole. If the performance can hold the listeners spell-bound and attentive throughout, it is deemed to have the quality of Lāgdāṁṭ. Lāgdāṁṭ depends not upon the quality of the voice or the sound of instruments but mainly on the choice of melodic phrases of a Rāga and the juxtaposition of such phrases to make them attractive and pleasing to hear. If on the contrary, the phrases, themselves pleasant, are used in such a way to make them unpleasant by being badly set against ill selected phrases, the whole performance would appear boring and often repulsive – therein lies the difference between a great and an ordinary artiste. Unexpected use of notes and phrases sometimes attracts notice and sometimes repulses the listeners. It can be compared to a well-written novel which holds the readers' interest till the end. Such a novel may be said to have Lāgdāṁṭ.

154. Laggī

A very fast Vistāra of a portion of Ṭukḍā, Kāyadā (Qāedā) or Gat in Tablā is called Laggī : e.g., Ḋhā-Teṭe Keṭetāk Ṅādhin-nā Tā-Teṭe Keṭetāk Ṅādhin-nā Tereketẹ Tāghin-Nā Dhā Tereketẹ Tākin-Nā Tā Ġhenedhāgi Ṅādhātereketẹ Kenetāki Ṅātā Tereketẹ.

155. Laghu Saṁgīta

Literally 'Light music'.
Ramya Gīti (q.v.), Ghazal, Bhajana, 'Modern' songs, Concert compositions, Laharā-Gats etc. are all considered light music in comparison with classical music.

156. Laharā

Lahar means waves. When percussion-playing becomes the principal item of music with the Bolas played in proper order, such a percussionist's programme is called Laharā. In this case the percussionists are accompanied by instrumental musicians (usually, a Sārangi or harmonium player) who play a type of Gat composition called Laharā-Gat to keep the Tāla and Laya constantly as a standard for the percussionists to do rhythmic variations freely. Here are the playing sequence of a percussion programme:

(1) Uṭhān	(2) Ṭhekā	(3) Pharāsbandī
(4) Peśkār	(5) Kāyadā (Qāedā)	(6) Gat
(7) Ṭukḍā	(8) Cakradāra	(9) Relā
(10) Laggī		

All these terms have been explained under their respective heads. The last two items are often excluded according to the inclination of the artistes.

157. Laharā-Gat

A Gat composition to be played in a Laharā programme as accompaniment. The characteristic feature of a Laharā-Gat is in its simplicity of Bolas, having one Mātrā each; another feature is that these Gats have neither 'Māṁjhā' nor 'Antarā' as such. Sometimes variations are made by introducing a higher octave to give out a show of Antarā.
Laharā-Gat composed in the Rāga Durgā in Tritāla:

P - P D M P D - M P D P M R S R
Ḍā - Ḍā Rā Ḍā Rā Ḍā - Ḍā Rā Ḍā Rā Ḍā Rā Ḍā Rā

Variation P - P D M Ṙ Ṡ D M P D P M R S R
Ḍā - Ḍā Rā Ḍā Rā Ḍā Rā Ḍā Rā Ḍā Rā Ḍā Rā Ḍā Rā

158. Lāsya

Vide 'Nṛtya (Maṇipurī').

159. Laya

According to Saṁgītaratnākara, the time interval between two Mātrās or beats is called Laya. It would be obvious if we consider the description of Saṁgītaratnākara annotation i.e., Ṭikā: viz.,

"If a strike is immediately followed by another without any gap or respite, there cannot be any Laya." According to this, Laya is an intervening period between two successive beats. If such periods are of small duration, the beats must be faster, hence we call them fast tempo. If the periods are twice the duration of the fast tempo, the beats become slower and we call them medium tempo, if four times the duration, we call slow tempo or Vilambita, meaning extended. It may be pointed out that if the medium tempo is considered the standard, then both slow and fast tempo can be better demonstrated in relation to the medium tempo. It is worthwhile, in this context, to refer to 'Mātrā' where this has been further explained.

It has been explained under Mātrā that if a Mātrā is extended to twice its duration, it is called 'Guru', if to thrice its duration, it is called 'Pluta' – that is, one and the same thing (Laya) has been classified in three ways, viz., fast, medium and slow.
Modern books classify Laya into seven groups viz.,

(1) Vilambita (2) Madhya or Barābar (3) Āḍi
(4) Kuāḍī (5) Perāḍī (6) Barāḍī (7) Suluph

These have been explained under their respective heads.
In the foregoing classification according to a book 'Tablā Sikṣā' by Durgādās Lālā, there is no mention of 'Fast' or 'Drut'. 'Suluph', which is very fast, has been mentioned though.
There are three other ways of classifying a Laya:
(1) *Sāraktā* – In this category a Bola has its two ends in slow and the middle portion in fast tempo.

(2) *Mṛdaṁgā* – The Bola under this category has its two ends in fast and the middle portion in slow tempo.

(3) *Gopuccha* – The Bola has its first part in medium, the middle portion in slow and the end in fast tempo.

For both vocalists and instrumentalists, if they are to do some Layakārī (q.v.) a standard Laya should be maintained by the percussion accompanist, so that they may do any extempore rhythmic variations freely. The listeners, having the occasion to follow the standardised Laya in the playing of the accompanists, can enjoy each and every variation that the vocalists or instrumentalists are capable of doing. Thus it is indispensable that a standard Laya should be maintained in the percussion instruments. Where the percussionists are the chief musicians, this standard Laya is maintained by string or wind instrumentalists who serve as accompanists to the percussion-players. The melody for these instrumentalists as composed in Rāgas, is known as Laharā-Gats (vide 'Laharā').

We are giving below the examples of medium, slow and fast tempo by Bolas as used in Gats and also the percussion Bolas in medium tempo which is considered to be normal Laya:

Percussion Bolas for Tablā in Barābara or Medium Tempo:	Dhā	Gi	Ne	Te	Nā	Ka	Dhi	N
Gat Bolas: Medium Tempo	Ḍā	Rā	Ḍā	Rā	Ḍā	Rā	Ḍā	Rā
Slow Tempo	Ḍā	–	Rā	–	Ḍā	–	Rā	–
Fast Tempo	ḌāRā	ḌāRā	ḌāRā	ḌāRā	ḌāRā	ḌāRā	ḌāRā	ḌāRā
Suluph Tempo (Extra Fast)	ḌāRā	ḌāRā	ḌāRā	ḌāRā	ḌāRā	ḌāRā	ḌāRā	ḌāRā
	ḌāRā	ḌāRā	ḌāRā	ḌāRā	ḌāRā	ḌāRā	ḌāRā	ḌāRā

It can be noticed that the percussion Laya is in the medium tempo and this being the standard background for the Gat Bolas, variations thereof can be better appreciated by the listeners.

160. Layakārī

Variations in different tempos and rhythms in relation to a standard tempo and rhythm are called Layakārī on the part of the musicians, vocal or instrumental; the standard tempo is usually maintained by an accompanist. All such variations as Vilambita, medium, fast, Āḍi, Kuāḍī, Perāḍī, Barāḍī, Suluph, Sama, Viṣama, Atīta, Anāgata and Anāghāta are to be shown against a standard tempo or medium Laya maintained by the accompanying percussionist. The act of doing these variations is called Layakārī, and may be called embellishments of Laya.

Five types of Layakārī have been mentioned in the book 'Tablā Vādana' published by the Gāndharva Mahāvidyālaya:

(1) Catasra (2) Tisra (3) Khaṇḍa
(4) Miśra (5) Saṁkīrṇa

Some mention another type called Divyasaṁkīrṇa.

(1) *Catasra* – When the basic Laya is divided in equal divisions it is called Catasra Layakārī. The basic Laya has been taken to be that of Tritāla having 16 beats or Mātrās divided into 4 groups of 4 beats each.

(2) *Tisra* – Keeping Tritāla of 16 Mātrās as the standard, if the variation is done in such a way that each beat interval of this variation is a quarter less than the original beat of the standard – this Layakārī is called Tisra and is the same as Āḍi (q.v.).

(3) *Khaṇḍa* – Keeping Tritāla of 16 Mātrās as the standard, if the variation is done in such a way that each beat interval of this variation is a quarter more than the original beat of the standard i.e., each beat interval in the variation is one and a quarter of the original beat interval, it is called Khaṇḍa Layakārī.

(4) *Miśra* – If the variation beat interval is of the value of one and three quarters of the original beat interval, it is called Miśra Layakārī.

(5) *Saṁkīrṇa* – If the variation beat interval is of the value of two and a quarter of the original beat interval, it is called Saṁkīrṇa Layakārī.

There are other interpretations of the first four of the foregoing types:

(1) *Catasra* – Tāla which is composed of groups of 4 Mātrās each e.g., Tritāla, Kaharvā etc.

(2) *Tisra* – Tāla which is composed of groups of 3 Mātrās each e.g., Ekatāla, Dādrā etc.

(3) *Miśra* – Tāla which is composed of groups of both 4 and 3 Mātrās e.g., Jhumrā (q.v.).

(4) *Khaṇḍa* – Tāla which is composed of groups of unequal distribution of Mātrās e.g., Jhāṁpatāla, Śūlatāla, Dhamāra etc.

In Layakārī, 10 features are admitted:

(1)	Kāla	:	Understanding of the Time continuum.
(2)	Mārga	:	Style, manner of progress.
(3)	Work	:	With or without sound.
(4)	Aṁga	:	The body, the groups in a Tāla.
(5)	Graha	:	Sama, Viṣama, Atīta, Anāgata, Anāghāta.
(6)	Jāti	:	Catasra, Tisra, Miśra, Khaṇḍa, Saṁkīrṇa, Divyasaṁkīrṇa.
(7)	Kalā	:	Beauty of the movement of palms or arms.
(8)	Laya	:	Progressing speed and rest.
(9)	Yati	:	The rules of the progress of Laya and inclination to rest – Samā, Srotagatā, Gopucchā, Mṛdaṅgā, Pipīlikā.
(10)	Prastāra	:	Vistāra of rhythm and Mātrās.

161. Madhya Laya

Literally, medium tempo. This is considered to be the natural tempo. Its half is considered to be slow and its double to be fast tempo. Madhya Laya is also called Barābara Laya. Actually the slow, medium and fast are all relative terms and there is no standard to determine tempo or Laya, yet Saṁgītaratnākara mentions some standard which has been fully dealt with under Laya (q.v.).

162. Madhya Saptaka

Vide 'Tāra Saptaka'.

163. Madhyama

The fourth note of the scale. As it is placed in the exact middle, it is called Madhyama. This note has four Śrutis viz., Vajrikā, Prasāriṇī, Prīti and Mārjanī and the note itself is placed on the last.

164. Madhyama Grāma

Vide 'Gāndhāra Grāma'.

165. Maṁca (Mañca)

The five-line-staff of the European notation system has been called Mañca in Bengali. About 1920, there had been some attempts to bring staff notations into currency in the Indian music but the attempts could not succeed.

The other meaning of Mañca is cycle or Āvardā (q.v.) or Āvarta, generally used with reference to percussion instruments.

166. Maṁdra Saptaka (Mandra Saptaka)

Vide 'Tāra Saptaka'.

167. Maṁjādār or Māṁjhādār

A type of Tukḍā (q.v.) or Gat and Relā (q.v.) to be played on Tablā – a percussion instrument. The chief characteristic of this is that, in a rather long composition, the beginning and the ending portion would differ from the middle portion in rhythm e.g.,

The beginning portion:

+| | 2| | 0| |
Dhāgete Rekeṭe Dhāgat Tākeṭe Dhāghene Dhātreket
3| |
Dhināga Dighene

The middle portion:

+| | 2| | 0|
Keḍenāg Dhāgtere Keṭetāg Dhā-teṭe. Gheḍenāg
| 3| |
Tegenāg Tākeṭedhā Trekeṭedhekeṭe

The ending portion:

+| | 2|
Dhāgeterekeṭe Dhāgat tākeṭe Dhāgenedhātreket
| 0| |
Dhināgadighene Keḍenagtāgtere Keṭetāgdhāteṭe
3| |
Gherenāgtegenāg Tākeṭedhākeṭdheteṭe

168. Māṁjhā or Māṁjā

A variety of Tuk (q.v.).

169. Mārga Saṁgīta

In the past, only the doxological songs in strict conformity with the rules given in the Śāstras used to be called Mārga Saṁgīta, but at present classical music, as such is known as Mārga Saṁgīta. Mārga Saṁgīta is that which strictly follows the Śastrīya rules. Mārga means 'The path shown by the sages'.

170. Masīdkhānī or Masitkhānī

Masīd Khān was the grandson of Karīm Sen who himself was a grandson of Bilās Khān, the son of Miyān Tānsen. It was Masīd who thoroughly renovated the Sitār by adding two more strings and by introducing a particular style of playing which has proved to be a lasting gift to the world of instrumental music. The style of Sitār playing prevalent before Masīd Khān had been devised by Amīr Khusro. At present, in almost all musical instruments, the style devised by Masīd Khān is followed. Masīd Khān taught his son Bahādur Khān (according to some, Bahādur Sen) and from Bahādur Khān the Jaipur Gharānā (cultural lineage) (q.v.) was established. Masīdkhānī style was created after the pattern of slow tempo Khayāls and Joḍ; Toḍā and Vistāra were used in this style. Amṛta Sen, the famous Sitār player of Jaipur, was the great grandson of Bahādur Sen. Amṛta Sen's nephew (sister's son) Amīr Khān was the court musician of Mysore. This, in brief, is the history of the Jaipur Gharānā.

Bahādur Sen had another pupil named Qutub Bukhsh, later known as Qutubuddaulā. He had composed innumerable Saragamas (q.v.) and Gats. Amīr Khān's pupil was Prof. Barkat U'l-lāh, the famous Sitār player of the Mysore Court. The recital of his Sitār had been recorded in the Gramophone disc in the Rāga Bhūpakalyāṇa (Bhūpālī). This is the only representative record of Jaipur style of Sitār playing. Barkat U'l-lāh's pupil was Āshiq Alī Khān, father of Mushtāq Alī Khān, one of the foremost Sitār players of contemporary India.

Masīd added two more strings to the Sitār of three strings, as known to Amīr Khusro, but he did not add Tarapha or Strings for sympathetic vibrations. Later, when the Seniyās of Jaipur used Tarapha strings, the Cikārīs were not added; these were added around 1930.

We are describing in a nutshell, the Amīr Khusro style and the Masīdkhānī style of Gats:

(1) *Amīr Khusro Bāj* or *playing style*: In this Bāj the Gats had only one stanza (Tuk) and some Toḍās (q.v.) were also used. The famous Gat composition of Amīr Khusro is still in currency although further stanzas have been added subsequently by different composers. It is in the Rāga Kāphī–

S RR R g - M P M P - P M g R S ṇ
Ḍā Ḍere Ḍā Rā - Ḍā Rā Ḍā Rā - Ḍā Rā Ḍā Rā Ḍā Rā
The Bolas are very simple, to be played in medium tempo.

According to Paṇḍit Sudarśanācārya Śāstrī, a pupil of Amṛta Sen of Jaipur, Masīd Khān's father was Firoz Khān and the latter's father was Amīr Khusro who was responsible for the name 'Sitār'.

This theory is not admitted by all, rather it goes against the current view. The original Amīr K͟husro, who is supposed to have given the name Sitār to Tritantrī Vīṇā, lived in the transition period of the thirteenth and the fourteenth centuries A.D. Firoz K͟hān's father Amīr K͟husro must have been a different person. The only reason to give credence to Sudarśanācārya's theory is that there is no mention of any Sitāriyā in the Court of Akbar, so Amīr K͟husro, the Sitār-protagonist, might have come later.

(2) *Masīdk͟hānī Bāj* or *playing style*: This is also called Pachāva Kā Bāj (Pachāva is West). Masīd K͟hān composed slow-tempo Gats after the slow K͟hayāl songs and he used to play Sitār in the style of K͟hayāl songs, as sung in his time. These Gats were also embellished with Tāna, Ṭoḍā and Vistāra in the K͟hayāl style. Here are given some sequences of Masīdk͟hānī Gat composed in Dhīmā Tritāla and without any complex Bolas. Only Bolas are given without the melody since Masīdk͟hānī Gat composition is chiefly recognised by the composition of Bolas:

```
    |      ³|   |    |    |  ⁺|   |    |    |
(Dere) Ḍā Ḍere Ḍā Rā Ḍā Ḍā Rā Ḍere
  ²|   |    |    |   ⁰|   |    |    |
Ḍā Ḍere Ḍā Rā Ḍā Ḍā Rā Ḍere
  ³|   |    |    |   ⁺|   |    |    |
Ḍā Ḍere Ḍā Rā Ḍā Ḍere Ḍā Rā
  ²|   |    |    |   ⁰|   |    |    |
Ḍā Ḍere Ḍā Rā Ḍā Ḍā Rā Ḍere
```

The first cycle or Āvardā (q.v.) of the foregoing Gat is called Sthāyī stanza and the second is now-a-days known as Māṁjhā, being the middle portion between Sthāyī and Antarā. Māṁjhā means "One in the middle."

Antarā:

```
    |      ²|   |    |    |  ⁰|   |    |    |
(Dere) Ḍā Ḍere Ḍā Rā Ḍā Ḍā Rā Ḍere
  ³|   |    |    |   ⁺|   |    |    |
Ḍā Ḍere Ḍā Rā Ḍā Ḍere Ḍā Rā
  ²|   |    |    |   ⁰|   |    |    |
Ḍā Ḍere Ḍā Rā Ḍā Ḍā Rā Ḍere
```

After Sthāyī, Māṁjhā and Antarā have been played, Vistāra is done around the Aṁśa (q.v.) note of the Rāga, then the same thing i.e., Vistāra is done around the Saṁvādī (q.v.) note of that Aṁśa note. After these have been played, particular phrases belonging to the same Rāga are taken and around those phrases

Vistāra is done. Then small and large Tānas are played. Most of the Tānas end on the 3rd beat of Viṣama symbolised in notation by 'O' and the Gat is resumed from the next beat i.e., the 4th beat of Viṣama. In percussion instruments, Tablā and Bāṁyā, only Ṭhekās (q.v.) used to be played as an accompaniment; Paraṇas (q.v.) were not played in those days. Nor was Jhāla (q.v.) played since there were no Cikārī strings. Masīdkhānī Gat used medium and fast Joḍ (q.v.) as played in Ālāpa (q.v.) and that was the ending piece of Masīdkhānī Gat.

Gholām Mohammad Khān invented the Surabahār and added Cikārī strings to it - copying this the Cikārīs were added to the Sitār also. Gholām Mohammad and his son Sajjād Mohammad used to play Surabahār mainly and all the techniques of Vīṇā-playing were applied in that instrument. Gholām Mohammad also composed many Gats for the Sitār, some of which are still in currency. Sajjād Mohammad also used to play the Sitār - but both the father and the son were chiefly Surabahār players. Imdād Khān using the twelve stages of Ālāpa (q.v.) in Masīdkhānī Gats, vastly changed the playing technique of Sitār and also vastly improved upon the Masīdkhānī Bāj. Hitherto Masīdkhānī Gats were chiefly in the Khayāl style, but Imdād Khān added the Dhrupada style through the twelve stages of Ālāpa. This was a bold step on the part of Imdād Khān to mix Khayāl and Dhrupada styles which remarkably enriched the playing technique of Sitār with due importance to Jhālā (q.v.). Imdād Khān added the Khayāliyā style in Surabahār also; as a result the technique of Surabahār playing improved greatly in the use of Tānas and Palṭās (q.v.). Since the playing technique of both Surabahār and Sitār has been so much improved and enriched, it cannot be called pure Masīdkhānī any longer. As such, some have called it 'Modern Masīdkhānī'. However, the present author named it 'Imdādkhānī Bāj' in 1940 A.D. and this name 'Imdādkhānī Bāj' has been accepted by the musical intelligentsia (vide 'Imdādkhānī').

171. Mata

There is a Bengali saying "Nānā Munir Nānā Mata" that is, "Different sages have different opinions." The saying holds good in the Indian musical field as well. Though the opinions of different Śāstras by different sages have been accepted by Indian musicologists, they hardly have any bearing upon the practice of music today. However, for historical research, these are indispensable.

The Rāgas and Rāgiṇīs as described in the Śāstras are quite different from the Rāgas and Rāgiṇīs of the same name at present in vogue. The chief scale as described in the Śāstras is similar to the Kāphī scale of today. The Bilāvala, i.e., the diatonic major scale of today has not been described in the Śāstras as the chief scale or Śuddha Ṭhāṭa. Nevertheless, while describing modern Rāgas, musicologists have a tendency to quote from the Śāstras, the description of the same Rāgas.

It would never do merely to refer to the Śāstras for Rāgas and Rāgiṇīs until and unless the Śāstrīya scale together with the Śāstrīya descriptions of Rāgas and Rāgiṇīs are fully analysed with a view to matching them with those in currency.

We are enumerating the opinions about different Rāgas with reference to their descriptions of the family of Rāgas and Rāgiṇīs, and according to one of the four sages, the sons and the daughters-in-law of the Rāgas have been included also.

There are chiefly four Matas or opinions of four sages viz., (1) Brahmā, (2) Bharata, (3) Hanumanta, (4) Kallinātha.

(1) *Brahmā* - According to Brahmā's opinion, there are six Rāgas having six wives or Rāgiṇīs each. There could not be found any Śāstra in support of Brahmā's opinion or Mata but later sages had referred to the same. Here are the descriptions of Rāgas and Rāgiṇīs according to Brahmā's opinion:

Rāga	**Rāgiṇīs**	**Rāga**	**Rāgiṇīs**
(i) Bhairava	(a) Bhairavī	(ii) Śrī	(a) Mālaśrī
	(b) Gurjarī		(b) Triveṇī
	(c) Rāmakalī		(c) Gaurī
	(d) Guṇakalī		(d) Kedārī
	(e) Saindhavī		(e) Madhu-mādhavī
	(f) Baṅgālī		(f) Pahāḍī
(iii) Megha	(a) Malhārī	(iv) Vasanta	(a) Deśī
	(b) Saurāṭī		(b) Devagirī
	(c) Sāverī		(c) Varāṭī
	(d) Kauśikī		(d) Toḍī
	(e) Gāndhārī		(e) Lalitā
	(f) Haraśṛṅgārī		(f) Hindolī

(v) Pañcama	(a) Vibhāsa	(vi) Naṭa	(a) Kāmodī
	(b) Bhūpālī		(b) Kalyāṇī
	(c) Karanāṭī		(c) Ābherī
	(d) Varahaṁsikā		(d) Nāṭikā
	(e) Mālavī		(e) Sāraṅgī
	(f) Paṭamaṁjarī		(f) Hamīra

(2) *Bharata* – Although not based on history, the Mata or opinion which passes in the name of the sage Bharata has six Rāgas having five Rāgiṇīs, five sons and five daughters-in-law each viz.,

Rāga	Rāgiṇīs	Sons	Daughters-in-law
(i) Bhairava	(a) Madhu-mādhavī	(a) Bilāvala	(a) Rāmakalī
	(b) Bhairavī	(b) Pañcama	(b) Suhāi
	(c) Baṅgālī	(c) Deśākhya	(c) Sugharāi
	(d) Barārī	(d) Devagā-ndhāra	(d) Paṭamañjarī
	(e) Saindhavī	(e) Vibhāsa	(e) Toḍī
(ii) Mālakauśa	(a) Guṇakalī	(a) Soma	(a) Suraṭhī
	(b) Khambāvatī	(b) Parāśana	(b) Triveṇī
	(c) Gurjarī	(c) Baḍahaṁsa	(c) Karnāṭī
	(d) Bhūpālī	(d) Kakubha	(d) Āsāvarī
	(e) Gaurī	(e) Baṅgāla	(e) Goḍagiri
(iii) Hindola	(a) Belāvalī	(a) Rekhaba-haṁsa	(a) Kedārā
	(b) Deśākhī	(b) Vasanta	(b) Kāmodī
	(c) Lalitā	(c) Lokahāsa	(c) Bihāgarā
	(d) Bhima-palāsī	(d) Gāndharva	(d) Kāphī
	(e) Mālavī	(e) Lalita	(e) Paraja
(iv) Dipaka	(a) Naṭa	(a) Śuddha-kalyāṇa	(a) Baḍahaṁsī
	(b) Malhārī	(b) Saurāṭha	(b) Desavarāṭī
	(c) Kedārī	(c) Deśakāra	(c) Vairāṭī
	(d) Kānaḍā	(d) Hamīra	(d) Devagirī
	(e) Bhārekā	(e) Mārū	(e) Sindharā

(v) Śrī	(a) Vāsantī	(a) Naṭa	(a) Śyama
	(b) Mālavī	(b) Chāyānaṭa	(b) Puriyā
	(c) Mālaśrī	(c) Kānaḍā	(c) Gurjarī
	(d) Sahānā	(d) Yamana	(d) Hambīrī
	(e) Dhanāśrī	(e) Saṅkarā-bharaṇa	(e) Aḍānā
(vi) Megha	(a) Sāraṅga	(a) Bahādurī	(a) Pahāḍī
	(b) Baṅkā	(b) Naṭanārā-yaṇa	(b) Jayantī
	(c) Gāndharva	(c) Mālava	(c) Gāndhārī
	(d) Malhārī	(d) Jayati	(d) Pūravī
	(e) Mulatānī	(e) Kāmoda	(e) Jayajayantī

(3) *Hanumanta* – There could not be traced any Śāstra to support this Mata or opinion but the sages of later age have referred to this. Some of the present musicologists consider this Mata to be in support of the present Rāgas and Rāgiṇīs.

Rāga	Rāgiṇīs	Rāga	Rāgiṇīs
(i) Bhairava	(a) Madhyamādi	(ii) Kauśika	(a) Toḍī
	(b) Bhairavī		(b) Khambāvatī
	(c) Baṅgālī		(c) Gaurī
	(d) Barāṭikā		(d) Guṇakirī
	(e) Saindhavī		(e) Kakubhā
(iii) Hindola	(a) Belāvalī	(iv) Dīpaka	(a) Kedarī
	(b) Rāmakirī		(b) Kānaḍā
	(c) Daśākhya		(c) Deśī
	(d) Paṭamañjarī		(d) Kāmodī
	(e) Lalitā		(e) Nāṭikā
(v) Śrī	(a) Vāsantī	(vi) Megha	(a) Malhārī
	(b) Mālavī		(b) Deśakārī
	(c) Mālaśrī		(c) Bhūpālī
	(d) Dhanyāsikā		(d) Gurjarī
	(e) Āsāvarī		(e) Ṭaṅka

(4) *Kallinātha* – No Śāstra written by Kallinātha could be traced. He was an annotator of Saṁgītaratnākara. Six Rāgas, with thirtysix Rāgiṇīs, according to his opinion, are as follows:

Rāga	Rāgiṇīs	Rāga	Rāgiṇīs
(i) Śrī	(a) Gaurī (b) Kolāhala (c) Dhavala (d) Barorājī or Radāraṅgī (e) Mālakauśa (f) Devagāndhāra	(ii) Pañcama	(a) Triveṇī (b) Hastāntaritahā or Stambhatīrthikā Khamāicī (c) Ābheri or Ahīrī (d) Kokabha (e) Barārī (f) Āsāvarī
(iii) Bhairava	(a) Bhairavī (b) Gurjarī (c) Belāvalī (d) Bihāga or Bādahaṁsī (e) Karnāṭa (f) Kānaḍā or Bhāṣā	(iv) Megha	(a) Baṅgālī (b) Madhurā or Mudrā (c) Kāmodī (d) Dhanāśrī (e) Devatīrthī (f) Devalī or Tīrthakī
(v) Naṭa-Nārāyaṇa	(a) Tarabaṅkī or Devalī (b) Tilaṅgī or Tilakī (c) Pūrvī (d) Gāndhārī (e) Rāma or Virāma (f) Sindhu Malhārī or Śuddha Malhārī	(vi) Vasanta	(a) Āndhālī (b) Gamakī (c) Paṭamañjarī (d) Gauḍagiri (e) Dhāmakī or Ṭankā (f) Devaśākha

From the foregoing descriptions it would appear that these systems of connecting Rāgas and Rāgiṇīs, their sons and daughters-in-law, are but the product of poetic imagination. Had there been any relevance of connecting one Rāga to another, it would have given impetus for further research. The same imagination leads one to draw visual pictures of Rāgas and Rāgiṇīs.

Furthermore, these Matas of the sages are being given some importance while their opinions with regard to the fundamentals of music are being ignored and violated.

172. Māṭhā

The name has come down to us from 'Manṭha Tāla' mentioned in Saṁgītaratnākara, though the meaning differs widely (vide 'Ālāpa').

173. Mātrā

Mātrā is a beat, a measuring unit of time interval. According to Saṁgītaratnākara, a Nimeṣa Kāla is called Mātrā or Kalā. Nimeṣa Kāla is that period of time which is required in uttering a short letter. It can also be explained as the twinkling of an eye. Saṁgītaratnākara also measures a Mātrā in an ingenious way. According to it, the time required to utter five short letters of the alphabet is called a Mātrā i.e., the interval between two Mātrās or beats. Five Sanskrit, letters Ka, Ca, Ṭa, Ta, and Pa should be uttered uninterruptedly and the time required would be one Mātrā and is called a Laghu Mātrā. Thus ten letters would require double of the time and it would be known as Guru Mātrā and if fifteen letters are uninterruptedly uttered the time required would be called Pluta Mātrā. In other words, a Guru Mātrā takes twice the time required for a Laghu Mātrā and a Pluta Mātrā takes thrice the time of Laghu Mātrā.

Tāla has been created to represent Mātrās by sound so that the time interval can be well appreciated. At present the sounded beats are being called Mātrās. Time is infinite. Man, for his own comprehension and use, has divided it into intervals of years, months, weeks, days, hours, minutes and seconds. The act of thus dividing time is called Mātrā.

174. Matsarikṛta

Vide 'Mūrcchanā'.

175. Mātu

The literary portion of a song is called Mātu whereas the melodic or Rāga composition in notations is known as Dhātu (q.v.).

176. Mela

Vide 'Ṭhāṭa'.

177. Melakartā

Āśraya Rāga – Vide 'Ṭhāṭa'.

178. Metronome

An European instrument for measuring beat intervals. It was invented in the seventeenth century A.D. but the instruments found at present were made in the beginning of the nineteenth century A.D. There is an indicator - a steel arm, which swings to and fro sidewise with a click in each movement. The speed of this movement can be controlled and adjusted by moving up and down the arm a weight. There is also an adjustable bell which rings once after a group of beats. For instance, if Tritāla is selected to be indicated in metronome, the bell can be adjusted to ring every three beats or clicks. Thus indicating Sama (q.v.). The bell is capable of being adjusted to ring after one to six beats and the speed of the arm can be adjusted to click forty to two hundred and eight times per minute. It is an ideal instrument for the students to develop the sense and uniformity of beat intervals or Laya (q.v.).

179. Mīḍ

One of the chief playing techniques of fretted pluck string instruments such as Vīṇā, Surabahār and Sitār. When the left forefinger or the middle finger, or sometimes both, press upon a fret on the main string which is struck once to produce a sound, the left fingers thus pressing the string on the fret pull it outwards, the note or notes higher in pitch than the usual note as indicated on the fret are produced before the vibration of the string caused by a single stroke dies out. This way of producing different notes by pulling the string outwards is called Mīḍ. It requires extreme accuracy in pulling the string to produce the accurate note or notes. Probably Mīḍ has been called 'Sphurita' in the Śāstras.

180. Mīḍakhaṇḍa

Vide 'Tāna'.

181. Mirāsī

The musicians who accompany a professional dancing girl or Bāī or Tayafā (q.v.) either with string or percussion instruments are called Mirāsīs.

182. Moḍedār

A Ṭukḍā (q.v.) or Gat to be played on Tablā. e.g.,

+| | | |
Krān Kerenāg Tāgtere Keṭetāg
2| | | |
Dhindhā Keṭetāg Tāgtere Keṭetāg
0| | | |
Ghintere Keṭetāg Tāgteṭe Krān
3| | | | +|
Terekeṭe Tāgdhere Keṭetāg Krān Dhā

183. Moharā

In instrumental or vocal Ālāpa a particular composition to indicate the end of a Tāna or Vistāra.

(a) Moharā for instrumental Ālāpa:

(1) Slow Tempo: S - - S - - - - - SṆ SṆ R - S -
Ḍā - - Ḍā - - - - - Ḍā Ḍā Ḍā - Ḍā-

The dashes are to be sounded in Cikārī strings with the Bola Rā. All the beat intervals should be uniform but rather long.

(2) Medium tempo (faster than the above).
S - - S - - SṆ SṆ R - S -
Ḍā - - Ḍā - - Ḍā Ḍā Ḍā - Ḍā-

(3) Fast tempo (yet faster):
S - S - SṆ SṆ R S -
Ḍā - Ḍā- Ḍā Ḍā Ḍā Ḍā-

(b) Moharā for vocal Ālāpa:

(1) Slow Tempo:
S S S S S S S S SṆ SṆ R S
Tā Nā Nā Tā Nā Nā Nā Nā Tā Nā Num Nā

(2) Medium tempo – faster than the above:
S S S S S S SṆ SṆ R S
Tā Nā Nā Tā Nā Nā Tā Nā Num Nā

(3) Fast tempo – yet faster:
S S S S Ṇ Ṇ R S
Tā Nā Nā Nā Tā Nā Nū Ūm
The time interval to articulate the Vāṇīs
Tā, Nā etc. should be uniform.

184. Mṛdu

Weak or soft. All the flattened notes are known as Mṛdu notes e.g., Mṛdu Madhyama is the natural Madhyama since it has only one other variety which is sharpened or Tīvra Madhyama. Mṛdu Ṛṣbha or flattened Ṛṣabha etc. In some Śāstras Tīvra Madhyama is referred to as Mṛdu Pañcama.

185. Mudi

In Tablā and Bāṁyā, those Bolas that require both the palms or fingers to be stuck to the Tablā Bāṁyā even after the production of the Bolas, are called Mudi Bolas. These are somewhat of muffled sound that is, they do not have free vibrations.

186. Mudi Bolas

Ta, Te, Tī, Tet, Tik, Dheḍnak, Ra,
Ṭa, Ṭe, Ṭi, Ṭuṁ, Diṁ, Tiṁ, Dī, Ke, Kī, Kiṁ,
Ka, Kat, Dhā, Dha, Dhe, Dhet, Dhit, Dhik.
(vide 'Mudi', vide 'Khuli' also).

187. Mudrā

Gestures are called Mudrās. If they are pleasant to look at, it is called Mudrā-Guṇa and if unpleasant, Mudrā-Doṣa. In the Nāṭyādhyāya i.e., chapter dealing with drama, of Saṁgītaratnākara, mention has been made of sixtyfour manual gestures or Mudrās. These are used in dance and dramatic performances.

188. Mukha

A portion of the Sthāyī stanza of a song or a Gat. In Tritāla, the portion containing five Mātrās immediately before Sama (q.v.) is generally known as Mukha. During a recital any Paraṇa (q.v.), Tāna (q.v.) or Vistāra (q.v.), either vocal or instrumental, ends in the 'Mukha' to resume the original composition— this is the usual way. It can be called a Gīta Bidārī or a Pada Bidārī (vide 'Bidārī').

189. Mukhaḍā, Mohaḍā or Moḍā

A type of Ṭukḍā for the percussion instrument Tablā. The Ṭukḍā composed to be started at Viṣama (q.v.) i.e., Phāṁk and to be ended at the Sama is called Mukhaḍā. Some hold that the Ṭukḍā composed in such a way as to be played thrice in one cycle of the Tāla from Sama to the next Sama is called Mohaḍā; they also say that the Ṭukḍā composed to be started at Phāṁk and to be ended at Sama is called Mukhaḍā, as mentioned earlier, but they treat Mohaḍā and Mukhaḍā to be different things.

0| | | |
Mukhaḍā: Dheredhere Keṭetāg Dhā - Katā Ged-di Ghen - nā
3| | | | +|
Kat - te Ṭe-dhā Dheredhere Keṭetāgtā-ān Dhā

190. Mūrcchanā

(1) Same as Mīḍ (q.v.). This interpretation is now obsolete.
(2) The Āroha (ascending) and Avaroha (descending) of a scale in proper order is called Mūrcchanā, but singly known as Krama and Vyutkrama respectively (vide 'Krama'). That is the difference in meaning between Mūrcchanā and Krama. Mūrcchanā somewhat resembles modulation of the Western music. We are describing Mūrcchanās of Ṣaḍja and Madhyama Grāmas. Since Gāndhāra Grāma has become obsolete, we refrain from dealing with Mūrcchanās belonging to that Grāma.

The difference between Ṣaḍja and Madhyama Grāma depends on the Śruti value of P and D (vide 'Gāndhāra Grāma'). The pure or Śuddha scale as described in the Śāstras approximately resembles the present Kāphī scale i.e., flattened G and N of the diatonic major scale.
There are four different types of Mūrcchanās in each Grāma, depending upon the Śruti value of G and N viz.,

(1) Śuddha Mūrcchanā
(2) Sakākalīka Mūrcchanā (vide 'Kākalī Niṣāda')
(3) Sāntara Mūrcchanā (vide 'Antara Gāndhāra')
(4) Sāntarakākalīka Mūrcchanā

In the above types:
(1) Uses flattened G and flattened N,
(2) Uses only sharpened N,
(3) Uses only Sharpened G,
(4) Uses both sharpened N and sharpened G.
In other words, the diatonic major scale.

We are giving in detail all the Mūrcchanās belonging to Ṣaḍja Grāma and only Śuddha Mūrcchanās of Madhyama Grāma with the Śāstrīya scales reduced to modern scales and pointing out the Ṭhāṭa names as known at present.

Ṣaḍja Grāma
Śuddha Mūrcchanā

According to Saṁgītaratnākara	*According to Nārada*	*Āroha*
(1)	(2)	(3)
(1) Uttaramandrā	Uttaravarṇā	SRGMPDN

(2) Rajanī	Abhirudgatā	ṆSRGMPD
(3) Uttarāyatā	Asvakrāntā	ḌṆSRGMP
(4) Śuddhaṣaḍjā	Saubīrī	P̣ḌṆSRGM
(5) Matsarīkṛt	Hṛṣyakā	ṂP̣ḌṆSRG
(6) Aśvakrāntā	Uttarāyatā	G̣ṂP̣ḌṆSR
(7) Abhirudgatā	Rajanī	ṚG̣ṂP̣ḌṆS

Avaroha	*Modern Scale*	*Present Ṭhāṭa Rāga name*
(4)	(5)	(6)
NDPMGRS	SRgMPDn	Kāphī
DPMGRSṆ	SRGMPDN	Bilāvala
PMGRSṆḌ	SrgMmdn	?
MGRSṆḌP̣	SRgMPdn	Jaunapurī (Āsāvarī)
GRSṆḌP̣Ṃ	SRGMPDn	Khamāj
RSṆḌP̣ṂG̣	SRGmPDN	Kalyāṇa
SṆḌP̣ṂG̣Ṛ	SrgMPdn	Bhairavī

It may be noted that according to the Śāstras, the Mūrcchanā should be written thus 'SRGMPDNDPMGRS'. But as we have shown the Āroha and Avaroha separately, so we have to write respective ending and initial note twice.

Madhyama Grāma
Śuddha Mūrcchanā

(1)	(2)	(3)
(1) Soubīri	Āpyāyanī	MPDNṠṘĠ
(2) Harināśvā	Visvahṛtā	GMPDNṠṘ
(3) Kalopanatā	Candrā	RGMPDNṠ
(4) Śuddhamadhyā	Hemā	SRGMPDN
(5) Mārgī	Kapardinī	ṆSRGMPD
(6) Pauravī	Maitrī	ḌṆSRGMP
(7) Hṛṣyakā	Candrāvatī	P̣ḌṆSRGM

(4)	(5)	(6)
ĠṘṠNDPM	SRGMPDn	Khamāj
ṘṠNDPMG	SRGmPDN	Kalyāṇa
ṠNDPMGR	SrgMPdn	Bhairavī
NDPMGRS	SRgMPDn	Kāphī
DPMGRSṆ	SRGMPDN	Bilāvala

PMGRSṆḌ	SrgMmdn	?
MGRSṆḌP̣	SRgMPdn	Jaunapurī (Āsāvarī)

Ṣaḍja Grāma

Sakākalīka Mūrcchanā

According to Saṁgīta-ratnākara	*Āroha*	*Avaroha*	*Modern Scale*	*Present Ṭhāṭa Rāga Name*
(1) Uttaramandrā	SRGMPDN	NDPMGRS	SRgMPDN	X
(2) Rajanī	ṆSRGMPD	DPMGRSṆ	SrgGmdn	X
(3) Uttarāyatā	ḌṆSRGMP	PMGRSṆḌ	SRgMmdn	X
(4) Śuddhaṣaḍjā	P̣ḌṆSRGM	MGRSṆḌP̣	SRGMPdn	X
(5) Matsarīkṛt	ṂP̣ḌṆSRG	GRSṆḌP̣Ṃ	SRGmdDn	X
(6) Aśvakrāntā	G̣ṂP̣ḌṆSR	RSṆḌP̣ṂG̣	SRGmdDN	X
(7) Abhirudgatā	ṚG̣ṂP̣ḌṆS	SṆḌP̣ṂG̣Ṛ	SRgMPDN	X

Sāntara Mūrcchanā

(1) Uttaramandrā	SRGMPDN	NDPMGRS	SRGMPDn	Khamāj
(2) Rajanī	ṆSRGMPD	DPMGRSṆ	SRGmPDN	Kalyāṇa
(3) Uttarāyatā	ḌṆSRGMP	PMGRSṆḌ	SrgMPdn	Bhairavī
(4) Śuddhaṣaḍjā	P̣ḌṆSRGM	MGRSṆḌP̣	SRgMPDn	Kāphī
(5) Matsarīkṛt	ṂP̣ḌṆSRG	GRSṆḌP̣Ṃ	SRGMPDN	Bilāvala
(6) Aśvakrāntā	G̣ṂP̣ḌṆSR	RSṆḌP̣ṂG̣	SrgGmdn	X
(7) Abhirudgatā	ṚG̣ṂP̣ḌṆS	SṆḌP̣ṂG̣Ṛ	SRgMPdn	Jaunapurī (Āsāvarī)

Sāntarakākalika Mūrcchanā

(1) Uttaramandrā	SRGMPDN	NDPMGRS	SRGMPDN	Bilāvala
(2) Rajanī	ṆSRGMPD	DPMGRSṆ	SrgMmdn	X
(3) Uttarāyatā	ḌṆSRGMP	PMGRSṆḌ	SRgMPdn	Jaunapurī (Āsāvarī)
(4) Śuddhaṣaḍjā	P̣ḌṆSRGM	MGRSṆḌP̣	SRGMPDn	Khamāj
(5) Matsarīkṛt	ṂP̣ḌṆSRG	GRSṆḌP̣Ṃ	SRGmPDN	Kalyāṇa
(6) Aśvakrāntā	G̣ṂP̣ḌṆSR	RSṆḌP̣ṂG̣	SrgMPdn	Bhairavī
(7) Abhirudgatā	ṚG̣ṂP̣ḌṆS	SṆḌP̣ṂG̣Ṛ	SRgMPDn	Kāphī

It should be noted from the foregoing tables that excepting Sakākalika Mūrcchanā all other Mūrcchanās but one have their counter-parts in the present day Ṭhāṭas. Rajanī Mūrcchanā as given in Saṁgītaratnākara is similar to the present day diatonic major scale or the Bilāvala Ṭhāṭa.

On the other hand, Sāntarakākalika Ṣaḍja Mūrcchanā is also similar to Bilāvala Ṭhāṭa. Thus it is possible to draw the present day diatonic major scale or Bilāvala Ṭhāṭa from the Śāstra reference in two different ways. As such, the arguments for wrong distribution of Śrutis contrary to the Śāstras are hereby refuted (vide 'Śruti').

191. Murkī or Murakī

Another name for Khaṭkā (vide 'Khaṭkā').

192. Nāda

In the Śāstras, Nāda has been mentioned as inseparable from Brahma and has been recognised to be Nādabrahma. Nāda is indivisible and is Ānanda or Supreme Joy itself. The root of the 'Praṇava' or 'Om' which is 'Parāvāk' and Nāda are one and the same and Nāda-worship leads to the realisation of Brahma. The Śāstras have cited an example – as a jewel and its radiance are so inseparable, so that one, trying to discover the source of radiance, gets the jewel itself, so is the relation between Nāda and Brahma. The root meaning of Nāda has been explained as this – 'Nā' is life (Vāyu or air) and 'Da' is fire (energy), these together form sound—expressed, which is called Nāda. There are two kinds of Nāda, one is Anāhata or unstruck i.e., not caused by any means but self sounding, and the other is Āhata or struck i.e., produced by some means or other. On the other hand three other categories of Nāda are to be considered viz., Anudātta or Bass or lower, Svarita or Tenor or medium and Udātta or Soprano or higher. Anudātta has its site in the thorax region, Svarita in the throat and Udātta in the head. The conception and the use of three gamuts viz., Bass, Tenor and Soprano have evolved out of these categories mentioned in the Śāstras. It has also been mentioned in the Śāstras that each of these three Nādas is sounded with double the effort as compared with the previous one (vide 'Vazan' and 'Saptaka').

193. Nāḍā

The meaning of this Hindi word is red string. Ustāds tie Nāḍā on the right wrist of their pupils before accepting them as such. This is a symbolic tie of honour that binds the Śiṣya to his Guru.

194. Nasṭa or Prohibited Bolas

In percussion instruments, the following Bolas are prohibited as unusable:
Dhāṭ, Tāṭ, Tarkaṭ, Tirkaṭ, Nākāṭe, Nākiṭ, Gaddi (Gadi or Gidi to be used), Tāṭe, Dharkaṭ, Dhāvā, Nāḍ, Nāḍā, Dhādhāḍā, Dhātikāyen, Dhātā.

195. Nauhāra Vāṇī

Vide 'Ālāpa' and 'Gīti'.

196. Nāyaka

A musician who is most proficient in all the departments of music is given the title of Nāyaka. In his book 'Madnūl Mausīqui' (1853 A.D.) Hakīm Mohammad Karam Imām has mentioned the names of the following twelve Nāyakas:-

(1) Bhānu, (2) Lohaṁga, (3) Ḍālu, (4) Bhagavān, (5) Gopāladās, (6) Baijū, (7) Pāṇḍe, (8) Cajjū, (9) Bakhshū, (10) Dhoṇḍu, (11) Mīrāmadh (Mīr Ahmad), (12) Amīr Khusro.

197. Nāyakī Tār or Main String

The main string of all the string instruments. Excepting the Vīṇā it is fixed on the right side from the onlooker's point of view; the main string of the Vīṇā (Sārasvat or North Indian Vīṇā) is on the left side.

198. Nibaddha

The musical composition which is bound by Mātrā, Tāla, Laya and rhythm. Songs, Tarānās, Dhrupadas, Gats are of the Nibaddha variety.

199. Niṣāda

The seventh note of the scale. Generally called Nikhāda also. Niṣāda or Ni contains two Śrutis viz., Ugrā and Kṣobhinī and is itself on the latter Śruti. This Niṣāda of two Śrutis as mentioned in the Śāstras is at present known as Komala Niṣāda (B flat), while the B natural or Śuddha Niṣāda was known as Kākalī Niṣāda in the Śāstras. Ṣaḍja has four Śrutis viz., Tivrā, Kumudvatī, Mandā and Chandovatī. When Niṣāda, according to the Śāstras, takes the initial Śruti of Ṣaḍja and itself sits on the Tivrā, it becomes known as Kaiśikī Niṣāda, at present called Tīvra-Komala Niṣāda or Sharpened-flat B. When the same Niṣāda takes two Śrutis off Ṣaḍja and thus sits on the Śruti - Kumudvatī and itself becomes a note of four Śrutis, it is known as Kākalī Niṣāda according to Śāstras and Śuddha Niṣāda according to the present usage (vide 'Śruti').

200. Nṛtya

In Bharata's Nāṭya Śāstra, Nāṭya has been divided into 3 branches: (1) Nāṭya, (2) Nṛtta, (3) Nṛtya. It is unnecessary to go into the details and differences in the meaning of these three words for the present purpose. In different provinces of India there are various types of Nṛtya i.e., Dance– Katthak, Kathākali, Maṇipurī etc. Besides these, there are different types of folk dances prevalent in different areas. It is not possible to describe all the different types of Dances in this dictionary. Broadly speaking there are two types of dances – (1) Tāṇḍava – a type of hilarious and unrestrained variety propagated by Taṇḍu, a follower of Lord Śiva, (2) Lāsya – a soft, delicate and to some extent lustful dance propagated by Uṣā, the daughter of Bāṇa. Some mixed varieties are also there. We are describing the main four varieties:

(1) *Bharatanāṭyam* – It is a Tāṇḍava dance and is mostly prevalent in South India. Mṛdaṅga and Mādala are the percussion instruments used as accompaniment and Bolas, such as Delāg, Digitakā, Tādhikitā etc. are used. Bharata Muni had learnt this dance from Taṇḍu, so this dance can be considered as Tāṇḍava.

(2) *Maṇipurī Nṛtya* – It is prevalent in the locality of Maṇipur (Assam). This dance mainly describes Śrī Kṛṣṇa's playful sports and is devotional in character. Although it belongs to the category of Lāsya – soft and delicate—but being devotional in nature, the lascivious spirit is absent. Mṛdaṅga is the percussion instrument used. It is said that Uṣā, the daughter of Bāṇa, had taught the milkmaids of Dvārakā the Lāsya dance and those milkmaids, in turn, had taught Lāsya to the women folk of Saurāṣtra.

(3) *Kathākali Nṛtya* – This dance is mostly prevalent in the province of Kerala in South India. It is mainly in the nature of Nāṭya-Nṛtya as described in the Nāṭya Śāstra. Kathākali, as seen at present, is the result of the gradual evolution of local folk-dance of Kerala. In this dance, the different and various sentiments belonging to Gods, demons and men are manifested through Tableau. Percus-

sion Bolas such as Thi Thi, Thoi Thoi, Tātāthoi, Hittā Tho etc., are used with this dance.

(4) *Katthak Nṛtya* – During the Mughal period, this dance was brought into being by an intermixture of Bharatanātyam, Maṇipurī Nṛtya and some amount of Persian Folk dances by the Katthaks of Upper India. Pakhāvaj and Tablā are the percussion instruments used as accompaniment. The Bolas such as Tat Thun Dṛge Thun, Tat Tat, Jhikiti etc. are used. In Katthak dance, the percussion Bolas of various rhythm are repeated in the foot-steps of the dancer and the use of Tihāī (q.v.) is to be especially noted.

The above four varieties are considered classical, and there are numerous types of folk dances known as Deśī Nṛtya such as Sāṁotāla Nṛtya, Nāgā Nṛtya, Devadāsī Nṛtya, Gājana Nṛtya etc.

201. Nyāsa

When the understanding of a Rāga seems to be complete and satisfying by resting on a particular note of the scale, that note is called the Nyāsa Svara of that particular Rāga. In the olden days, before the conception of a Rāga name came into being, Jāti, produced out of the seven notes, was in vogue; the use of Graha, Nyāsa, Apanyāsa, Sanyāsa and Vinyāsa notes was indispensable in the description of Jāti. At present sometimes, some references are made of Graha and Nyāsa notes with regard to classical music but most of the musicians do not use these notes as indispensably as in olden days. However, Nyāsa Svaras are still indispensable in some of the Rāgas e.g., lower N in Tilaka Kāmoda, middle R in Deśa etc. Many Rāgas take S as the Nyāsa Svara. In most of the Rāgas, Aṁśa notes and their consonant i.e., Saṁvādī notes are used as the Nyāsa notes, for instance G in Rāga Yamana can be considered its Nyāsa Svara. Before resting on the Nyāsa note, no Rāga-phrase can be considered satisfying and relieving to either the musician or the audience.

202. Pada

The meanings 'Word' and 'Phrase' out of various meanings of this Sanskrit word Pada have been considered here. In Sanskrit Grammar, Pada means a word also. As in literature, Svara Varṇa (Vowels) and Vyañjana Varṇa (Consonants) combine to make a word or a phrase, so in music, various Padas or words are framed by arranging the musical alphabets, which are known as Varṇas (q.v.), in different orders to make a Pada, i.e., word or phrase, to signify the concept of a Rāga. The sequence of notes, by the way, is the main factor of Indian Rāga music as in all other purely melodic music. Various Padas belonging to a particular Rāga are artistically arranged in a proper sequence to make a musical demonstration. A pertinent question may arise – how many notes can make a Pada? The answer is – from two notes to the entire seven notes – can make different Padas of a Rāga using seven notes. For example 'rg' is a two-note Pada used in Rāga Toḍī whereas mNDNmDP is a Pada or phrase using seven notes. It matters little if the notes are repeated, they can be equally used in Rāga Yamana, Rāga Hamīra or Rāga Kedārā. This common phrase would reveal a particular Rāga by the use of other Padas according to a particular Rāga. This seven-note phrase can be divided into parts e.g., mNDN, and mDP. Here two separate phrases can point to a particular Rāga, Yamana, Hamīra or Kedārā, but if the seven-note phrase is divided thus mND, NmDP, the first Pada mND is a particular recognised Pada for Hamīra but NmDP is an arbitrary Pada and indicates no particular Rāga. Of course this Pada can be used in recognized Yamana, but conventionally it is not a phrase for Yamana.

Every Rāga has various Padas of its own e.g., dnP, ḍṇSR etc. for Darbārīkānhaḍā, GRMG for Gauḍasāraṅga, GMRG for Bilāvala, PmGMG for Bihāga etc. In modern musical books, while mentioning Pakaḍa for a Rāga, Padas are often separated by commas(,). Pada is also called 'Rāga Pada', or 'Svara-Śabda' i.e., 'Note-word'. In literature a 'Word' signifies a concept; in music 'Word' or Pada signifies a Rāga and in case of such an arrangement of notes, which does not signify a Rāga, it cannot be called either a Pada or a word, e.g., RgG, mDgM etc. Arrangement of notes in a proper order to form a Pada and composition of Padas in a proper order to delineate a Rāga are the main features of pleasant Rāga-music.

203. Pada Bidārī

Vide 'Bidārī'.

204. Paḍāla

The way in which the Bolas of a percussion instrument are produced by the hand is called Paḍāla. In another meaning: the Bolas of a percussion instrument, if composed in conformity with

the rhythm of a Sanskrit Śloka or couplet, then such Bolas are called the Paḍāla of that particular Śloka e.g.,
Śloka : Taddehabhuṣita Ahirika Phaṇā
Paḍāla : Dhet Dhere Keṭetāk Dregedhene Tānā.

205. Pakaḍa

The meaning of this Hindi word is 'To catch'. In musical terminology, it means the phrases, composed of the smallest number of notes, by which a particular Rāga can be distinctively recognised. For instance the phrase PmGRGmP can be considered Pakaḍa of Rāga Yamana, because this phrase can point only to Yamana and to no other Rāga; Pakaḍa phrases of Tilaka Kāmoda are RMPDMG, SRGSṆ; those of Sohanī - G - mDNṠṙṠ – the phrase includes G separated by a dash i.e., a time gap of a second or so, the rest of the notes are sounded in quick succession.

206. Palṭā

Vide 'Tāna'.

207. Pañcama

'Pañcama', a Sanskrit word meaning 'Fifth'; so the fifth note of the scale is called Pañcama. In Ṣaḍja Grāma (q.v.) the fifth note Pañcama, commonly known as Pā or P has four Śrutis allotted to it viz., - Kṣiti or Kṣamā, Raktā, Sandīpinī and Ālāpinī and P is precisely placed on the fourth. When Madhyama or M takes over two Śrutis of P viz., Kṣiti and Raktā and sits on the latter, M becomes sharpened and is known as Kaḍi M or m of the present time, although it should have been known as flattened P. However, in this case it is an exception, as in the case of Ṣaḍja (vide 'Niṣāda'). Since both Ṣaḍja and Pañcama are Acala Svaras, they cannot be moved either flat or sharp. Pañcama is a very important note of the scale because according to the laws of Harmonics, Pañcama, as a self-emanant note, closely follows Ṣaḍja. The Sanskrit meaning of self-emanant is Svayambhū (q.v.). This theory of self-emanation is commonly known in Indian music as Ṣaḍja-Pañcama Bhāva. Pañcama is the main consonant note i.e., Saṁvādī of Ṣaḍja (vide 'Vādī', 'Śruti').

208. Paraṇa

In Saṁgītaratnākara, a compound word 'Tāla-Pūraṇa' meaning 'Filling the gap of Tāla' has been used. Pūraṇa means 'Filling the gap'. So it can well be imagined that 'Paraṇa' is a modern rendering of the old word 'Pūraṇa'. When the Ṭhekā of a percussion instrument is played, sometimes the precomposed Ṭhekā-Bolas of a few Mātrās (q.v.), before 'Sama' (q.v.), are replaced by some other Bolas, either freelance or precomposed. This replacement of original Ṭhekā Bolas is called Paraṇa. It can also be called 'Ṭhekā-Paraṇa' or 'Tālaparaṇa'. Some have referred to Paraṇa as 'Parama'; some have again referred to Paraṇa as 'Prakramaṇikā' in chaste Bengali. But 'Paraṇa' as a colloquial rendering of 'Pūraṇa' is more justifiable as evident from its use. Broadly speaking, anything played on a percussion instrument excepting Ṭhekā can as well be called 'Paraṇa' (vide 'Tāraparaṇa', 'Ālāpa').

209. Pardūna

In speed, the double of the double i.e., four times the original Laya, is called Pardūna. If two sounds are produced in a beat, the act is called Dūna and double of this i.e., if four sounds are produced in a beat, it is called Pardūna. In Bengali this is generally called 'Caudūna' i.e., fourtimes Dūna - which becomes eight sounds per beat. Although this has obtained currency, it is etymologically incorrect.

210. Parkhāda or Parkhāja

This is a Hindi word. The octave lower than the usual lower octave is known as Parkhāda, 'Par' is 'After' and 'Khāda' is just the lower octave. In Bengali it is called Atimandra.

211. Parmāṭhā

Vide 'Ālāpa'. This word seems to have been derived from the Sanskrit word Pratimanṭha mentioned in Saṁgītaratnākara, although not in the same meaning.

212. Pāṭa

The alphabets used in percussion Bolas are called Pāṭas (vide 'Bola').

213. Perāḍī

A variation of rhythm. If in a rhythm of sixteen beats, ten and a half Bolas are sounded in equal intervals, then that rhythm is called Perāḍī. In this case each Bolas will be of $1^{11}/_{21}$ times the duration of a beat (vide 'Laya').

214. Peśkār (Peshkār)

Variations of a Ṭhekā of a percussion instrument are called Peśkārs. After a Ṭhekā has been introduced, to present it in various ways, the Bolas of that particular Ṭhekā are presented with various accents and in various ways; it would contain both Khuli and Mudi Bolas e.g.,

| | | | | | | |
Dhāteṭe Keṭedhi Nāg Dhenā Ghenā Dhāge Tenā Kenā
| | | | | | | |
Tateṭe Keṭeti Nāk Tenā Ghenā Dhage Dhenā Ghenā

215. Phāṁk

The most accented beat of a Tāla is called 'Sama' and the beat which is altogether unaccented is called 'Phāṁk'. If the beats of a Tritāla are equally divided into two groups, each containing 8 beats, it would be seen that the particular beat representing Phāṁk would be exactly opposite to the beat representing Sama, so the Phāṁk is also known as Viṣama i.e., opposite to Sama (q.v. 'Tāla').

216. Pharad

This word appears to be onomatopoeic. As used in the percussion instrument Tablā, it is that variety of Tukḍā, which terminates in the phrase 'Katdhereketetāk Dhā, and is usually played twice faster than the rest of the Bolas. For example, look at the following Pharad:

+| | | | 2|
Dhā-teṭe Teṭe dhāge Teṭeghaḍā-ṇ Dhāge Teṭeteṭe
| | | 0| |
Kaḍdhāteṭe Ghenetetẹ Ghenetunā Tāteṭetā Teṭekaḍdhā
| | 3| | |
Teṭeteṭe Dhāteṭedhā Teṭedhāgi Nadhagin Trekeṭtaktā
| +|
'Katdhereketetāk Dhā'.

217. Pharāsbandī

In percussion instruments viz., Tablā etc. a type of Tukḍā played as a prologue to a programme of the same instrument in solo or in accompaniment, is called 'Pharāsbandī' (q.v. 'Salāmī Tukḍā' and 'Uṭhāna').

218. Phirat

Alternative name of 'Phirkat', some hold this to be an alternative name of 'Palṭi' (q.v. 'Tāna').

219. Prakāra Bheda

Different types . In the field of north Indian classical music, there are, broadly speaking two types viz., Anibaddha and Nibaddha. Anibaddha is that type of music which is absolutely free from any rhythmic bounds in the form of Tāla, metre etc. such as the first portion of Ālāpa. On the other hand, rhythmic or Nibaddha music is bound by rhythm, metre, Tāla etc. such as songs, Gats, Saragam compositions and Tarānās etc. In all these compositions, Tāla plays an indispensable role.

Ālāpa has in itself both the Anibaddha and the Nibaddha varieties. The first portion of Ālāpa is an extempore composition free from Tāla or metre and is known as the Anibaddha portion, while the second portion is bound by rhythm and metre and some portion of it is bound by Tāla also. In the Tāla portion, percussion accompaniment is provided with Pakhāvaj or Tablā in a particular Tāla. This is known as the Nibaddha portion. The bridge or link between the Anibaddha and Nibaddha portions is provided by a middle portion known as Joḍ (q.v.).

Apart from the above types, there are the Rāga varieties. In Indian musical Gharānās, different varieties of the same Rāga can be found. It is not possible to deal fully with each variety nor have all the Rāgas been dealt with in this dictionary. For the convenience of inquisitive readers, a list has been prepared only to mention the numbers of varieties of the same Rāgas. This list, prepared from the personal collection of the present author, is by no means the last word. There are innumerable varieties which could not be collected. Here also is supplied a list of different Rāgas belonging to the same category. For instance, Rāga Toḍī is a genus, in other words, a category and the names of Rāgas belonging to this category such as Darbārī, Gurjarī, Lācārī etc. have also been enlisted. No attempt has been made to go into the details of each Rāga; only the name and the number of varieties have been mentioned. It will be observed that in mentioning varieties of a Rāga category, some mixed Rāgas have been included just as an attempt to make the list complete as far as possible.

Apart from this, some musicians try to categorize the Rāgas according to the number of notes in each, such as Auḍuva or pentatonic i.e., Rāgas using five notes, Ṣāḍava or hexatonic i.e., Rāgas using six notes and Sampūrṇa or heptatonic i.e., Rāgas using all the seven notes of the scale.

(A). Number of varieties of the same Rāga prevalent in different Gharānās:

(1)	Āḍambarīkānhaḍā	...2
(2)	Āśā	...2
(3)	Āsāvarī	...2
(4)	Baḍahaṁsa Sāraṅga	...4
(5)	Bāgeśrī	...2
(6)	Bahādurī Toḍī	...2
(7)	Barvā (Bāroāṁ)	...2
(8)	Basavarā	...2
(9)	Bhavasākha (Bhusākha)	...2
(10)	Bhīma	...2
(11)	Bhinna Ṣaḍja	...2
(12)	Bhūpāla Toḍī	...2
(13)	Bihāga	...2
(14)	Bihāgaḍā	...2
(15)	Cañcalasasamalhāra	...2
(16)	Candrakauśa	...2
(17)	Chāyātoḍī	...2
(18)	Citragaurī	...2
(19)	Darbārīkānhaḍa	...2
(20)	Deśagauḍa	...2
(21)	Deśakāra	...2
(22)	Devagiri Bilāvala	...5
(23)	Dhanāśrī	...2
(24)	Dhavalaśrī	...2
(25)	Dhuliyā Sāraṅga	...2
(26)	Dīpaka	...2
(27)	Durgā	...2
(28)	Gāndhārītoḍī	...2
(29)	Gauḍamalhāra	...2
(30)	Gaurī	...6
(31)	Gorakha Kalyāṇa	...4
(32)	Guṇakrī	...2
(33)	Haridāsī Malhāra (Haradāsī Malhāra)	...2
(34)	Hema	...2

(35) Hindola ...2
(36) Jaṅglā ...3
(37) Jayajaya Bilāvala ...2
(38) Jayanta Bihāga ...2
(39) Jayet (Jaita) ...4
(40) Jayet (Jaita) Kalyāṇa ...2
(41) Jilaph (Zilaf) ...2
(42) Jogiyā ...2
(43) Kāphī ...2
(44) Kaukabha Bilāvala ...2
(45) Khamāj ...2
(46) Khaṭ ...2
(47) Kṣema Kalyāṇa ...2
(48) Lācārī Toḍī ...5
(49) Laṅkādahana Sāraṅga ...4
(50) Madhumādhavī Sāraṅga ...5
(51) Mālaśrī ...2
(52) Māligaurā ...3
(53) Māṁjha ...2
(54) Maṅgala Bhairava ...3
(55) Māru ...2
(56) Māru Kedāra ...2
(57) Meghamalhāra ...2
(58) Miyān Kī Sāraṅga ...5
(59) Nārāyaṇī ...2
(60) Nāyakī Kānhaḍā ...4
(61) Nīlāmbarī ...2
(62) Pahāḍī ...2
(63) Palāśrī ...2
(64) Pañcama ...7
(65) Paṭamañjarī ...3
(66) Phirozkhānī (Firozkhānī) Toḍī ...2
(67) Pīlū ...2
(68) Prabhātabhairava ...3
(69) Pratāpalaṅkeśvara ...2
(70) Pūravī ...2
(71) Pūrvā ...2
(72) Rāmakalī (Rāmakelī) ...4
(73) Sāmanta Sāraṅga ...2
(74) Śaṅkarā Aruṇa ...2
(75) Sáṅkarābharaṇa ...2

(76) Śaṅkarākaraṇa ...2
(77) Sāvanī ...2
(78) Sāverī ...2
(79) Śivamata Bhairava ...2
(80) Sohanī ...3
(81) Śuddha Kauśa ...2
(82) Śuddha Malhāra ...2
(83) Śuddha Sāraṅga ...2
(84) Śuklabilāvala ...2
(85) Sūradāsī Malhāra ...2
(86) Surāṭī Kānhaḍā ...2
(87) Śyāma Kalyāṇa ...3
(88) Tilaka Kāmoda ...3
(89) Triveṇī ...2
(90) Varāṭi or Vararī ...2
(91) Vasanta ...6
(92) Vibhāsa ...4
(93) Vṛndāvanī Sāraṅga ...2
(94) Yamana ...4

(B). Different Rāgas belonging to the same category:

I. Bahār

(1) Aḍāṇā
(2) Bāgeśrī
(3) Bhairava
(4) Bhairavī
(5) Hindola
(6) Jaunapurī
(7) Lalita
(8) Mālakauśa
(9) Sohanī
(10) Śuddha
(11) Sūhā

II. Bhairava

(1) Ādi
(2) Ahīra
(3) Ānanda
(4) Auḍuva
(5) Baṅgāla
(6) Bilāskhānī
(7) Kallinātha
(8) Komala
(9) Maṅgala
(10) Naubadkhānī
(11) Palāśrī
(12) Pañcamukhī
(13) Prabhāta
(14) Ṣāḍava
(15) Sāmanta
(16) Sarasvatī
(17) Śivamata
(18) Śrī

(19) Śuddha
(20) Ṭaṁka
(21) Vairāgī
(22) Vasanta
(23) Viṣṇu

III. Bhairavī
(1) Ānanda
(2) Āśā
(3) Kasaulī
(4) Kauśī
(5) Palāsrī
(6) Sāmanta
(7) Sindhu
(8) Sindhurā
(9) Sohana
(10) Śuddha
(11) Toḍī

IV. Bihāga
(1) Deva
(2) Hema
(3) Jayanta
(4) Komala
(5) Mālava
(6) Māru
(7) Naṭa
(8) Paṭa
(9) Rainī
(10) Śuddha

V. Bilāvala
(1) Ahīrī
(2) Ahīrī Bhairava
(3) Alhaiyā
(4) Auḍuva
(5) Auḍuva Devagiri
(6) Baṅgāla
(7) Devagiri
(8) Haṁsa
(9) Hema
(10) Jayajaya
(11) Kṣema
(12) Kukubha
(13) Lacchāsākha
(14) Māru
(15) Mudrā
(16) Mudrika
(17) Naṭa
(18) Sarpardā
(19) Śuddha
(20) Śukla
(21) Vibhāsa

VI. Gaurī
(1) Citra
(2) Lalitā
(3) Māligaurā
(4) Māravā
(5) Śuddha
(6) Ṭaṁkī

(22) Yamanī

VII. Jhiṁjhiṭa (Jhiṁjhoṭī)
(1) Deva
(2) Gārā
(3) Kasaulī
(4) Lūma
(5) Nūrapurī
(6) Pahāḍī
(7) Śuddha

VIII. Kalyāṇa
(1) Bhoga
(2) Bhūp
(3) Bilās<u>kh</u>ānī
(4) Candra
(5) Chāyā
(6) Dīpaka
(7) Gorakha
(8) Guṇa
(9) Hamīra
(10) Hema
(11) Jaita
(12) Kāmoda
(13) Kedāra
(14) Kṣema
(15) Miyān Kī
(16) Pūrvā
(17) Pyāra
(18) Rainī
(19) Ravi
(20) Śaṅkara
(21) Śaṅkarā
(22) Sāvanī
(23) Śuddha
(24) Śyāma
(25) Yamana

IX. Kāmoda
(1) Gopī
(2) Hema
(3) Karuṇa
(4) Śrī
(5) Śuddha

X. Kānhaḍā
(1) Āḍambarī
(2) Bāgeśrī
(3) Bhupa
(4) Bilās<u>kh</u>ānī
(5) Candramukhī
(6) Darbārī
(7) Daulatī
(8) Devasākha
(9) Husaynī
(10) Jayajayantī
(11) Kauśīka

(12) Khamājī
(13) Kolāhala
(14) Mudrā Kī
(15) Nāgadhavani
(16) Naubadkhānī
(17) Nāyakī
(18) Palāśrī
(19) Pañcamukhī
(20) Sindūrā
(21) Śuddha
(22) Sughrāī
(23) Sūhā
(24) Sūhā-Sughrāī
(25) Surathī
(26) Vāsantī

XI. Kauśa
(1) Bhava
(2) Candra
(3) Māla
(4) Maṅgala
(5) Rava
(6) Śuddha
(7) Sūrya

XII. Kedāra
(1) Cāṁdnī
(2) Jaladhara
(3) Komala
(4) Maluhā
(5) Manohara
(6) Māru
(7) Sāvanī
(8) Śuddha

XIII. Khamāj (Khambāj)
(1) Ahaṁ
(2) Gārā
(3) Hamīra
(4) Jhiṁjhiṭa (Jhiṁjhoṭī)
(5) Lūma
(6) Śuddha
(7) Tilaṁga

XIV. Malhāra
(1) Aruṇa
(2) Bilāsī
(3) Cañcalasasa
(4) Carjū Kī
(5) Deśa
(6) Dhuṁdhi Kī
(7) Dhuriyā
(8) Gauḍa
(9) Hā-Hā-Hū-Hū
(10) Haridāsī
(11) Jāja
(12) Jayajayantī
(13) Kāmoda

(14) Madanamañjarī
(15) Mathurādāsakī
(16) Megha
(17) Mīrābāī Kī
(18) Miyān Kī
(19) Naṭa
(20) Naubadk͟hānī
(21) Purānī
(22) Rāmadāsī
(23) Rūpamañjarī
(24) Sat Kī
(25) Sohana
(26) Śuddha
(27) Sūradāsī
(28) Suraṭha

XV. Naṭa
(1) Bṛhannaṭa
(2) Chāyā
(3) Gauḍa
(4) Kāmoda
(5) Kedāra
(6) Naṭakindra
(7) Naṭakurañjikā
(8) Naṭanārāyaṇa
(9) Śuddha

XVI. Rāmakalī or Rāmakelī
(1) Komala
(2) Paraja
(3) Śuddha

XVII. Śaṅkarā
(1) Aruṇa
(2) Bharaṇa
(3) Karaṇa
(4) Śuddha
(5) Śudhaṁkarā
(6) Varaṇa
(7) Yamana

XVIII. Sāraṅga
(1) Baḍahaṁsa
(2) Bhīma
(3) Dhuliyā
(4) Gauḍa
(5) Gaurahāra
(6) Laṅkādahana
(7) Luma
(8) Madhu-mādhavī
(9) Māru
(10) Miyān Kī
(11) Raktahaṁsa
(12) Sāmanta

(13) Sāraṅgī
(14) Sarpa
(15) Śuddha
(16) Śukla
(17) Suraṭhī
(18) Suta
(19) Vṛndāvanī

XIX. Toḍi
(1) Adāraṅgī
(2) Ahīrī
(3) Añjanī
(4) Āsāvarī
(5) Bahādurī
(6) Bhūpāla
(7) Bilāskhānī
(8) Chāyā
(9) Chāyālī
(10) Darbārī
(11) Deśī
(12) Devagāndhāra
(13) Firozkhānī
(14) Gāndhārī
(15) Gāndrikā
(16) Gurjarī
(17) Jaunapurī
(18) Kāphī
(19) Khaṭa
(20) Komala Deśī
(21) Lācārī
(22) Lakṣmī
(23) Mārgī
(24) Miyān Kī
(25) Prabhātapaṭa
(26) Rāma
(27) Śuddha
(28) Turkī
(29) Varārī

XX. Vasanta
(1) Gopī
(2) Lalita
(3) Pañcama
(4) Paraja
5) Śrī
(6) Śuddha
(7) Vasantabahār
(8) Vasantabhairava
(9) Vasantamukhārī
(10) Vasanta-nārāyaṇī

220. Pramāṇa Śruti

Both Bharata and Śāraṅgadeva mentioned Pramāṇa Śruti specifically to determine the value of one Śruti as it sounds in the ear. Inter alia it must be remembered that in their time there was no other determining factor to evaluate or to understand the Śruti except by the perception of hearing. Hence the name 'Śruti' has been selected, the only word to cover the entire connotation of Śruti, which literally means "What is heard". In the Ṣaḍja Grāma, the note Pañcama has four Śrutis viz., Kṣiti or Kṣa, Raktā, Sandīpinī and Ālāpinī and the note P is precisely placed on this last. This Pañcama is a Saṁvādī note of Ṣaḍja and is located on the thirteenth Śruti counting from Ṣaḍja and the other Saṁvādī note Madhyama is on the ninth Śruti from Ṣaḍja. The Saṁvādī note of Ṛṣabha is Dhaivata being placed on the thirteenth Śruti counted from Ṛṣabha, but the other Saṁvādī note which should have been placed on the ninth Śruti is missing in Ṣaḍja Grāma. On the other hand, in the Madhyama Grāma, Pañcama being placed on its third Śruti Sandīpinī, becomes a Saṁvādī note of Ṛṣabha, being placed on the ninth Śruti from Ṛṣabha. The other Saṁvādī note Dhaivata is placed on the thirteenth Śruti as in the Ṣaḍja Grāma. So in both the Grāmas, Dhaivata is a Saṁvādī note of Ṛṣabha, although in Madhyama Grāma, it has become a note of four Śrutis, having taken from Pañcama its last Śruti Ālāpinī.

Now Pañcama, as a Saṁvādī note of Ṣaḍja in the Ṣaḍja Grāma, is diminished by a Śruti to make it as Saṁvādī note of Ṛṣabha in the Madhyama Grāma. If these two scales are heard simultaneously, the difference between the Pañcamas of Ṣaḍja Grāma and Madhyama Grāma would be clearly manifest - and this difference in pitch is the Pramāṇa Śruti i.e., the value of one Śruti as perceived by the ear.

221. Prastāra

Means elaboration of musical notes by permutations. In music, the fundamental notes are seven in number and in different permutations these seven-note-scales can be re-arranged in 5040 different ways. This whole process is called Prastāra, and each of those 5040 arrangements is called a Tāna. If only six notes out of seven are taken into account, then the group of six notes is called Ṣāḍava (q.v.) and can be re-arranged in 720 different ways; a group of five notes – known as Auḍuva (q.v.), can be re-arranged in 120 ways; a group of four notes known as Svarāntara (q.v.), can be re-arranged in 24 different ways; a group of three notes known as

Sāmika (q.v.), can be re-arranged in 6 different ways; a group of two notes known as Gāthika (q.v.), can be re-arranged in two different ways and lastly the unit of one note known as Ārcika (q.v.), has no re-arrangement, so, it has to be satisfied with only one way (vide 'Tāna').

222. Purvāṁga

Vide 'Aṁga'.

223. Rāga

The root meanings of Rāga according to Saṁgītaratnākara are as follows : 'Rañjayati Iti Rāgaḥ'.

(a) The sound, produced out of Svaras (q.v.) i.e., notes and Varṇas (q.v.) i.e., cluster of notes, to which people's mind is attracted is called a Rāga.

(b) The sound, produced out of Svaras and Varṇas which attracts the mind of people, is called a Rāga.

The above definitions or rather descriptions do not lead anybody anywhere; the descriptions are so widely general that any type of pleasing sound can be called a Rāga, including the Western music. The definition can be formulated in the following manner:

"The juxtaposition of notes, according to some particular rules, when sounded to produce a pleasing perception in the listeners can be called a Rāga." Juxtaposition of notes is different from a harmonic composition where chords are sounded simultaneously. Rāga is a composition solely depending upon the juxtaposition of notes, sounded in sequence. We can explain by citing an example. 'SGP', if sounded simultaneously, would produce a major chord of the Western harmonic music, but if sounded in a sequence, would reveal a short phrase of Rāga Saṅkarā. That is the only difference between harmonic and melodic music. But all melodic compositions are not Rāgas. In order to compose a Rāga-melody, one has to follow strictly the rules of a particular Rāga in such a careful manner that while listening the same, no other Rāga melody seems to appear even for a short while, unless intended by the musician himself. The Rāga melody is entirely Indian in origin; no where in the world is there anything like Rāga melody, although there are pure melodic music in various parts of the world. Innumerable different Rāgas have been created so far based upon the use of twelve notes (seven pure and five either flattened or sharpened) in ascending and descending orders, the use of a number of notes of a scale and the inter-relation of juxtaposed notes. The whole edifice of the Rāga melody stands on this juxtaposition of notes. Various precise and meticulous rules have been devised solely to keep one melody separate from all others.

A Ṭhāṭa is simply an enumeration, in natural sequence, of notes to be used in a particular Rāga composition. A Ṭhāṭa has neither an Āroha nor an Avaroha. All the ten Ṭhāṭas that have obtained currency since 1930 or so, use seven notes of the scale i.e., they are Sampūrṇa (q.v.) in nature.

By omitting one or two notes from a Ṭhāṭa, and arranging the six or five notes in particular and different ways, various Rāgas have been formed; so from each Ṭhāṭa, various Rāgas may be formed. That is the difference between a Ṭhāṭa and a Rāga. A Ṭhāṭa is a general enumeration of notes in their natural sequence whereas a Rāga is a specific juxtaposition of notes belonging to a particular Ṭhāṭa. In short, Ṭhāṭa is the enumeration of 7 Śuddha (q.v.) or Vikṛta (q.v.) notes, and Rāga is the enumeration of 5, 6 or 7 Śuddha or Vikṛta notes according to a particular way of Āroha and Avaroha, e.g.,

'Ṭhāṭa' - SRgMPDnṠ

'Rāga' - Āroha – ṇSgMPnṠ

Avaroha – nDPMgRS

In the above example, enumeration of the 'Kāphī Ṭhāṭa' is given using flattened G and N i.e., E flat and B flat (Western) respectively. Then the Āroha and Avaroha of a Rāga, Bhīmapalāśrī, using the same notes as Kāphī Ṭhāṭa, but in some particular arrangement viz., in ascending i.e., in Āroha, it starts from B flat (Western) of the lower octave and omitting D and A and in Avaroha, it uses all the notes upto C and does not necessarily touch B flat of the lower octave.

In olden times, Hindustāni classical music was based upon the 'Jāti' (q.v.) system, but for the last five or six centuries, the 'Rāga' system has been used in place of the former. Later, references had been made of Rāgas, their Rāginīs (wives), sons and daughters-in-law (vide 'Mata') but this imaginary relationship cannot be supported by logic.

Generally there are three types of Rāgas:

(1) Sampūrṇa (Heptatonic or using 7 notes)

(2) Ṣāḍava (Hexatonic or using 6 notes)

(3) Auḍuva (Pentatonic or using 5 notes)

By an intermixture of the above, according to Āroha and Avaroha, 9 types of Rāgas can be created (vide 'Jāti'). There is yet another way of classifying the Rāgas viz.,

(1) Śuddha – Pure Rāga

(2) Sālaṅka or Chāyālaga – Mixture of two Rāgas

(3) Saṁkīrṇa – Mixture of more than two Rāgas.

Besides the above the Rāgas can also be classified according to season or Ṛtu (q.v.).

Paṇdit Viṣṇunārāyaṇa Bhātakhaṇḍe has classified the Rāgas thus:

(1) Day Rāgas

(2) Dawn and Dusk Rāgas

(3) Night Rāgas.

Furthermore, Paṇditjī, after examining and analysing the Rāgas, has formulated the following rules in respect of their classification:

(1) Rāgas are of 3 types according to the use of 7, 6 or 5 notes.

(2) At least 5 notes are required for a melody to be called a Rāga. There is an exception, namely, a variety of the Rāga Mālaśrī using 4 notes.

(3) No Rāga would leave out both P and M at the same time.

(4) Generally, a note cannot be used in both Śuddha and Vikṛta form together in a Rāga - there is an exception viz., Śuddha and Tīvra M in Rāga Lalita.

(5) In Upper India Bilāvala Ṭhāṭa or the diatonic major scale is to be known as the Śuddha scale.

(6) Generally, in the Hindustānī system, Rāgas have been classified in three main categories viz.,

(a) Rāgas using Śuddha R and Śuddha D

(b) Rāgas using Komala R and Komala D

(c) Rāgas using Komala G and Komala N

(7) In every Rāga, there will be one Vādī (Aṁśa) note and it will be used in a distinguished manner.

(8) A Rāga will be called Uttarāṁga (q.v.) or Pūrvāṁga (q.v.) on the basis of Vādī note.

(9) The time factor as determined for each Rāga appears to be based upon psychological reasons.

(10) In determining the time factor, the role of Tīvra M is very important.

(11) Rāgas for dawn and dusk are known as 'Sandhiprakāśa' (i.e., manifestation of transition between day and night) Rāgas, and usually belong to the category using Komala R and Komala D.

(12) Generally, Rāgas using Komala G and Komala N are used at noon and at mid-night.

(13) Rāgas using Śuddha R, G, D & N are used immediately after the 'Sandhiprakāśa' Rāgas.

(14) An evening Rāga can easily be rendered a morning Rāga by shifting the Vādī note from Pūrvāṁga to Uttarāṁga i.e., from lower tetrachord to upper tetrachord respectively. For example an evening Rāga having the Vādī Svara G, which is on the lower tetrachord of the scale, can be changed to morning Rāga by treating D as the Vādī note which is in the upper tetrachord.

(15) The Hindustāni musicians of India, by their personal dexterity, use the Vivādī note of a Rāga.

(16) Pūrvāṁga Rāgas express their beauty fully in Āroha while Uttarāṁga Rāgas in Avaroha.

(17) Rāgas used immediately before 'Sandhiprakāśa' Rāgas, prolong the use of the notes, S, M and P and these notes are used as Vādī in them.

(18) There is scope for inter-mixture of Rāgas in North India while such a thing is unthinkable in the South.

The following aspects of a Rāga are to be noted carefully:

(1) Name

(2) Āroha and Avaroha

(3) Ṭhāṭa

(4) Laya (time interval), whether slow, medium or fast tempo

(5) Pūrvāṁga or Uttarāṁga

(6) Aṁśa or Vādī note

(7) Graha etc. i.e., the initial and the ending note

(8) Region of the scale – whether lower, middle or upper octave should preponderate

(9) Jāti – Sampūrṇa, Ṣāḍava or Auḍuva

(10) Classification – Śuddha, Chāyālaga or Saṁkīrṇa

(11) Calana i.e., progress, whether Śuddha (or straight) or Vakra (or crooked)

(12) Time – Season and hour
(13) Pakaḍa – Important short phrases to recognise a Rāga
(14) Goṣṭhī – i.e., Group.

It can be said with regard to this last i.e., Goṣṭhī or group that Rāgas which belong to one Ṭhāṭa may not be of the same group, e.g., Toḍī and Multānī both belong to Toḍī Ṭhāṭa but they are widely different from each other in spirit or sentiment; obviously they belong to different groups. Likewise Bhairavī and Mālakauśa, although of a common Bhairavī Ṭhāṭa, belong to different groups in sentiment (vide 'Prakārabheda').

The following have been considered as the basic Rāgas:

(1) Kānhaḍā	(11) Mālakauśa
(2) Kāphī	(12) Mālaśrī
(3) Kāmoda	(13) Megha
(4) Khamāj	(14) Lalita
(5) Gauḍa Sāraṅga	(15) Śaṅkarā
(6) Naṭa	(16) Śuddha Kalyāṇa
(7) Vṛndavanīsāraṅga	(17) Śuddha Malhāra
(8) Bilāvala	(18) Śrī
(9) Bihāga	(19) Sindhu
(10) Bhairava	(20) Hindola.

The time schedule of Rāgas, according to Indian Standard Time, as accepted by the Seniyā Gharāna:

4 to 5-30 a.m.	–	Vasanta, Paraja, Sohanī, Lalita, Pañcama, Bhāṭiyāra, Vibhāsa, Bhākāra etc.
5-30 to 7 a.m.	–	Megharañjanī, Vibhāsa, Jogiyā, Kāliṁgaḍā, Prabhāta, Rāmakalī, Guṇakalī or Guṇakarī, Bhairava etc.
7 to 10 a.m.	–	Hindola, Mālasrī, Gauḍasāraṅga etc.
10 to 11-30 a.m.	–	Bhairavī, Āsāvarī, Toḍī, Jaunapurī, Deśī, Khaṭa, etc.
11-30 a.m. to 1 p.m.	–	Sūhā, Sughrāī, Devasākha, Sāraṅga etc.
1 to 4 p.m.	–	Haṁsakiṁkiṇī, Paṭamañjarī, Pradīpikā, Dhānī, Bhīmapalāśrī, Dhanāśrī, Pīlū, Multānī etc.
4 to 5-30 p.m.	–	Pūravī, Puriyā, Dhanāśrī, Jayaśrī, Revā, Śrī, Triveṇī, Taṁka, Mālavī, Gaurī, etc.

5-30 to 7 p.m.	–	Puriyā, Māravā, Jayet, Mālīgaurā, Sājagiri, Varāṭī.
7 to 10 p.m.	–	Yamana, Bhūpālī, Śuddha Kalyāṇa, Jayet Kalyāṇa, Candrakānta, Hamīra, Kāmoda, Śyāma, Chāyānaṭa, Bihāga, Hemakalyāṇa, Naṭa, Maluhā, Saṅkarā, Durgā, Māṁḍ, Pahāḍī etc.
10 to 11-30 p.m.	–	Khamāj, Jhiṁjhoṭī, Tilaṁga, Khambāvatī, Durgā, Rāgeśrī, Gārā, Suraṭha, Deśa, Tilaka Kāmoda, Jayajayantī etc.
11-30 p.m. to 1 a.m.	–	Kāphī, Saindhavī, Sindūrā, Bāgeśrī, Bahār, Śahāna, Megha, Malhāra etc.
1 to 4 a.m.	–	Darbārīkānhaḍā, Aḍāṇā, Nāyakī-kānhaḍā, Kauśika Kānhaḍā, Mālakauśa, etc.

There are many books recommending different timings for different Rāgas but the foregoing timings are well established and generally accepted by musicians and musicologists.

224. Rāga–Citra

The anthropomorphic representation of different Rāga through paintings and their relevant description speak of poetical imagination. However, there is a scope for research along this line.

225. Rāgiṇī

No where is there any law to differentiate a Rāga from a Rāgiṇī. Some hold that only 6 Rāgas had been created to suit the Indian six seasons, and the rest are Rāgiṇīs. Some, on the other hand, hold that Rāgas are of masculine nature and Rāgiṇīs feminine, but this seems to be untenable. It appears that Rāgas and Rāgiṇīs have been so named in conformity with the names used for each. According to Sanskrit Grammar, the melodies with masculine names are called Rāgas and with feminine names called Rāgiṇīs. Yet Toḍī and Gurjarī, though grammatically feminine names, are Rāgas, according to Saṁgītaratnākara. Naming of a melody as Rāgiṇī must have been a later creation. It requires further research.

226. Rajanī

Vide 'Mūrchanā'.

227. Rakti

Sweetness or charm. Usually used with reference to a Rāga.

228. Ramya Gīti

Pleasant melodic songs composed free from Rāga rules.

229. Rañjakatā

Pleasantness as used with reference to a Rāga.

230. Rasa

The meaning of Rasa, according to Saṁgītaratnākara, is the emotional change in body or mind caused by the perception of a thing or a quality. Although there is a difference of opinion about the exact number of Rasas, there is a general consensus about nine varieties of Rasas:

(1) Ādi or Śṛṁgāra Rasa - or primordial emotion arising out of love or sexual pursuit.
(2) Hāsya Rasa - or the Rasa arising out of laughter.
(3) Karuṇa Rasa - or the melancholy emotion.
(4) Raudra Rasa - or the emotion arising out of temper or anger.
(5) Vīra Rasa - or the emotion arising out of prowess.
(6) Bhayānaka Rasa - or the emotion arising out of terror.
(7) Vībhatsa Rasa - or the emotion arising out of loathsomeness or aversion.
(8) Adbhuta Rasa - or the emotion arising out of the wonderful.
(9) Śānta Rasa - or the emotion arising out of the quest for the ultimate truth.

Those, in favour of eight Rasas, hold Śānta Rasa to be the cessation of all emotions which is the neutral and natural condition of the mind.

Those who are in favour of ten Rasas hold Vātsalya i.e., parental love to be a separate Rasa. Some include three more, Bhakti (devotion), Sneha (affection) and Laulya (greed) Rasas.

We are describing in some details the Rasas and their Bhāvas (q.v.) etc.

Śṛṁgāra Rasa has been called the Ādi Rasa since creation itself is based upon this Rasa.

Rasa	Sthāyī Bhāva	Sañcārī Bhāva	Anubhāva	Vibhāva
(1) Śṛṁgāra	Love or the sexual act.	Thoughts, curiosity, exhaustion, labour etc.	Side-glance, swinging of arms, biting of upper lips etc.	Spring season, flower, garden, song and dance, sandelwood paste, looking at a picture etc.
(2) Hāsya	Laughter		Trembling of the eye, cheek or lips, closing of eyelids, winking of eyes, pressing at the sides etc.	Shamelessness, copying others, aversion in things, indiscreet words, deceit etc.
(3) Karuṇa	Grief, mourning	Exhaustion, labour, terror, stupefaction, defection, anxiety, curiosity, distress, madness, hoarseness, fainting etc.	Shedding of tears, feeling of anguish, stunning, paleness, sigh, outburst, wasting of the body, striking at the head or heart.	Loss of wife, children or friends and well-wishers, danger, mischief, exile etc.
(4) Raudra	Anger	Anxiety, fortitude, violence, agility, standing on end of body hair etc.	Puckering of brows, red eyes, biting of lips, tightening of jaws, squeezing of the palms, pursuing the enemy, pounding, striking with the arms, beating, bleeding etc.	Ferocious creature, lies, anger, illicit pursuit of others' wives, calumny of customs or education etc.
(5) Vīra	Fortitude	Standing on end of body hair, anxiety, violence, etc.	Charity, sacrifice, speaking of deep and thoughtful words etc.	Ethics, modesty, glory, the ability to wage war, dauntlessness etc.

Rasa	Sthāyī Bhāva	Sañcārī Bhāva	Anubhāva	Vibhāva
(6) Bhayānaka	Terror	Wretchedness, anxiety, restlessness, fear, stupefaction, terror, fainting, death etc.	Trembling or rigidity of hands, feet and eyes, standing on end of the body hair, dryness of lips, tongue and the palate, hoarseness, worries.	Looking at dreadful animals or persons, hearing queer sound, terror, hearing the death news of near and dear ones etc.
(7) Vībhatsa	Hatred, Aversion	Stupefaction, anxiety, fainting, disease, death etc.	Tremor of the body, wrinkling of lips, nose and jaws, faltering steps etc.	Disagreeable things, forbidden things, disagreeable things owing to satiety, things causing anxiety etc.
(8) Adbhuta	Astonishment	Stupefaction, sweating, standing on end of body hair, anxiety reverence etc.	Widely opened eyes, steady and fixed gaze, thrill, praise, joyful uproar, voice choked by intense feeling, delight etc.	Achievement of rare object, vision of space travellers, vision of air ships, witnessing magical feats or unearthly palaces etc.
(9) Śānta	Indifference owing to higher wisdom	Madness caused by extreme delight, delhight knowledge of the ultimate truth, retentive faculty of the mind etc.	Conversations relating to higher knowledge, to look at the tip of nose, thinking of implications of the Śāstras dealing with the liberation of the soul, initiation to the knowledge of Divine spirit etc.	Aversion to the world, finding fault with worldly things, cultivating the company of sages, discussing spiritual things, pilgrimage etc.

Saṁgītaratnākara contains a detailed interpretations of the above (vide 'Bhāva').

231. Razākhānī (Rezākhānī)

Gats composed after the Tarānā style are called Rezākhānī. Some hold that the Rezākhānī style was created by one Gholām Rezā, a pupil of Masīd Khān of Miyān Tānsen Gharānā, while others think that it was Masīd Khān himself who composed the Rezākhānī Gats and named them after his devoted pupil Gholām Rezā. Masīd Khān's own generation did not know the Rezākhānī Gats; they knew Masīdkhānī style only. Rezākhānī Gats are also known as Pūrvī Bāj or the eastern style since Gholām Rezā's home was to the east of Delhi i.e., Patna. Likewise, Masīdkhānī Gats are also known as Pachāvī or Pachāha Bāj or the western style since Jaipur is to the west of Delhi. Unlike Masīdkhānī Gats, which are composed in simple Bolas and in slow tempo, Rezākhānī Gats use complex Bolas and in a faster tempo. In truth both Masīdkhānī and Rezākhānī are complementary to each other. After playing the Masīdkhānī Gat in slow tempo one has to play a Rezākhānī fast tempo Gat, as it is the practice with vocal music wherein a slow Khayāl is followed by a fast Khayāl or a Tarānā. In Masīdkhānī Gats, no particular importance is given to the Bolas whereas in Rezākhānī Gats the Bolas play more important part. We are comparing a Tarānā Vāṇī with a Rezākhānī Bola. The melodic notations are not given, as they are redundant in this context:

3| | | | +| | | | 2| | | | o| | | | 3|
\- Tā - Nā Dī - - - M Tā - Nā Dī - - - M
Ḍā r Ḍā Ḍā - - - r Ḍā r Ḍā Ḍā - - - r

| | | +| | | | 2| | | |
Tā - Nā Tu - - - M Tā - Nā
Ḍā r Ḍā Ḍā - - - r Ḍā r Ḍā

o| | | | 3| | | |
Der Der Der Der Der Der Tum Der
Ḍere Ḍere Ḍere Ḍere Ḍere Ḍere Ḍā Ḍere

+| | | | 2| | | | o| | | |
Tre Dā - Re Tā Nā De - R Nā De - R Nā
Dre Ḍā r Ḍā Ḍā Rā Ḍā - r Ḍā Ḍā - r Ḍā

3| | | |
De - R Nā Tā
Ḍā - r Ḍā Rā

This is a famous Tarānā composition and equally famous Gat composition in Rāga Yamana; obviously the Gat was composed on the Vāṇīs of a Tarānā.

After the Rezākhānī Gats have been played, Bāṁtas (q.v.) are done, then Ṭukḍās (q.v.) are played. The distinguishing feature of a Bāṁta and a Ṭukḍā lies in the use of complex Bolas, though at present simple Bolas are being played with Rezākhānī Gats. Imdād Khān had added some stages of Ālāpa, a stage called 'Jhārā' (q.v.) and varieties of 'Jhālā' (q.v.) in the old style of Rezākhānī Gats and thus created a style of playing called Imdādkhānī style both for Masīdkhānī and Rezākhānī Bāj.

232. Relā

Literally, the word means 'Forceful showers'. In Tablā, speedy yet simple Bolas are called Relā. A Relā has both Khuli and Mudi Bolas e.g.,

	+|	|	|	|
Khuli:	Dhā-Tere	Gheḍenāk	Dhā-Tere	Gheḍenāk
	2|	|	|	|
	Dhā-Tere	Gheḍenāk	Tun-Nā	Keḍenāk
	0|	|	|	|
Mudi:	Tā-Tere	Keḍenāk	Tā-Tere	Keḍenāk
	3|	|	|	|
	Dhā-Tere	Gheḍenāk	Tun-Nā	Keḍenāk

'Gheḍenāk', 'Dheredhere Keṭetāk' etc. Bolas are used in Relā.

233. Ṛṣabha

The second Svara or note of the scale beginning with S. According to some, the name has its origin in the supposed fact that its sound resembles the bellow of a bull. Ṛṣabha, popularly known as Re, has three Śrutis allotted to it viz., Dayāvatī, Rañjanī and Raktikā and is placed precisely on the Raktikā Śrutī. The modern tendency has been to place Re on the initial Śrutī Dayāvatī (vide 'Śruti').

234. Ṛtu

Season. There are six seasons prevalent in India viz., Grīṣma (Summer), Varṣā (Rains), Śarada (Autumn), Hemanta (Dewy season), Śisira or Śīta (Winter), Vasanta (Spring). They correspond with the months as follows:

Vaiśākha and Jaiṣtha (mid April to mid June) – Summer
Āṣāḍha and Śrāvaṇa (mid June to mid August) – Rains
Bhādra and Āsvina (mid August to mid October) – Autumn

Kārtika and Agrahāyana (mid October to mid December) – Dewy Season
Pauṣa and Māgha (mid December to mid February) – Winter
Phālguna and Caitra (mid February to mid April) – Spring

The following are the names of Rāgas corresponding to the seasons, according to the system known as 'Hanumanta Mata' (q.v.):

Dīpaka for Summer
Megha for Rains
Bhairava for Autumn
Mālakauśa for Dewy
Śrī for Winter
Hindola for Spring.

It is commonly believed in India that these seasonal Rāgas appear in their best in the corresponding seasons. So much so that in their own seasons these Rāgas do not have to follow the usual hours enjoined for them. Mālakauśa, for instance, is a Rāga enjoined to be performed in the midnight or a little later, but in the dewy season, it can be performed at any time.

This theory of seasonal or hourly Rāgas, has enormous scope for deeper research. Whether this theory has any logical or scientific justification or is merely a creation of poetic imagination, like the imaginary anthropomorphism attached to each Rāga as has been expressed in so many paintings of Rāgas, is yet to be determined.

235. Śabdālaṁkāra

Vide 'Alaṁkāra'.

236. Sacala Svara

Excepting S and P, the other five notes in a scale are known as Sacala Svaras as they undergo change in being sharpened or flattened. S and P are known as Acala Svaras (vide 'Acala Svara').

237. Sacala Ṭhāṭa

In this context, a Ṭhāṭa means a fret of any string instrument. In instruments having 17 frets, the flattened notes are produced by shifting the frets, i.e., the frets are Sacala or movable. These instruments are known as Sacala Ṭhāṭa instruments (vide 'Acala Ṭhāṭa').

238. Sādarā

A Dhrupada song, composed in Jhāṁpatāla, is called a Sādarā. As Dhrupada is generally composed in Cautāla, Dhamāra is also a Dhrupada composed in Dhamāra Tāla. In the village of Śāhdarā, near Delhi, two brothers Śivamohana and Śivanātha, the disciples of the generation of Baijū Bāvrā, lived. They composed Dhrupadas in Jhāṁpatāla in a distinctive way and called them Sādarā after the name of their village. Sādarā is neither a Dhrupada nor a Jhāṁpatāla singly, but a combination of the two.

239. Ṣāḍava

When a note is omitted from the scale of 7 notes, it becomes a scale of six notes and is called a Ṣāḍava scale or Ṣāḍavita Krama (q.v.). It is to be noted that S can never be omitted. The Rāgas based on the Ṣāḍava scale are known as Ṣāḍava Rāgas.

240. Sādhāraṇa Gāndhāra

When the Śāstrīya G i.e., flattened G (flattened E of the Western Scale) takes a Śruti from M (F of Western scale) and becomes a three-Śruti note, it is known as Sādhāraṇa Gāndhāra according to Saṁgītaratnākara (vide 'Śruti').

241. Sādhāraṇī Gīti

Vide 'Gīti'.

242. Ṣaḍja

Vide 'Kharaja'.

243. Ṣaḍja Grāma

Vide 'Gāndhāra Grāma'.

244. Sākārī

Attending note or Svara. When a note is shifted to the Śruti next to the Śruti occupied by the previous note, the shifted note is called Sākārī note of the previous note, e.g., Ati Komala R (vide 'Svara'). The word is a contraction of the word 'Sahakārī' meaning attending.

245. Salāmī Ṭukḍā

Saluting Ṭukḍā. At the start of a percussion programme, a Ṭukḍā with a Tihāī (q.v.) is played; the Tihāī is composed in such a way that after every portion of the Tihāī, there is enough gap to salute the audience; it is done thrice. After this, the actual programme begins according to Silsilā or proper sequence (vide 'Laharā').

246. Sālaṅka Śreṇī

Another name for Chāyālaga or Sālaga Śreṇī (vide 'Chāyālaga').

247. Sama

Vide 'Tāla'.

248. Sāma

Sāma Veda. The portion of a Veda meant to be sung is called Sāma. When the Mantras of Ṛk (Vedic hymns) are sung, they are called Sāma. Sāma song was in vogue even 4 or 5 thousand years ago. Some say that Sāma was sung with only 4 notes, while others say that all the seven notes of the scale were used. But according to Saṁgītaratnākara, only 3 notes were used. As such a Tāna (q.v.) composed of 3 notes is known as Sāmika Tāna. In a Sāma song, Udātta (q.v.) i.e., high tone, Anudātta (q.v.) i.e., low tone and Svarita (q.v.) i.e., middle tone are used.

249. Samaya

Time. A particular time of the day (and night) has been allotted to a particular Rāga. But there are some Rāgas which can be sung or played at anytime e.g., Kāphī, Pilū, Bhairavī etc. Then there are some day-Rāgas which are actually sung at night, such as Sūhā and Sughrāī Kānhaḍā. Gauḍasāraṅga, for instance, is sung during the day, as a part of the Sāraṅga class, but Sāraṅga is not at all present in the constituents of this Rāga; it is rather fit to be sung during night. It is interesting to note that in common practice among the Ustāds (virtuosi), it is called "Din-kā-Bihāg" that is, Bihāga for the day. Whether this allocation of time to Rāgas has any logical reason or not, cannot be definitely said. However, long use has given this tradition a definite sanctity. At present the time factor is not very rigidly followed. There is another convention that the Rāgas allotted to a particular season of the year can be sung or played at any time throughout that particular season. Paṇḍit Viṣṇunārāyaṇa Bhātakhaṇḍe had examined this allotment of time and codified certain rules in this respect (vide 'Rāga').

250. Saṁgat

Literally meeting. The percussion accompaniment to a vocal or instrumental music is called Saṁgat and is always treated as secondary. Whenever percussion becomes the primary item, it is called Laharā and the instrument played as an accompaniment to the percussion is then called Saṁgat. There are two types of Saṁgat (vide 'Sāth Saṁgat' and 'Javāb Saṁgat').

251. Saṁgīta

Vocal and instrumental music, and dance when combined is called Saṁgīta. At present Saṁgīta generally means either vocal or instrumental music, but specifically it means only vocal music. Usually it means vocal or instrumental music accompanied by percussion instruments. Dance or Nṛtya has been separated from its original role in the word Saṁgīta and is treated as one of the major five arts.

252. Sāmika

A Tāna composed of 3 Svaras or notes. It is so called since the Sāma songs used only 3 notes (vide 'Tāna' and 'Sāma').

253. Saṁkīrṇa Śreṇī

The Rāga in which a Śuddha and Chāyālaga Rāgas have been mixed is called Saṁkīrṇa Śreṇī (class) Rāga (vide 'Rāga').

254. Sampūrṇa

When a Rāga uses seven or more notes of a scale, it is known as Sampūrṇa Rāga. The Mūrcchanā, Krama or Tāna using seven notes are also Sampūrṇa. The literal meaning is 'Complete'.

255. Saṁvādī

Vide 'Vādī'.

256. Sañcārī Tuk

One of the stanzas of Ālāpa or Dhrupada and limited between the Gāndhāra of middle register and the extreme lower register of the gamuts (vide 'Tuk' and 'Dhātu').

257. Sañcārī Varṇa

Vide 'Varṇa'.

258. Sandhi Prakāśa

Rāgas fit to be sung at dawn or at dusk are known as Sandhi Prakāśa Rāgas. Generally Rāgas using Komala R and Komala D, belong to this class. Literally, Sandhi here means the meeting of day and night. Prakāśa here means manifestation (vide 'Rāga').

259. Sanyāsa

Vide 'Bidārī'.

260. Sapāṭa Tāna

Vide 'Tāna'.

261. Saptaka

The scale of 7 notes is called Saptaka. Generally Mandra (lower), Madhya (middle) and Tāra (higher) Saptakas are used but in Ālāpa, 'Ati Mandra Saptaka' i.e., still lower scale, is also used. The Saptakas are also known as Grāmas when Udārā (lower), Mudārā (middle) and Tārā (higher) Grāmas are often mentioned.

262. Saragam

The Rāga composition of Svaras or notes without the literary portion of a song, or the Vāṇīs of Tarānā, is called Saragam. This expression is a contraction of Sā, Re, Gā, Mā – the lower tetrachord of the scale. Saragam is chiefly meant to be sung but can also be used as an instrumental piece as Laharā-Gat (q.v.). There are innumerable famous and worthwhile compositions of Saragams in Upper India. Sometimes it is sung as a part of a Khayāl (q.v.) or Ṭhumrī (q.v.). Saragam forms a necessary portion of Trivaṭa (q.v.), Caturaṅga (q.v.) and Tarānā (q.v.).

263. Sāraṇā

'Sāraṇā' is 'To move'. According to Saṁgītaratnākara, an ingenious method has been devised to prove that the Śruti-intervals are equal in pitch, although the purpose has not been revealed in so many words.

The following experiment is suggested. Let two identical Vīṇās be constructed having 22 strings each. The strings of both are to be tuned with a gradual rise in pitch of equal value according to one's own auditory perception. As both the Vīṇās are lying parallel, the notes are to be marked on the strings of both thus: S on the 4th, R on the 7th, g on the 9th, M on the 13th, P on the 17th, D on the 20th and n on the 22nd string counting from the left. After marking the notes identically on both the Vīṇās, one is to be considered 'Dhruva' or 'Unalterable' Vīṇā while the other 'Cala' or 'Alterable' Vīṇā. Now, one is ready to start the process of movement thus: on the 'Cala' or 'Alterable' Vīṇā, the pegs are to be loosened in such a uniform way that the sound of the second string of the same coincides with that of the first string of the 'Dhruva' or 'Unalterable' Vīṇā. Similarly, each of the strings of the 'Cala' Vīṇā coincides with each of the preceding strings of the 'Dhruva' Vīṇā. This is the first movement. But the first movement does not prove anything. In the second movement, the strings of the 'Cala' Vīṇā are further loosened in such a way that its third string coincides with the first string of the 'Dhruva' Vīṇā and so on with all other strings. In this second movement in the 'Cala' Vīṇā, the notes having 2 Śrutis each viz., g and n, merge in their respective preceding notes viz., R and D of the 'Dhruva' Vīṇā. In the third movement, the notes R and D, having 3 Śrutis each, of the 'Cala' Vīṇā, merge in S and P of the 'Dhruva' Vīṇā. In the fourth movement the notes S, M and P, having 4 Śrutis each, of the 'Cala' Vīṇā, merge in lower n (non-existent in the present Dhruva Vīṇā) g and M respectively of the 'Dhruva' Vīṇā. The process of 'Sāraṇa' stops with this last movement, all the notes having been covered. It should be noted that the scale used is the Śuddha or pure scale of the Śāstras having Komala G and Komala N and approximates to the modern Kāphī scale.

To sum up, the twentytwo strings of each Vīṇā represent 22 Śrutis or units of pitch measurement according to the ancient Śāstras (vide 'Śruti'). There are three types of notes used viz., two notes g and n having 2 Śrutis each, two notes R and D having 3 Śrutis each and three notes S, M and P having 4 Śrutis each. In the first 'Sāraṇā', no note of the 'Cala' Vīṇā merges into any other note of the 'Dhruva' Vīṇā. In the second 'Sāraṇā', the notes g and n having two Śrutis each of the 'Cala' Vīṇā, merge in their preceding notes R and D respectively of the 'Dhruva' Vīṇā. In the third 'Sāraṇā', the notes R and D, having three Śrutis each of the 'Cala' Vīṇā, merge in their preceding notes S and P respectively of the 'Dhruva' Vīṇā. In the fourth 'Sāraṇā', the notes S, M and P, having four Śrutis each, of the 'Cala' Vīṇā merge in their preceding notes viz., lower n, g and M respectively of the 'Dhruva'

Vīṇā. It may be noted that the present 'Dhruva' Vīṇā does not have the extra string for the lower n, the existence of which is assumed for the present purpose. Thus ends the 'Sāraṇā' which points to the definite conclusion that the Śruti intervals are equal in pitch. If this were not so, the notes of the alterable Vīṇā would not have merged into their respective preceding notes of the unalterable Vīṇā with such perceivable precision.

264. Sārikā

Frets.

265. Sāth Saṁgat

When the accompanying percussionist plays his Relā, Kāyadā (Q̱āedā) etc. simultaneously with the Tāna, Bāṁta or Vistāra of a vocalist or an instrumentalist, such accompaniment is called Sāth Saṁgat (vide 'Saṁgat', 'Javāb Saṁgat', 'Ālāpa').

266. Savārī

The bridge in a stringed instrument. Literally– 'On which the strings ride'.

267. Seniyā Gharānā

Generally speaking the descendants of Tānsen are known as the 'Seniyās'. But the two main lines of Tānsen through his son and daughter do not use this term 'Seniyā', they simply call themselves 'The descendants of Tānsen'. The descendants of Sūrat Sen (one of Tānsen's sons) and the descendants of Masīd Kẖān, the famous Sitāriyā, migrated to Jaipur and came to be known as the 'Seniyā Gharānā'. The Seniyās of Jaipur took up the Sitār as their chief instrument. The famous Sitār player of this Gharānā, Amīr Kẖān, was a court musician of Mysore and made Prof. Barkat U'l-lāh Kẖān his worthy pupil. The style of Sitār playing followed by them was Masīdkẖānī Bāj or Pachāvī (Western) Kā Bāj.

268. Silsilā

Sequence. Any composition, whether musical, literary or otherwise, is based on well formulated sequences without which no analysis or classification or codification of rules is possible. Ālāpa, Dhrupada, Kẖayāl, Ṭhumrī, Ṭappā, instrumental Gats, all have well formulated sequences. A traditional virtuoso knows the Silsilā and teaches his pupils accordingly. Musicians who do not know the proper sequences, but have merely acquired certain inadequate dexterity of presentation by blindly copying worthwhile musicians are called 'Ātāi' (q.v.). It is beyond the scope of this dictionary to treat in details the Silsilā of all forms of music, yet, the Silsilā of an Ālāpa has been given as an example (vide 'Ālāpa').

269. Sparśa

Literally, it means 'Touch'. A technique of playing a string-instrument with frets. While the forefinger of the left hand is on a fret, the string is struck and before the sound dies out, the middle finger of the same hand touches the next fret and is immediately lifted away. This is called 'Sparśa'. It is a variety of Śabdālaṁkāra (vide 'Alaṁkāra') and is almost like a Kṛntana (q.v.). In the latter the finger is laterally moved away while in Sparśa it is simply lifted.

270. Śruti

Anything heard can be called a Śruti in a general manner. In Indian musical parlance, a Śruti is a unit of measurement of the pitch of notes. It is to be particularly noted that Śruti, as a unit of the measurement of pitch, is not based on any scientific theory – it is rather based on the perception of the sages of old.

The reason for such a unit being called a Śruti appears to be this: A sound can only be heard by the ears and cannot be perceived through any other means or by any other organ. So it has been called a Śruti.

That there are innumerable different pitches of sound within the span of usual 7 notes, is admitted by the ancient Śāstras. Then the question may be raised as to why only twentytwo points have been chosen to be known as Śrutis. Some explain that only twenty-two points of sound can be differentiated from one another, hence the choice of twentytwo Śrutis. But this theory is evidently too wide to be considered, since the capability of picking up the small difference of sound varies with each individual. Saṁgītaratnākara explains that out of three Nāḍis or nerves namely, Iḍā, Piṅgalā and Suṣumnā that pass along the spinal chord, two Nāḍis namely, Iḍā and Piṅgalā give out twentytwo invisible side Nāḍis which are placed one above the other and through these Nāḍis twentytwo Śrutis are perceived. So the number of Śrutis has been fixed at twentytwo. The above explanation, however speculative, cannot satisfy an investigating mind. But perhaps all 'Whys' cannot be satisfactorily answered. As there is no particular reason to divide a foot rule into twelve inches, so there may not be any specific reason to divide the scale of 7 notes into twentytwo divisions or Śrutis – all that we have to do is to accept them if we want to put any value to the ancient Śāstras.

The ancient sages classified the twentytwo Śrutis into five classes or Jātis as will be found in the tables given hereunder. European scientists have measured the pitches in terms of number of vibrations of the vibrating string in a second. The pitch of a Śruti can be determined in terms of the number of vibrations (vide 'Vazan').

Some Indian scholars hold that the Śrutis are not equal in pitch, but they have not established their theory logically. We are in favour of treating all the Śrutis to be equal. Otherwise a Śruti cannot be a measuring unit nor can there be any ground to refer to the number of Śrutis a note contains. The pitch of a Śruti depends upon the pitch of the initial note of a scale i.e., S. In this context it is to be particularly pointed out that Indian notes S, R etc. are not standardised by allotting fixed number of vibrations to each Svara; any single sound can be the initial note i.e., S of a scale of seven notes. So, if the number of vibrations of any note is A, then the higher octave of that note will be 2A and each Śruti would be of the value of A ÷ 22, since the number of vibrations which is A is uniformly spread out upon the scale of seven notes. But the Śruti value thus arrived at may not be scientifically accurate since the sages depended upon their perception only in fixing a Śruti to be a unit of measurement of pitches of notes. Doubts have been cast in the scientific world as to the fixed value of an inch as a measuring unit after the discovery of the Theory of Relativity by Prof. Einstein. Then how can a Śruti be absolutely determined by scientific methods when Śrutis never depended upon science? Modern musical scholars have a queer tendency of sounding metaphysical objects by modern science just like dissecting a stone idol to see if the heart beats inside. This tendency of putting the inside concept of Śruti under scientific microscope has given the modern scholars the wisdom that Śrutis are unequal and this wisdom unnecessarily complicates the problem instead of resolving it. If the Śrutis are not equal then ceases the question of refering to a particular note having a particular number of Śrutis – and such a reference is not only irrelevant but ridiculous also.

The details of Śrutis are given in the following Table:

S.No.	Name	Jāti or Class	Svaras of Saṁgīta-Pārijāta	Svaras of Saṁgīta-ratnākara	Modern Svaras	Vibration Number according to E. Clements
4.	Chandovatī	Madhyā	S	S	S	240
5.	Dayāvatī	Karuṇā	Pūrva R	–	Ati Komala R	250
6.	Rañjanī	Madhyā	Komala R	–	Komala R	256
7.	Raktikā	Mṛdu	R or Pūrva G	R	R	$266^2/_3$
8.	Raudrī	Dīptā	Tīvratara R or Komala G	–	Tīvra R	270
9.	Krodhā	Āyatā	G	G	Komala G	$284^4/_9$
10.	Vajrikā	Dīptā	Tīvra G	Sādhāraṇa G	Tīvra Komala G	288
11.	Prasāriṇī	Āyatā	Tīvratara G	Antara G	G	300
12.	Prīti	Mṛdu	Tīvratama G	Cyuta M	Tīvra G	$316^4/_{81}$
13.	Mārjanī	Madhyā	M or Ati Tīvratama G	M	M	320
14.	Kṣiti	Mṛdu	Tīvra M	–	–	$333^1/_3$
15.	Raktā	Madhyā	Tīvratara M	–	Tīvra M	$337^1/_2$
16.	Sandīpinī	Āyatā	Tīvratama M	Madhyama Grāmokta or Kauśika P	Tīvratara M	$345^3/_5$
17.	Ālāpinī	Karuṇā	P	P	P	360
18.	Madantī	Karuṇā	Pūrva D	–	Ati Komala D	375
19.	Rohiṇī	Āyatā	Komala D	–	Komala D	384
20.	Ramyā	Madhyā	D or Pūrva N	D	D	400
21.	Ugrā	Dīptā	Tīvra D or Komala N	–	Tīvra D	405
22.	Kṣobhiṇī	Madhyā	N or Tīvra-tara D	N	Komala N	$426^2/_3$
1.	Tīvrā	Dīptā	Tīvra N	Kauśikī N	Tīvra Komala N	432
2.	Kumudvatī	Āyatā	Tīvratara N	Kākalī N	N	450
3.	Mandā	Mṛdu	Tīvratama N	Cyuta S	Tīvra N	$474^2/_{27}$
4.	Chandovatī	Madhyā	Ṡ	Ṡ	Ṡ	480

Now we are giving below the vibration number together with the Western symbol of each Śruti according to Mr. Arthur Moore and K.K. Varmā. The Śrutis have been tabulated in the same order as above:

Sl.No. and name of Śrutis	Vibration Number	Western Symbol
4. Chandovatī	264	C
5. Dayāvatī	275	C sharp
6. Rañjanī	286	D flat
7. Raktikā	297	D
8. Raudrī	309.375	D sharp
9. Krodhā	319.6875	E flat
10. Vajrikā	330	E
11. Prasāriṇī	341	E sharp
12. Prīti	346.5	F flat
13. Mārjanī	352	F
14. Kṣiti	371.25	F sharp
15. Raktā	384	G flat
16. Sandīpinī	396	G
17. Ālāpinī	412.5	G sharp
18. Madantī	426.25	A flat
19. Rohiṇī	440	A
20. Ramyā	454.66	A sharp
21. Ugrā	462	A double sharp
22. Kṣobhiṇī	469.332	B flat
1. Tīvrā	495	B
2. Kumudvatī	506	B sharp
3. Mandā	517	C flat
4. Chandovatī	528	C

(*The Statesman*, Aug. 21 and Sept. 5, 1961).

For the sake of convenience and parity with the vibration numbers according to E. Clements, we have doubled the numbers of vibration as published in the Statesman.

According to Arthur Moore, A sharp on Ramyā Śruti had 449.776 and A double sharp on Ugrā Śruti had 459.554 vibration numbers but their relations to A, in that case, gave rise to high dissonance, so those frequencies have been changed to the ones given above by K.K. Varmā.

Their efforts are undoubtedly praiseworthy but cannot be said correct according to ancient Śāstras since G (of Western scale), which bears a relation of 3/2 to C, (of Western scale), has been placed on Sandīpinī Śruti when it should have occupied the Ālāpinī Śruti. According to E. Clements, G has been placed on

Ālāpinī as will be seen in the table. Counting the Śrutis from C, it will be seen that G occupies the 13th Śruti which is Ālāpinī, but in Moore and Varmā's experiment, G occupies the 12th Śruti counting from C. Perhaps both Moore and Varmā, in counting the Śrutis, took the Śruti occupied by C into account but in counting the 13th Śruti one occupied by C must be left out.

The foregoing descriptions of notes are according to Ṣaḍja Grāma of Saṁgītaratnākara. Neither Madhyama nor Gāndhāra Grāma has been considered here as they are unnecessary (vide 'Grāma'). It has been found indispensable to examine and analyse the notes or Svaras as they occupy the Śrutis at present. The distribution of Śrutis according to ancient Śāstras is given below with the serial numbers of Śrutis starting from Tīvrā given on the heads of the lines representing Śrutis:

1	2	3	4	5	6	7	8	9	10	11	12	13
|	|	|	|	|	|	|	|	|	|	|	|	|
			S			R		G				M
14	15	16	17	18	19	20	21	22	1	2	3	4
|	|	|	|	|	|	|	|	|	|	|	|	|
			P			D		N				Ṡ

It will be seen that S has 4 Śrutis, R 3, G 2, M 4, P 4, D 3, and N 2. Bharata Muni, Śārṅgadeva and other sages have definitely enjoined that the Svaras must occupy the last of their Śrutis.

Sir William Jones, Captain N. Augustus Willard and others studied the Sanskrit Śāstras on music and apparently, by error, had placed the four Śrutis occupied by S between S & R and similarly for other notes. In those days the error could not be detected, probably because they had found certain similarity between the Western diatonic major scale and the Śuddha scale of the Śāstras, the notes of which have the following distribution of Śrutis:

4	3	2	4	4	3	2	
S	R	G	M	P	D	N	Ṡ

In the diatonic major scale, the intervals between the notes are almost of the same nature viz., the intervals between E and F and also between B and C are the smallest, likewise the intervals between F and G, C and D and also between G and A are the largest while the intervals between D and E, and between A and B are medium. It may well be supposed that the interval between E and F i.e., G and M of the Indian scale had led the Western scholars to place the two Śrutis occupied by G between G and M and so on with the other Śrutis also. The error of this nature on the part of the Western scholars cannot be treated as a serious blunder since they had been satisfied to see the apparent similarity between the Śāstrīya scale and Western scale. Naturally, no doubt as to the veracity of such a distribution of Śrutis on their part was ever raised. Those scholars produced a number of dependable books on Indian music which satiated the thirst for musical knowledge of those Indian scholars for whom the Sanskrit Śāstras were unapproachable.

It is regrettable that Indian musicologists had written a number of books on music considering the Western error to be the correct interpretation of Śāstras without even consulting the original Śāstras themselves. As a result, the error, two hundred years old, is being called the 'Modern distribution of Śrutis' and is confusing the students of today. Even the great musical scholar Paṇḍit Viṣṇunārāyaṇa Bhātakhaṇḍe, who wrote a number of Sanskrit Śāstras, not only committed the same error but himself composed Sanskrit Ślokas to tinge the error with an ancient glory and said that the notes should occupy their first Śruti.

This, apparently a small error, has done a great harm to Indian music. Although there appears an apparent likeness of modern Śuddha scale or Bilāvala Ṭhāṭa to the Śāstrīya Śuddha scale, yet the Rāgas in the Śāstras appear widely different from the Rāgas of the same name that are current today. The modern musicologists, instead of examining and analysing the Rāgas of the Śāstras, have simply cast them away as obsolete.

It is now upto us to understand the Śrutis and Svaras in their proper place and perspective. Only then would it be possible to start the worthwhile research work on the Śāstrīya Rāgas and compare them with the modern Rāgas.

Some European Scientists have measured the pitch of notes by 'Cents' but we have not included it here. We have mentioned the frequencies of notes as determined by scientific experiments and accepted by all so as to examine the inter-relationship of notes in their numerical value.

In the following table we have shown the inter-relationship of notes taking the frequency of middle S to be 240:

S = 240	R:S = 9/8,	G:S = 5/4,	M:S = 4/3	P:S = 3/2
		D:S = 5/3,	N:S = 15/8	$\dot{S}$:S = 2

R = 270	G:R = 10/9,	M:R = 32/27,	P:R = 4/3,
	D:R = 40/27,	N:R = 5/3,	Ṡ:R = 16/9
G = 300	M:G = 16/15,	P:G = 6/5,	D:G = 4/3,
		N:G = 3/2,	Ṡ:G = 8/5
M = 320	P:M = 9/8,	D:M = 5/4,	N:M = 45/32
			Ṡ:M = 3/2
P = 360	D:P = 10/9,	N:P = 5/4,	Ṡ:P = 4/3
D = 400	N:D = 9/8,	Ṡ:D = 6/5	
N = 450	Ṡ:N = 16/15		
Ṡ = 480			

In India, a Svara or note does not have a fixed number of vibrations; any Svara can be S whereas European C is bound by a fixed frequency (vide 'Svara').

271. Śruti - Harmonium

This has not been included in the descriptions of the other musical instruments given elsewhere since it was a personal contrivance of a Maharashtrian gentleman, Mr. K.V. Devala, a Deputy Collector and a connoisseur of music. He passed his retired life in musical research. This Śruti-Harmonium was made by Messrs. Moore and Moore Co. of London under the instructions of Mr. Devala and it was patented in London (15548/11).

The harmonium had 23 keys with reeds tuned to 22 Śrutis. Mr. Devala did various experiments and also published a few books. Mr. E. Clements also, in collaboration with the famous Khayāliyā, the late Abdul Karīm Khān, did a lot of research work on Śrutis with this instrument. The frequencies of the Śrutis were found to be somewhat different from those of the present day notes.

272. Sthāyī Tuk

Vide 'Tuk' and 'Dhātu'.

273. Sthāyī Varṇa

Vide 'Varṇa'.

274. Śuddhā Gīti

Vide 'Gīti'.

275. Śuddha Jāti

Vide 'Rāga'.

276. Śuddha Śreṇī

Vide 'Śuddha Jāti' and 'Rāga'.

277. Śuddha Svara

The five notes of a scale or gamut – excepting S and P — can either be flattened or sharpened i.e., they are capable of being shifted from their normal place. But when they are in their normal place, they are known as Śuddha Svaras. S and P are always Śuddha since they do not undergo any change. Because of this, these are also known as Acala Svaras. It is to be noted here that G and N, as they are in the diatonic major scale or Bilāvala Ṭhāṭa, are known as Śuddha Svaras at present, and the flattened G and N are known as Vikṛta Svaras, whereas, according to the ancient Śāstras, flattened G and N were considered Śuddha Svaras and Śuddha G and N of the Bilāvala Ṭhāṭa were considered Vikṛta Svaras. So the Śuddha Ṭhāṭa, according to the ancient Śāstras, was the modern Kāphī Ṭhāṭa, having flattened G and N (vide 'Svara').

278. Śuddha Tāna

Vide 'Tāna'.

279. Śuddhaṣaḍjā

Vide 'Mūrchanā'.

280. Śuluph

When Laya acquires the speed of more than four times the speed of medium or Madhya Laya, it is known as Śuluph Laya. This term is used with reference to percussion instruments only. If in Tritāla of 16 Mātrās, more than 64 Vāṇīs are sung or Bolas played, then that would be in Śuluph Laya, e.g.,

| | | | | | | | | | | | | | | |

Dhere Dhere Keṭe Tāk Tāk Tere Keṭe Tāk. Here are 16 Mātrās normally distributed among the percussion Bolas. But if they are distributed thus:

| |

Dhere Dhere Keṭe Tāk Tāk Tere Keṭe Tāk i.e., eight Mātrās compressed into one, it would be a case of Śuluph Laya, the speed would be double of 4 times.

281. Suraparaṇa

The various ways of playing rhythmic Paraṇas (q.v.) composed of notes and Bolas on instruments is called Suraparaṇa. Unlike Tāraparaṇa where the rhythm of percussion Bolas is played on string instruments, Suraparaṇa does not follow the percussion Bolas but plays rhythmic Bolas of a free nature. That is precisely the difference between Tāraparaṇa and Suraparaṇa (vide 'Ālāpa', 'Tāraparaṇa' & 'Paraṇa').

282. Svara

There are infinite varieties of sounds in the world but all sounds are not Svaras or notes. Saṁgītaratnākara defines a Svara thus:

"The sound which has a vibrational (Anuraṇanātmaka) quality of a pleasing nature (Snigdha) and also has Śrutis immediately before it, and pleases the mind of the listeners without depending on any other factor is called a Svara."

This definition requires clearer annotations. The mention of 'Śrutis immediately before it' points to the fact that there are other sounds also, separated by intervening Śrutis, and the sounds that have intervening Śrutis can point only to a scale. Then we are to formulate that to be called a Svara, a sound in addition to the foregoing qualities, must be a note in the scale of seven notes. Therefore, we can define a Svara thus: If between a musical sound and its double in pitch, there are other musical sounds separated from each other, with gradual rising of the pitch following a particular law, then those sounds can be called Svaras and all such Svaras taken together can be called a scale.

It should be remembered that an Indian Svara is not fixed by any particular frequency; any note can be a key note to a scale. A musical sound, bereft of a scale, is no Svara in Indian music. It can only be called a Svara or a note if it belongs to a scale i.e., its relation to the tonic must be established before it can be called a Svara. Singly, it is only a pleasing sound.

Anuraṇanātmaka means 'Of persisting vibrations' – a piece of wood when thrown on the ground, gives out a sound which is not Anuraṇanātmaka. Therefore, it cannot be a musical or 'Snigdha' sound. On the other hand, a broken piece of glass, if struck with a stick, gives out a sound that can be called a Svara if the identity of this sound can be fixed in relation to a scale.

In our own definition of a Svara as mentioned above, a

reference has been made to the gradual rising of the pitch following a particular law. Now, we can measure this gradual rising of the pitch in two ways (vide 'Śruti'):

(1) In the Indian way by Śruti units.
(2) In the Western way by frequencies.

Usually the notes are written with the initials of the names of Svaras:

Ṣaḍja, Ṛṣabha, Gāndhāra, Madhyama, Pañcama, Dhaivata and Niṣāda i.e., S, R, G, M, P, D, N.

These are the Śuddha or pure notes of the scale. Then there are five Vikṛta (q.v.) Svaras which are but the changed forms of R, G, M, D and N. S and P cannot be changed and they are known as Acala Svaras (q.v.). Such change can be brought about by two methods:

(1) By the use of Mūrcchanā (q.v.).
(2) By shifting the notes from their own Śrutis to other unoccupied Śrutis in the scale.

(1) Change by the use of Mūrcchanā: We are once again writing out the scale showing the interval of Svaras:

S Tone R Tone G Semi-Tone M Tone P Tone D Tone N Semi-Tone Ṡ. Tone and Semi-tone divisions are borrowed from temperamental scale for convenience. This is the original Bilāvala Ṭhāṭa and is called Ṣaḍja Mūrcchanā. The descending portion of the Mūrcchanā has been left out as unnecessary here. The second or the Ṛṣabha Mūrcchanā would be:

R Tone G Semi-Tone M Tone P Tone D Tone N Semi-Tone Ṡ Tone Ṙ.

Let us see what happens if this Ṛṣabha Mūrchanā is played on an instrument from the S fret:

S Tone R Semi-Tone G Tone M Tone P Tone D Semi-Tone N Tone Ṡ.

The Semi-Tones are between the R and G frets and also between D and N frets — this gives us Kāphī Ṭhāṭa with flattened G and N.

Thus the changes of other notes can also be brought about in the similar way. Usually this is shifting of the key note or in other words, Kharaja Parivartana (q.v.).

(2) Change by the shifting of the notes from their original Śruti.

The distribution of Śrutis on notes according to all the ancient Śāstras is as follows:

IIII III II IIII IIII III II IIII
S R G M P D N Ṡ

This is Śāstrīya Śuddha Ṭhāṭa but known as Kāphī Ṭhāṭa at present with flattened G and N.

If the notes G and N are shifted from their original Śrutis as above to the second Śrutis of M and S respectively:

II III IIII II IIII III IIII II
S R G M P D N Ṡ then these shifted G and N are known as Antara G and Kākalī N according to the Śāstras. Now a days they are known as Śuddha G and N. By the above shifts the scale changes to Sāntarakākalika which is almost identical with our Bilāvala Ṭhāṭa or Diatonic major scale.

In the above scale with the Śrutis shown by vertical lines, if the R is shifted to its first Śruti, it is called Ati Komala or Sākārī R (q.v.) and if shifted to its second Śruti, it is called Komala R. Similarly, D also takes the name of Ati Komala or Sākārī and Komala D if shifted to its first and second Śruti respectively. When M takes away two Śrutis from P by being shifted from its own Śruti, it is changed into Kaḍi or Tīvra M i.e., sharpened M.

We are giving below the notes of the Bilāvala Ṭhāṭa, otherwise known as Sāntarakākalika Ṣaḍja Mūrcchanā, in all their variations according to shifts:

Sl. No. of Śrutis	**Notes**
1	Tīvra Komala N
2	N
3	Tīvra N
4	S
5	Ati Komala or Sākārī R
6	Komala R
7	R
8	Ati Komala or Sākārī G, according to some – R
9	Komala G
10	Tīvra Komala G
11	G
12	Tīvra G
13	M
14	x

15	Tīvra or Kaḍi M
16	x
17	P
18	Ati Komala or Sākārī D
19	Komala D
20	D
21	Ati Komala or Sākārī N, according to some D
22	Komala N

All the foregoing changes of notes are being used at present though, theoretically, only five changes are admitted viz., Komala R, Komala G, Kaḍi M, Komala D and Komala N.

Lastly, we are describing the original distribution of Śrutis among the notes according to the ancient Śāstras and the modern, about 200 years old, erroneous distribution:

```
Original:           IIII III  II  IIII IIII III  II   IIII
                       S   R  G     M    P   D  N       Ṡ
Modern erroneous:   IIII III  II  IIII IIII III  II   IIII
                    S    R    G   M    P    D    N    Ṡ
```

A comparison will reveal that each note will have the same number Śrutis in both the scales i.e., in the identical order of the cluster of Śrutis viz., 4, 3, 2, 4, 4, 3, 2, 4, but in the second scale the notes occupy the first of their Śrutis, instead of the last, as enjoined by the Śāstras. The erroneous distribution would apparently conform to the modern Bilāvala scale; that is the scale with intervals of Semi-Tones between G and M and between N and Ṡ.

283. Svara Jñāna

The knowledge of Svaras. Paṇḍit Viṣṇunārāyaṇa Bhātakhaṇḍe has formulated two tests to assess the knowledge of Svaras

(1) The capacity of uttering any note at any moment,

(2) The capacity to recognise any note immediately after hearing it.

Passing these two tests a person would be known to have the knowledge of svaras.

284. Svaralipi

Notations – Saṁgītaratnākara contains some notations but these are more of an academic nature than practical. Undoubtedly the system of notations that is at present found in India came into existence in the last quarter of the last century or so, drawing inspiration from the Western system of notations. Kṛṣṇadhana Bandyopādhyāya, a renowned musicologist, tried to introduce the staff notations in Indian music but could not succeed. India stuck to her tradition in using Svara-name initials of alphabets similar to Western Tonic-solfa. We are describing the three main systems of notation in currency in India at present:

(1) *Daṇḍa Mātrika* i.e., the beats are represented by vertical lines precisely above the note on which the beat is supposed to strike. This system was invented by Kṣetramohana Gosvāmī.

(2) *Ākāra Mātrika* i.e., the beats are represented by "Ākāra" (ı) – a symbol for the vowel Ā (long) is joined to the note followed by a number of such symbols, if there are other beats for the same note, independently i.e., unattached to any note. This was invented by Dvijendranāth Ṭhākura, elder brother of world poet Rabīndranāth Ṭhākura and was popularized by his another brother Jyotirindranāth Ṭhākura. This system has been in existence since about 1920 in Bengal.

(3) *Bhātakhaṇḍe System* – In this system the beats or Mātrās are not shown but the notations are separated by vertical lines according to the divisions of a Tāla. This system was invented by Paṇḍit Viṣṇunārāyaṇa Bhātakhaṇḍe and has become the most popular of all the systems since about 1930.

Since Indian music is being appreciated by the Western nations more than ever before, a new system of notations using the English alphabets is being ushered into the musical world – which has been followed in this dictionary throughout.

We are citing some examples of each of the above:

(1) *Daṇḍa Mātrika*:

```
|  |  |  |  |  |  |  |  |  |  |  |  |  |  ·|  |  |
      Δ     Δ        μ     Δ     Δ        Δ     Δ
Ṇ  S  R  R  G  G  M  M  P  D  D  N  N  Ṡ  Ṙ  Ṙ  Ġ
```

In this system the lower octave is represented by a dot below the notes, the upper octave by a dot on the head of the notes and the middle octave is without any sign. The beats are represented by short vertical lines above the notes; a note can have as many such lines as there may be Mātrās or beats on that note. Half Mātrās are represented by the sign ∪ and quarter by x. The flattened notes are indicated by the sign of a triangle Δ above such notes and sharpened note by μ. In Tāla, this system and all other systems, use + (or x) for Sama, 3 for the next, then 'O' and lastly l. In Bhātakhaṇḍe system this order is a little different as will be explained hereafter.

(2) *Ākāra Mātrika*:

The different Sanskrit alphabets are used to indicate sharp and flats:

Ṇı Sı rı Rı gı Gı Mı mı Pı dı Dı nı Nı Śı ŕı Ŕı ǵı

We have used English in place of Sanskrit alphabets for printing convenience and we have used small letters for both the sharp (in case of M only) and flats. The beats are represented by the Ākāra sign ı which can be multiplied according to the number of beats such as Sıııı. This means that 'S' has four beats or Mātrās. If several notes jointly share a Mātrā or beat then the last of such notes will have the sign attached to it e.g., SRGMÔ which means each of the notes has a quarter of a Mātrā and jointly they have one Mātrā. The half Mātrās are indicated by " : " and quarter by " ā̃ " on the right of a note. The Sama is represented by 2, then 3, then o and lastly 1. The lower octave is indicated by "\" under a note, the upper by " / " over a note, the middle octave is without any sign.

(3) *Bhātakhaṇḍe system*:

Ṇ | S R̲ R G̲ | G M Ṁ P | D̲ D N̲ N | Ṡ Ṙ̲ Ṙ Ġ̲ |

The flats are indicated by a dash below the note and sharp by a vertical line above. The lower octave has a dot below and the upper on the head of a note. No signs are used for beats but the divisions of Tāla are indicated by long vertical lines beside the notes. If a few notes are intended to be of one Mātrā duration, then these are joined together and a sign ‿ is placed under them e.g., S R G M. Otherwise the notes are written separately to indicate that they have one Mātrā each – as shown above. The Sama is indicated by X and numerically it is considered 1. The other Tālas are 2, o, and 3. There is no sign for a half Mātrā or a quarter Mātrā.

The late Brajendrakiśor Rāyacaudhurī, musicologist, for his

own use, invented a system of notation using lesser number of symbols and this is considered convenient by many -

Ṇ S r R g G M m P d D n N Ṡ ṙ Ṙ ġ

Letters of the Sanskrit alphabet are used as in the Ākāra Mātrika but Mātrās are not indicated, a note having one Mātrā is written separately and a cluster of notes of the same duration are written together. The Tāla divisions are indicated as in Bhātakhaṇḍe system but sometimes the '|' signs for Tāla divisions are omitted. Only the Tāla figures are written as in other systems on the head of notes. The octaves are indicated by dots placed below for lower and on the head for upper octaves leaving the middle one without any sign.

When a note contains more than one Mātrā the articulation of that note is prolonged by the vowel sound attached to that particular alphabet e.g.,

N D - Ṙ - Ṡ N D P m - P G R S -

This, if articulated would sound like this:

Ni Dhā ā Re e Sā Ni Dhā

Pā mā ā Pā Gā Re Sā ā

This articulation of vowel sounds such as 'ā', 'e' or 'ī' after the pertinent notes is found to be most convenient for all.

For international use with English alphabets, the notations would be like this:

Ṇ S r R g G M m P d D n N Ṡ ṙ Ṙ ġ

Each note has one Mātrā.

All the foregoing notations would use the grace note or a cluster of grace notes as this:

^{SṆRS}Ṇ ^{MG}R ^{m}P

The grace note or a phrase i.e., cluster of notes are put in smaller types on the left corner above of the principal note.

285. Svarāntara

Vide 'Tāna'.

286. Svarita

The middle tone between a higher and a lower tone (vide 'Udātta' and 'Anudātta').

287. Śvāsa

The period in which a free vibration of a note in an instrument dies out is called its Śvāsa. In a good instrument the Śvāsa is longer. To prolong the Śvāsa, the wood is hollowed out and gourd fixed. The drier the wood, the longer is the possibility of its Śvāsa. Modern instrument makers of India are trying to prolong the Śvāsa by making various scientific experiments.

288. Svayambhū Svara

Literally – a self emanating note. Actually a self emanating Svara is the Anāhata Nāda (q.v.) but in stringed instruments it is a manifestation of harmonics. Usually it can be seen that when an open string of a Tamburā is sounded, the fifth note of that open string emerges almost simultaneously, sometimes the third note is also produced. When the open string is tuned to R, the fifth note D i.e., the Saṁvādī note is sounded likewise. Mr. K.V. Devala had done much research work with this Svayambhū Svara. In a diatonic scale, if experiments are carried out, they would reveal the meaning of Ṣaḍja clearly, which is, 'Out of which six notes are born'.

The following tables would establish the above theory. The present day diatonic scale has two types of note-intervals, (a) major (b) minor i.e., a tone and a semi-tone respectively. Thus:

S major R major G minor M major P major D major N minor Ṡ

Between S and P, which have Vādī Saṁvādī relationship to each other, there are three major and one minor Svara–intervals. For the sake of convenience, we shall use the term 'large' for major and 'small' for minor interval and in the following table we shall use the initials only:

S (l l s l) P	G (s l l l) N	d (s l l l) ġ
R G M P	M P D N	D N ṙ ġ
P (l l s l) Ṙ	Ṇ (s l l l) m	g (l l l s) n
D N S Ṙ	S R G m	M P D n
R (l s l l) D	m (s l l l) ṙ	ṇ (l l l s) M
G M P D	P D N ṙ	S R G M
Ḍ (l s l l) G	.r (s l l l) d	M (l l l s) Ṡ
Ṇ S R G	R G m d	P D N Ṡ

289. Syuṁt

Vide 'Āśa'.

290. Tāla

This has been derived from the root 'Tal' having the meaning of 'Being established'. In rhythmic music, vocal instrumental or dance, Tāla carries almost the same meaning. Tāla is that by which music is established or regulated in time. Time is infinitely continuous and when a section of it, so to say, is made apparent by intervals of sounds struck heavy or light, slow or fast, accented or unaccented, so that this section stands out with individuality from the great continuum known as 'Time', it may be called a musical time. It is bound by a number of beats, which we call 'Tāla'. This musical time or Tāla can have infinite number of variations according to the various characteristics of rhythm and the number of beats in each. In the present work, only a few of the Tālas, some rare and some more commonly used in Hindustāni classical music, are given. In this case the word 'Tāla' is used in a general sense. In a specific sense it means only the accented beats on the Mātrās, of which there are several in a rhythmic composition. To allay the possible confusion arising out of the words 'Beat' and 'Mātrā' it is necessary to make the meaning of the words more explicit. Mātrā (vide) is a division of time with regular intervals either sounded or otherwise, while beat is that particular Mātrā which is sounded either with claps or with one solid object struck against another. The existence of a Mātrā may be felt rather than heard. But a beat must be heard, and this beat also we call Tāla. Now, for example, here is a rhythm bound by sixteen Mātrās and three beats or Tālas (in a specific sense) and the pattern of rhythm is called 'Tritāla', (this time Tāla in a general sense). The syllables to be played on a percussion instrument are called the Bolas (vide). The notation below contains the Mātrās represented by vertical strokes, the Tālas (specific) represented by the digits or a cross:

x|	|	|	|	2|	|	|	|
Dhā	Dhin	Dhin	Dhā	Dhā	Dhin	Dhin	Dhā
0|	|	|	|	3|	|	|	|
Dhā	Tin	Tin	Tā	Tā	Dhin	Dhin	Dhā

The percussionist plays the syllables on his instrument and naturally sounds all the Mātrās but puts accents on the Mātrās with numerals, keeping in mind the place of loudest accent which is known as Sama and is marked by a cross and that of the softest accent marked by a naught. This is called Viṣama or 'Opposite of Sama'. It is commonly known as 'Phāṁk' i.e., 'Void' or 'Khālī', i.e., 'Empty' or without sound. Actually 'Phāṁk' is never kept unsounded as such since it is a Bola to be played on the Tablā, yet it must be played most softly to mark the difference from other beats. (Vide 'Sama', 'Viṣama', 'Atīta', 'Anāgata' and 'Graha'). It is in the nature of a human body to sway with a rhythm heard and felt, but in this Tritāla, there is hardly any rhythm to cause any swaying. It is uniformly flat in divisions of three beats and a Phāṁk. However, it has been accepted as the fundamental or basic Tāla with reference to which other rhythmic variations in other Tālas are made to appear different and are appreciated as such. In the Śāstras everything regarding Tāla has been described keeping this Tritāla in view. For example, sign x is called the Sama (meaning 'Together'), '2' is called Atīta (i.e., the Sama having passed by) 'o' is Phāṁk or Viṣama i.e., opposite of Sama, 3 is Anāgata (i.e., Sama having not come yet). These terms have been fully treated under their respective heads.

The whole composition cited above is called a Ṭhekā (vide). Some call it 'Gat' also.

Some of the 'Ṭhekās' are given hereunder.

In all cases, the sign x indicates the Sama or the principal accent, a single or a cluster of letters known as 'Bola' represents one Mātrā; a dash also represents the same. When a letter is closely preceded or followed by a hyphen, they together represent a Mātrā and in all cases the Mātrā falls precisely on the initial letter or the hyphen as the case may be. To avoid visual confusion in reading a Tāla, the phrases have been divided by vertical lines.

(1) Āḍā Cautāla – 14 Mātrās

x 2 o 3 o
Dhin Terkeṭ | Dhi Nā | Tu Nā | Kat Tā | Terkeṭ Dhi |
4 o
Nā Dhi | Dhi Nā.

(2) Bharatāṅga – 12 Mātrās

x 2 o 3
Ghe Ne Nā | Ge Dhe Ne | Ke Ṭe Tā | Ge Dhe Ne

(3) Brahma – 28 Mātrās

x o 2 3 o
Dhā Dit | Thun Nā | Dhā Ge | Teṭe Tāg | Thun Nā |
4 5 6 o 7
Dhā Keṭe | Tā Dhā | Keṭe Tā | Thun Nā | Dhā Ge |
8 9 10 o
Din Tā| Keṭe Tāg | Tāg Teṭe | Di in

(4) Brahmayoga – 17 Mātrās

x o 2 o 3 4
Kat | Tere | Keṭe | Dhāge | Dhātā | Keṭedhāge |
5 6 o 7 8
TāgTere | Keṭedhāg | Dhā | TerkeṭTāk | Tāktere |
9 10 0 11 12 0
KeṭeTāk | Katāghene | Dhāgdet | Kadhen | Tā | Kat |

(5) Cautāla – 12 Mātrās

x 0 2 0
Dhā Dhā | Dhin Tā | Kat Teke | Dhin Tā
3 4
Teṭe Katā | Gadi Ghene

(6) Chapkā – (Two varieties)

x 0
(a) 8 Mātrās: Dhik Nāte Keṭe Tāg | Tik Nāte Keṭe Tāg
x 2 0
(b) 12 Mātrās: Dhā Tik Dhin | Nā Tin Tin | Tā Tik Dhin|
3
Nā Dhin Dhin

(7) Dādrā – 6 Mātrās (Two varieties)

x 0
(a) Dhā Dhi Nāk | Nā Ti Nāk
x 0
(b) Dhi Dhi Nā | Nā Tu Nā

(8) Dhamāra – 14 Mātrās

x 0 2 0 3 0
Ka Dhe Ṭe | Dhe Ṭe | Dhā - | Ga Di Ne | Di Ne | Tā -
x 2 0 3
or Ka Dhe Ṭe Dhe Ṭe | Dhā - | Ka Ti Ta | Ti Ta Tā -

It appears to the present writer that, at some point of time in the past, there had crept in some misrepresentation in the distribution of the syllables of this Tāla. The main accent or Sama appears on a syllable 'Ka' meant to be kept unaccented and the Mātrā of least accent or Phāṁk is given on a syllable 'Ga' meant to be accented. Over a period of time, this doubtful way of distribution has gained firm roots. The present writer humbly recommends the following altered distribution of syllables for consideration of the enlightened and discerning percussionists.

x	0	2	0	3	0
Dhā - Ga	Di Ne	Di Ne	Tā - Ka	Dhe Te	Dhe Te

In this distribution, the main accent or the Sama is given on 'Dhā', the only right phrase for the Sama in this composition, and the beat of least accent or Phāṁk is on Tā, again the only right phrase for Phāṁk here. The argument that there are two more signs of Phāṁk in the above is untenable since the major unaccented beat or Phāṁk should be at a syllable exactly opposite of the major accented one i.e., the Sama (which is also known as Viṣama- vide). In this case the Phāṁk is placed on the seventh Mātrā from the Sama and is exactly opposite to it.

The famous Dhamāra in Rāga Puriyā viz, "Merī Aṁgiyā Raṅga Se Bhigoī" is better suited to this altered distribution than to any other.

(9) Dīpacandī – 14 Mātrās

x	2	0	3
Dhā Dhin -	Dhā Ge Tin -	Tā Tin -	Dhā Ge Dhin -

In reading aloud or playing on a percussion instrument, the lingering sound of the syllable just preceding the dash, in all cases like this, is allowed to cover the unaccented Mātrā indicated by a dash. To make it more clear, it may be written thus:

x	2	0	3
Dhā Dhi īn	Dhā Ge Ti īn	Tā Ti īn	Dhā Ge Dhi īn

(10) Dobāhāra – 13 Mātrās

The divisions represent 1 Mātrā each

x	0	2	3
Dhā Keṭe	Tet Dhā	Ghene Nāk	Gadi Ghene

4	0	5	0
Tā Dhā	Din Tā	Trekeṭ Tāk	Trekeṭ Tāk

6	7	8	9	0
Tet Dhāge	Dhen Tāg	Dhe Tāge	Katā Katā	Gadi Ghene

(11) Ekatāla – 12 Mātrās (Two varieties)

x 0 2 0
(a) Dhin Dhin | Dhāge Terkeṭ | Tun Nā | Kat Tā |
3 4
Dhin Terkeṭ | Dhen Dhādhā

x 2 0
(b) Dhin Dhin Dhā | Dhā Thun Nā | Kat Te Dhāge |
3
Terkeṭ Dhin Dhā

(12) Farodast – 7 Mātrās

x 2 3 4
Dintāk | Dhettāk | Terkeṭ | Keṭedin |
0 5 0
Dingredin | Dhādin | Dhātet

(13) Gaja Jhampha – 15 Mātrās

x 2
Dhā Dhin Nāk Tāk | Dhā Dhin Nāk Tāk |
0 3
Tin Nāk Tāk Keṭe | Tāk Gadi Ghene

(14) Jayamaṅgala – 13 Mātrās for Pakhāvaj (Two varieties)

x 0 2 0 3
(a) Dhā Dhā | Dhā Dhin | Tā Kiṭ | Dhā Dhin | Tā Tiṭ|
4 0 5
Katā | Gadi | Ghene

x 0 2 0 3
(b) Dhā Dhā | Kiṭ Dhā | Tiṭ Katā | Genā Getā | Genā Kiṭ|
4 0 5
Dhā | Dhin | Tā

(15) Jhāṁpatāla – 10 Mātrās

x 2 0 3
Dhi Nā | Dhi Dhi Nā | Ti Nā | Dhi Dhi Nā

(16) Jhumrā – 14 Mātrās

x 2
Dhin Dhā Terkeṭ | Dhin Dhin Dhāge Terkeṭ |
0 3
Tin Tā Terkeṭ | Dhin Dhin Dhāge Terkeṭ

(17) Kaharvā – 4 Mātrās

x 0
Dhāge Nāte | Nāk Dhin

(18) Kāśmīrī Khemṭā – 6 Mātrās

x 0
Dhi ig Nā | Dhā Ti Nā

(19) Kavvālī or Qawwālī (Two varieties) – 8 Mātrās

x 0
(a) Dhā Dhā Keṭ Tāg | Nā Dhi Dhā Terkeṭ
x 0
(b) Tāk Dhin Dhāgi Nak | Tāk Tin Tāki Nak

(20) Khāmshā – 8 Mātrās

x 0 2 3 0
Katteṭe | Dhādhā | Dhintā | Kredhākeṭe | Dhādhā
4 5 0
Dhintā | Katdhā | Dintā

(21) Khemṭā – 12 Mātrās

x 2 0 3
Dhā Ke Ṭe | Nā Dhi Nā | Te Ṭe Dhi | Nā Dhi Nā

(22) Lakṣmī – 18 Mātrās

x 2 3 4 5 6 7 0
Kat | Dheṭe | Din | Tā | Dhet | Dhāge | Din | Tā |
8 9 10 11 12 13 14 15
Dhumā | Keṭe | Keṭe | Dhātā | Din | Tā | Dhet | Ḍin
16 0
Tā | Dhet

(23) Līlā-Vilāsa – 18 Mātrās

x 2 3
Dhā Dhi in Dhā | Dhin Dhā | Dhā Ti Na ak |
0 4
Nā Ti in Tā | Tā Dhi in Dhā

(24) Madhyamāna – a name for Pañjābī Ṭhekā (No.28)

(25) Matta – 18 Mātrās

x 0 2 3 0 4
Dhā - | Dhe Re | Nā Ka | Dhe Re | Nā Ka | Te Ṭe |
5 6 0
Ka Tā | Ga Di | Ghe Ne

(26) Mohana – 12 Mātrās

x 2 0 3 0
Katteṭe | DhetTā | DhinDhā | DheṭeTā | DhinDhā |

4 0 5 6 0
DheṭeDhā | DheṭeDhā | DheṭeDhā | Tādhā | DinTāk |
7 0
TerkeṭTātā | Gadighene

(27) Pañcama Savārī – Six varieties – 15 Mātrās

x 0 2 0
(a) Kat Dhi | Dhi Nā | Dhi Nā | Titrek Tinā |
3 0 4 5
Kattā DhiDhi | NāDhi DhiNā | DhiNā GaDhi | Nāg
"Kattā" is pronounced separately as Kat Tā but quickly in one Mātrā.

x 0 2 0
(b) Katā Dhinā | GaDhi Nāg | Dhā Dhin | Dhin Nā |
3 0 4 5
Tin Tin | Nā Ti | Nā Ti | Nā

In slower tempo:

x 0 2
(c) Dhā-Keṭe Tāg | Thun Nā KeṭeTāg | TereKeṭe Tāg Dit|
0 3 0
Tākeṭe DinTā | TāgTeṭe TeṭeTāg | NeDhā KeṭeTāg |
4 5
TāgDit - | Tāg Dit

In the bar preceding the last, the phrase should be pronounced TāgDi ītTāg, the elongation of the vowel sound 'i' followed by 't' taking the place of dash.

x 0 2 0
(d) Dhin Dhā | Dhin Dhā | Terkeṭ Dhin | Dhāge Terkeṭ|
3 0 4
Ti-iKre Tinā | Tinā Kat-tā | TereKeṭe Dhinādhāge |
5
Nādhātereket

x 2
(e) Dhā Dhin | Dhāge Nāge | Ti-ikre Tinnā | Tinnā Tinnā |
0
Kat-tā Dhi-Dhi | Nā-Dhi Dhinā |
3
Dhā-Kre Dhet-Dhet |Dhā-tit

x 2
(f) Dhi Nā | Dhidhi Kat | Dhidhi Nā | Dhidhinā |

0 3
Ti-ikre Tinā | Tirkit Tunā | Kat-tā Dhidhi Nādhi | Dhin

(28) Pañjābī Ṭhekā or Madhyamāna – 16 Mātrās
x 2
Ghi - Dhā - Ghi Dhā | Ghi - Dhā - Ghi Dhā |
o 3
Ghi -Tā -Ki Tā | Ki - Dhā - Ghi Dhā

As has been explained earlier, each letter or a cluster of letters, written separately, represents one Mātrā. Here Ghi is one Mātrā and -Dhā one Mātrā, the hyphen represents 1/2 Mātrā and the rest i.e., Dhā 1/2 Mātrā. Thus the whole cluster '-Dhā' represents one full Mātrā and it falls precisely on the hyphen, as has been mentioned elsewhere.

(29) Paṭa – 8 Mātrās
x 0
Dhā Ge Dhā Ge | Din Tā Ka Tā

(30) Posta – 5 Mātrās
x 0
Din Tāk | Dhin Dhā Dhā

(31) Rāśa – 12 Mātrās
x 0 2
Katdheṭedhā | Katāghene | Katākatākatā |
3 0 4 5
Dhumākete | Gadighene | TereketṬātā | Gadighene |
6 0 7 8 0
TāDhā | NeDhā | Tākeṭe | Tādhā | Dhintā

(32) Rudra - 16 Mātrās
x 0 2 3 0
Dhāterkeṭ | Dhādhā | Katdhā | Dheṭetā | Katdhā |
4 5 6 0 7
Terkeṭdhā | Terkeṭdhā | Terkeṭdhā | Katdhā | Katdhā |
0 8 9 10 11 0
Dheṭetāg | Dhātā | Kat | Dheṭedhā | Katdhā | Dheṭedhā|

(33) Rūpaka – 7 Mātrās (Two varieties)
x 2 3
(a) Dhin Dhā Terkeṭ | Dhin Dhin | Dhā Terkeṭ
x 2 3
(b) Tin Tin Tāge | Dhin Dhāge | Dhin Dhāge

(34) Saṅkaṭa – 12 Mātrās, a name for Mohana Tāla (26)

(35) Śaśāṇka – $5^{1}/_{2}$ Mātrās (Composed by Ustād 'Alī Akbar K͟hān).

x 0 $^{1}/_{2}$
Tin Tin Nā | Dhin Dhāge Nā

(36) Sātti – 10 Mātrās

x 0 2 3 0
Katteṭe | Dhāgaddhi | GheneNāk | Gaddi | DheneTāg |
4 5 6 7
Tāteṭedhā | Dheneteṭe | DheṭeDheṭe | Dhāgateṭe |
0
Gadighene

(37) Savārī – 15 Mātrās

x 2 0
Dhintā Kadhin Tāk | Kat Thunā | Teṭe Thunā |
3 0 4
Dhā Thunā | Terkeṭṭāk Thunā | Keṭe Dhādhi |
0
Dhidhā Terkeṭṭāk

(38) Śikhara – 17 Mātrās

x| | | | | |
Dha Terkeṭ Dhin Nak Thun Nā |
0| | | | | |
Dhin Nak Dhuma Keṭe Tak Dhet |
2| | 3| | +
Dhā Teṭe Katā Gadi Ghene

(39) Śūlatāla – 10 Mātrās (Two varieties)

x 0 2 3
(a) Dhā Dhā | Din Tā | Keṭe Dhā | Teṭe Katā |
0
Gadi Ghene |

x 0 2
(b) Dhā Ghere Nāg | Di Ghere Nāg Gad Di | Ghere Nāg

(40) Suraphāṁktā – 10 Mātrās

x 2 3
Dhā Ghene Nag Di | Ghene Nag | Ga ddi Ghene Nag

(41) Tevaṭa – 14 Mātrās, a name for Jhumrā (16)

(42) Tevrā – 7 Mātrās

x 2 3
Dha Ghene Nāg | Gad di | Ghene Nāg

(43) Tilavāḍā – 16 Mātrāṣ

x 2
Dhā Terkeṭ Dhin Dhin | Dhā Dhā Tin Tin
0 3
Tā Terkeṭ Dhin Dhin | Dhā Dhā Dhin Dhin

(44) Tritāla – 16 Mātrās

x 2
Dha Dhin Dhin Dhā | Dhā Dhin Dhin Dhā
0 3
Dhā Tin Tin Tā | Tā Dhin Dhin Dhā

(45) Uparāla – 8 Mātrās

x 0
Tā Tā Kene Kat | Dhā Ghene Terket Ghene

(46) Vīrapañca – 16 Mātrās

x 0 2
Dhāge etdhā | Dhin Ghene | Tere Keṭe
3
Tunnā Teṭe |
0 4 0
Kredhe etdhā | Gin Dhā | Katā Katā |
5
Gadi Ghene

(47) Yat (Two varieties)

x 2
(a) 14 Mātrās – Dhā Dhi in | Dhā Ge Ti in |
0 3
Na Ti in | Dhā Ge Dhi in

x 2 0
(b) 8 Mātrās – Dhā Dhin | Dhāge Tin | Nā Tin
0
Dhāge Dhin

291. Tālīm

An Urdu word meaning 'Lessons'.

292. Tāna

Derived from the root 'Tan' meaning 'To be spread'. Whatever 'Spreads' a Rāga, is called a Tāna. How can a Rāga be spread? In a figurative sense, this word can be employed to mean 'To unroll extempore' or 'To compose extempore'. In musical parlance, it is known as Vistāra in a general sense. The description of Tānas is always given in terms of the gamut of notes. According to the Śāstras, there are broadly two types of Tānas: (1) Śuddha, (2) Kūṭa. Whenever the notes are used in their natural order in a Tāna composition, such a composition is called Śuddha (generally, it means 'Pure' but here it means 'Straight'). When, on the other hand, the notes are used in any other order in a Tāna composition, such a composition is known as Kūṭa Tāna (meaning 'Crooked' or 'Not straight'). For example, SRGP is a Śuddha Tāna. Although M is omitted, the natural order is there in this four-note Śuddha Tāna. SGRP is a Kuṭa Tāna. Here the natural order of SRGP has not been maintained as G precedes R. As such, it is called a Kūṭa Tāna.

Different names have been allotted to different Tānas depending upon the number of notes used in each. A Tāna of one note is called an Ārcika Tāna. The word 'Ārcika' has been taken from the uttering of Mantras during oblations. These Mantras are uttered in one note.

A Tāna of two notes is called Gāthika from Gāthā rhythm. A Tāna of three notes is called Sāmika since Sāmas are chanted in three notes. A Tāna of four notes is called Svarāntara derived from the middle note of a gamut i.e., the fourth note. A Tāna of five notes is called Auḍuva (vide). A Tāna of six notes is called Ṣāḍava (vide). A Tāna of seven notes is called Sampūrṇa (vide). Every gamut of seven notes can have seven Mūrcchanās, one for each note, no matter whether the gamuts have sharps or flats (vide Mūrcchanā). Likewise, every gamut of seven notes can undergo various combinations in the arrangement of notes - and each of the combinations is called a Śuddha or Kūṭa Tāna. This laying out of such combinations is known as Prastāra. Even this laying out process follows definite rules.

It is unnecessary to enter into the laying out rules in this dictionary. In a gamut of seven notes, there can be as many as 5040 different Prastāras having a gamut of seven notes, each arranged in a different combination. As with the diatonic major scale or

Biḷāvala Ṭhāṭa, it is the same with any other scales having sharp or flat notes. In the same way, as we are mainly concerned with the Ṣaḍja Grāma (vide), it holds equally good with the Madhyama Grāma. Taking everything together, we can have 3,17,927 number of different combinations of seven notes which we call Kūṭa Tānas. Although this figure includes 88 Śuddha Tānas also, but for the sake of calculating convenience, these have been included among the Kūṭa Tānas.

We have said elsewhere that the laying out of notes in their natural and ascending order is known as Krama. We are now examining the process of Prastāra. For the present, we are using the name Tāna for Krama. The Ārcika Tāna, having only one note, does not have any other Prastāra, i.e., we have 1 Prastāra.

The Gāthika Tāna having two notes (e.g., SR and RS)can have 2 Prastāras.

The Sāmika Tāna having three notes can have (SRG, RSG, SGR, GSR, RGS, GRS) 6 Prastāras.

The Svarāntara Tāna, having four notes, can have the following 24 Prastāras:

(1) SRGM	(7) SRMG	(13) SGMR	(19) RGMS
(2) RSGM	(8) RSMG	(14) GSMR	(20) GRMS
(3) SGRM	(9) SMRG	(15) SMGR	(21) RMGS
(4) GSRM	(10) MSRG	(16) MSGR	(22) MRGS
(5) RGSM	(11) RMSG	(17) GMSR	(23) GMRS
(6) GRSM	(12) MRSG	(18) MGSR	(24) MGRS

The Auḍuva Tāna of five notes can have 120 Prastāras.
The Ṣāḍava Tāna of six notes can have 720 Prastāras.
The Sampurṇa Tāna of seven notes can have 5040 Prastāras.

It will be seen that the first and the last Tānas are Śuddha since they are in their natural ascending and descending order e.g., SRGM and MGRS; all the rest are Kūṭa Tānas. The process of laying out strictly follows a rule so that each of the combinations has a number allotted to it. This process has its own academic merit also. Supposing someone wants to know a particular Tāna by mentioning the serial number or may want to know the serial number of a particular Tāna. Both these questions can be at once answered with the help of a process using a table called Khaṇḍameru. Curiously enough, this name 'Khaṇḍameru' has lately been changed into 'Mīḍkhaṇḍa' by musicians and is being used in a meaning contrary to the original one. By 'Mīḍkhaṇḍa' the musicians refer to Prastāra itself and this usage has already come to stay.

This much for the Tānas as described in the Śāstras. Now we shall examine the Tānas in their present use in Khayāls etc. There are, generally speaking, two types of Tānas:

(1) *Bola-Tāna* – Vocal Tānas using articulated syllables or Instrumental Tānas in which the Bolas occupy a prominent place to draw listeners' attention to them as well as to the melody.

(2) *Svara-Tāna* – Vocal Tānas using the vowel sounds only and Instrumental Tānas using the necessary Bolas but keeping them entirely in the background, the melody being the only thing that holds interest. Although some hold that Vistāra and Tāna are the same, but it is convenient to put a different meaning to each. The present author is in favour of using the term Vistāra for all Tānas not having any rhythmic pattern as are used mostly in Ālāpa as well as in rhythmic music for the sake of variety. Tānas should be so called when they are composed within a rhythmic pattern, and are never to be used in Ālāpa either in the a-rhythmic or in the rhythmic parts (vide 'Ālāpa').

In instrumental music specially, a variety of Tāna is called Toḍā. It is undoubtedly a Bola-Tāna but using the same Bola-phrases that are already in the Gat that is being played. From this the rhythmic performance in the instruments is sometimes called 'Gat-Toḍā'. The patterns of Tānas are innumerable and only a few are being described here below:

A note or a cluster of notes has one beat each.

The sign	=	Under a note means a greater accent is to be given there.
The sign	–	beside a note indicates a beat but is left unused or unaccented.
The sign	◡	is to indicate the use of Mīḍ or rolling from the previous note to the next one.
The sign	*ɯ*	is for Gamaka (vide). =

Name		***The Pattern***
(1) Āśa	–	DG like Mīḍ but the interval between two notes is longer.
(2) Bakrā	–	Each note uttered separately in a muffled voice resembling the bleating of a goat.

(3) Bal – GMPM GMPM RGṆS.

(4) Balsapāṭa – DNṠṘ ĠṘDĠ ṘṠND PMGR S.

(5) Bharat – SRGM RG GMP GMGR S.

(6) Biḍār – SRG ḌṆS PMG RSṆ GRS PḌṆ S. Unexpected. In pure Biḍār 'S' and 'P' are omitted.

(7) Bijalī – ṖṀĠṘ ṠNDP MGRS – it is a variety of Sapāṭa (53) but faster.

(8) Bolatāna – Uttering the words of a song.

(9) Caḍti – SRS GRG PDP Ṡ.

(10) Cakkara – SGRS RMGR GPMG MDPM.

(11) Chūṭ – ṠṘĠ SRG NDPM GRS.

(12) Dhaḍkā – SS RR GG MM PP DD N DP MG RS.

(13) Ḍolnā – ṠṠ DD NN PP DD MM PP GG MG RS.

(14) Gajatāna – SGR RMG GPM MDP in slower tempo.

(15) Gamakī – GGR NND MM GRS – in Gamaka.

(16) Ghis – Like Suṁt (56), with no accent.

(17) Guthāva – Ġ - ĠṘ ṠN, Ṙ - ṘṠ ND, N – ND PM, D- DP MG PM GR S.

(18) Halaka – Tānas uttered deep from the throat.

(19) Halkā – ND PM GR S, DP MG RS, PM'GR S, MG RS, GR S, RS.

(20) Havāī – SR GM GR, MP DN DP, NṠ ṘĠ ṘṠ, ND PM GR S.

(21) Joḍ – SSRR SSGG RRGG RRSS.

(22) Kaḍkā – GG RG GG, MM GM MM, PP MP PP, DD PD DD, NN DN ṠṠ.

(23) Kadmā or Phulajhuḍī – ṠṘṠN DNṠṘ ṠN DNṠṘ ĠṘṠN DNDN ĠṘṠN.

(24) Kākī – Rendering resembles the cawing of a crow.

(25) Kampita – ĠĠĠĠ ṘṘṘṘ ṠṠṠṠ NNNN uttered in Gamaka (vide).

(26) Khaṭaka – SR GG RS, MM RG RS, PD PM RG RS.

(27) Khaṭkā – SR RG GM MP DN ṠN ND DP PM MG GR RS.

(28) Kheḍ – Omission of a note or more by mistake.

(29) Khuli – Using the vowel sounds of 'Ā' and 'O'

(30) Koyel – S G -, G P -, P N -, N Ṡ -.

(31) Kūṭa – S R - R, G M - M, P D - D, N Ṡ - Ṡ.

(32) Laḍī – GR GM PM GR, GM PG MG PM GR, GM GR PM GR S.

(33) Laḍī-Lapeṭ – SRGM PMGR GMPM GR GMGR GRSṆ S.

(34) Laḍī-Phirat – GMGR MGR MGR GMGR DPMG RS.

(35) Laḍī-Sapāṭa – SRGS RGSR GMPM GRSṆ DPMG RS.

(36) Lapaka – SG RM GP MD PN DṠ.

(37) Lapeṭa – SR GM GR, GM PD PM, DN ṠṘ, ṠN, DN DP MP MG RG RS.

(38) Mār – SRGM RGMP GMPD MPDN - Slow and serpentine in exposition i.e., in gesture.

(39) Mīḍ – RGMP MGRS with rolled uttering.

(40) Mīḍkhaṇḍī – DNṠṘ DṘNṠ NDṠṘ DNṘṠ DṘṠN ṘṠND.

(41) Miskī – Uttered in a muffled voice.

(42) Miṭ – Uttered syllables and notes are rolled into one another losing all separate identity.

(43) Mudi – With vowel sounds 'A', 'I', 'U' and 'AU'.

(44) Mūraka – ṠNṘṠ NDṠN DPND MGPM GRMG RSGR S.

(45) Mūrkī – ṠNṘṠ NṠ PMDP MP GRMG RG SṆRS ṆS.

(46) Nākī – Uttered with nasal sound; it is a defect.

(47) Paṭaka – S - R, R - G, G - M, M - P.

(48) Pālṭi – SRGM MGRS GMPD DPMG.

(49) Phandā – NN DP MG RS, ṠṠ NN DP MG RS, ĠĠ ṘṠ ND PM GR S.

(50) Phikrābandī – PM GP MG RG RM RG MP PM P MP MG; unexpected use of combinations.

(51) Phirkat – SR GM GR, GM PM GR, GM PD ND PM GR.

(52) Reraka – ṢN ND DP PM; Gamaka separates it from Khaṭkā (27).

(53) Sapāṭa – ṠNDP MGRS ; ṖṀĠṘ ṠNDP MGRS ṆḌP̣

(54) Sphurita – S - S R - - , R - R G - - , G - G M- - .

(55) Sumiṭa – A name for Miṭ (42).

(56) Suṁt – SP PMGR S. Like Mīḍ but also resembles Āśa for long interval between S and P.

(57) Suṁtkārī – ṠṘ ṠṠ ND PM GR S. The Exhalation uttered using the palate.

(58) Ṭākī – Uttered with the vowel 'E'.

(59) Ṭāṅgan – Resembles the neighing of a horse.

(60) Ṭhoka – ĠĠ - Ġ - Ṙ Ṡ N, ṠṠ - Ṡ - N D P.

(61) Ulṭi – GM RG SR ṆS ḌṆ P̣Ḍ ṂḌ P̣.

(62) Upaja – PMGRS, RGMGRS.

(63) Uṭ – DD PP MGRS ṆS - to be started with closed lips and blowing very hard.

(64) Utarti – ṠNṠ DPD GRG S.

(65) Vartaniā – SRG RGM GMP MPD.

(66) Yugala Bandha – (a) A variety of Bola-Tāna (8).
(b) ṠNDP ṠNDP NDPM NDPM GRSṆ GRSṆ S.

(67) Zābḍā – In which the jowl are prominently moved.

(68) Zamzamā – SRSR SGRG SRSR SMGM PPPP MMMM GGGG RR S.

(69) Zhapak – S R G M DPMG RS - the first half slow, the rest fast.

(70) Zhar – PP GG DD MM GG NN DD PP GG RR SS RR GG.

(71) Zhaṭak – SR GM DPMG RS, P MGRS, N DPṂG RṆS.

(72) Zhaṭkā – GGG GGG GGRS ṆS.

The above names and descriptions are not accepted universally. The names may differ in each Gharānā or School of music but the characteristics are more or less the same.

293. Ṭappā

One of the four major forms of classical music, viz., Dhrupada, Khayāl, Ṭhumrī and Ṭappā. Formerly the camelriders of Punjab used to sing Ṭappā as their folk song but Gholām Nabī of Ayodhyā improvised the old form to a great degree by incorporating various Alaṁkāras and brought it to the standard of classical music. The Ṭappā songs composed by him contain the name of Śhaurī, his wife. Some hold that Shaurī was his own pseudonym. The songs composed in the name of Shaurī are still recognised to be the best. In Bengal, Rāmanidhi Gupta (1741-1828 AD) composed Bengali Ṭappās which are equally famous and are known as Nidhu Babu's Ṭappā.

Gholām Nabī was childless but his tradition continued through his pupil Gammū. Some authors hold that Shaurī was also a creator of the Rāga known as Ṭhumrī (vide 'Ṭhumrī'). The characteristics of Ṭappā lie in the abundant use of the Alaṁkāras, Zamzamā (vide) and Giṭkārī (vide) by which almost every word of the song is ornamented.

294. Tarānā, Telenā or Tillānā

A vocal, rhythmic and melodic composition employing phrases without meaning. Some authors had denounced the composition of Tarānās by imputing illiteracy to the composers. It is to be appreciated from the rhythmic beauty of such compositions that the composers were far from illiterate and that Tarānās were composed with a definite purpose. Besides the exposition of melody, these compositions have some meaning to communicate to the listeners and thus they captivate the attention of the listeners. In instrumental music it is only the melody that is enjoyed with undivided attention and Tarānās were composed precisely with the same purpose for vocal music. Vocal Ālāpa also uses articulated phrases without meaning such as 'Nom Tom'. The preponderance of dental and palatal sounds in the composition of a Tarānā allows it to be uttered very fast. Tarānā is an onomatopoeic word derived from the sounds of syllables used. Lately it has become a practice for some musicians to declare that the meaningless syllables of a Tarānā are but misrepresentation of a doxological phrase 'Ananta Hari Nārāyaṇa' meaning 'Hari Nārāyaṇa is infinite'. The present author does not put the slightest credence to this assertion. In instrumental music the Gats known as 'Rezākhānī' have been composed on the structure of Tarānās (vide 'Rezākhānī').

295. Tāraparaṇa

The rhythmic phrases composed for percussion instruments are generally known as Paraṇa (vide). This rhythmic pattern or Paraṇa played on a stringed instrument is called Tāraparaṇa. While playing it, the Bolas or strokes of instrumental music are used.

We are giving here an example of this:

Percussion Bolas -	Kredhā - Ne Dheṭe Dheṭe Dhāge
	Trekeṭ Tunā Katā
Instrumental Bolas -	Ḍreḍā - Rā Ḍere Ḍere Ḍārā
	Ḍreḍā Rāḍā Ḍārā

The melodic portion is not mentioned here as it is of no particular consequence in this context (vide 'Ālāpa' and 'Paraṇa').

296. Tarapha or Tarhap

The meaning of 'Tarapha' is 'Side' and 'Tarhap' is 'To vibrate'. The sympathetic strings that are added to some of the stringed instruments may be called either Tarapha-strings (i.e., side strings) or Tarhap-strings (i.e., vibrating strings). The present author prefers the latter. The instruments with such strings are called Taraphdār or Tarhapdār i.e., having Tarapha or Tarhap.

297. Tārasptaka

The upper gamut of seven notes indicated by "•" sign on top of every note of a notation. In the human body there are three regions of importance to music viz., (i) the heart, (ii) the throat and (iii) the head, and the Śāstras refer to these regions as (i) Mandra (deep or low) (ii) Madhya (middle) and (iii) Tāra (high). The notes that come out deep from the heart are known as Mandra or low, those from the throat as Madhya or middle and those from the head as Tāra or high. The pitch of a note in the middle region is double of the corresponding note in the low region and half of the same in the high region. If the low S has 128 as its number of vibrations per second, the middle S will have 256 and the high S 512 as the numbers of vibrations (vide

'Vazan'). The low gamut uses "•" sign under the notes in notations and the middle gamut uses none.

298. Tauryatrika

Taurya literally means the sound of a trumpet but it has been used in the broadest sense meaning music in general. 'Trika' means three and the combination 'Tauryatrika' means the three arms of music viz., Song, Instrumental music and Dance (vide 'Saṁgīta'). Tauryatrika includes both theoretical or Aupapattika Tauryatrika and practical or Kriyāsiddha Tauryatrika. Aupapattika is an adjective from Upapatti meaning 'Origin'. 'Kriyā' is work, 'Siddha' here means 'Perfected'. 'Kriyasiddha' means 'Perfected by practice', so to say.

299. Tayafā, Tavāyaph or Tawaif

Persian word meaning a 'Dancing girl'. Tayafās also used to sing Ṭhumrīs and G͟hazals besides dancing. During religious or other ceremonial occasions, these Tayafās used to be employed to sing and dance for the guests. Colloquially they are known as Bāīs, e.g., Bāī-Nāca or Bāī-dance.

300. Thāpiyā

Another name for 'Ṭhekā' (vide) of Mṛdaṅga and Pakhāvaj. Ṭhekā is commonly used with reference to Tablā-Bāṁyā.

301. Ṭhāṭa

When the seven notes are articulated or written in their natural ascending order, the whole of the gamut is called a Ṭhāṭa, Krama, Mela or Scale. The descending order is not so called, it is simply a descent or Avaroha. Including the sharps and flats we have twelve notes. Out of these twelve, a selection has been made of seven notes only to form a Ṭhāṭa. Caturdaṇḍiprakāśikā, written by Vyaṅkatamukhī, mentions 72 Ṭhāṭas but all of these Ṭhāṭas are not used in Hindustāni music. Paṇḍit Viṣṇunārāyaṇa Bhātakhaṇḍe has selected only 10 out of these 72 Ṭhāṭas and has tried to fit in all the common Rāgas (about 195 in number) of Hindustāni music within these ten, but all musicians do not agree with him on this. At present, the diatonic major scale has been accepted as the fundamental scale or Śuddha Ṭhāṭa viz., SRGMPDN and is called the Bilāvala Ṭhāṭa. Each of the ten Ṭhāṭas has a number of Rāgas using those particular notes. In order to keep in easy memory the notes that are used in each Ṭhāṭa, Paṇḍit Bhātakhaṇḍe has named each after the most common Rāga falling under it. It should be clearly borne in mind that the Rāgas thus grouped under a Ṭhāṭa have nothing in common excepting the notes used in that Ṭhāṭa. In vain do some of the musicologists try to establish a sort of kinship among the Rāgas falling under a Ṭhāṭa.

Here is the description of ten Ṭhāṭas as propounded by Paṇḍit Bhātakhaṇḍe:

Hindustāni	*Carnatak*	*Ṭhāṭas according to notes used*	*Total number of Rāgas under the Ṭhāṭa according to Bhātakhaṇḍe*
(1) Kalyāṇa	Mecakalyāṇī	SRGmPDN	15
(2) Bilāvala	Dhīraśaṅkarā-bharaṇam	SRGMPDN	36
(3) Khamāj	Harikāmbhojī	SRGMPDn	14
(4) Bhairava	Māyāmālavagaula	SrGMPdN	18
(5) Pūravī	Kāmavardhanī	SrGmPdN	15
(6) Māravā	Gamanaśrama	SrGmPDN	16
(7) Kāphī	Kharaharapriya	SRgMPDn	53
(8) Āsāvarī	Naṭabhairavī	SRgMPdn	14
(9) Bhairavī	Hanumattoḍī	SrgMPdn	7
(10) Toḍī	Śubhapantuvarālī	SrgmPdN	7
		Total:	195

The total number of Rāgas given above contains some uncommon Rāgas and also some Dhunas (vide) and the number given is approximate.

Rāga Māravā does not take P yet the Ṭhāṭa as described above, has P. As has already been said these names have been given to the Ṭhāṭas for memorising them easily rather than for any other reason. On the basis of the notes used, these Ṭhāṭas would have to be known respectively as:

(1) Scale using M sharp
(2) Śuddha Scale
(3) Scale using flattened N
(4) Scale using flattened R and D
(5) Scale using flattened R, D and sharpened M
(6) Scale using flattened R and sharpened M
(7) Scale using flattened G and N

(8) Scale using flattened G, D and N
(9) Scale using flattened RGD and N
(10) Scale using flattened RGD and sharpened M

Obviously, it is better that these Ṭhāṭas have been named after Rāgas. Otherwise, they would have to be memorised with the above connotation.

The above Ṭhāṭas can be further subdivided into three groups viz., Sampūrṇa, Ṣāḍava and Auḍuva according to the number of notes viz., seven, six or five used in a particular Rāga. It is possible that all such subdivisions do not have corresponding Rāgas for each. Musicologists hold that a Rāga cannot be formed of a scale using fewer than five notes, the only exception being Rāga Mālaśrī, using only four notes. By using the notes in their proper sequence, each of the above ten Ṭhāṭas of seven notes each, can be used to indicate the Rāga after which that Ṭhāṭa has been named. But for any other Rāgas falling under that Ṭhāṭa, the variation of the sequence would be needed to mark the difference between them and the principal Rāga which lends its name to the Ṭhāṭa. This principal Rāga has been called 'Melakartā' (i.e., lord of the scale) or 'Āśraya Rāga' (i.e., Rāga giving shelter) or 'Janaka Rāga' (i.e., the father Rāga). Rāgas grouped under a Ṭhāṭa are known as 'Āśrita' (sheltered) or 'Janya' (begotten) Rāgas. These relative terms such as sheltering and sheltered, or father and begotten etc. have proved themselves grounds for easy misunderstanding. Since no relation between a pair of Rāgas falling under a Ṭhāṭa can be traced either emotionally or intellectually - they are simply different Rāgas using the same notes.

The principal Rāga as per the Ṭhāṭa-name is rightfully presumed to use all the seven notes. Any other Rāga using fewer than seven notes cannot be treated as the principal Rāga or sheltering Rāga. In this sense, it is not justified to call Rāga Māravā, using six notes only and known as a Ṣāḍava Rāga, as the Principal Rāga or a Melakartā. Instead, the present author recommends to name the Ṭhāṭa Pūrvā Kalyāṇa, since this uses all the seven notes of the scale. Although a mixed Rāga, Pūrvā Kalyāṇa is no less popular than Māravā among the musicians, Since the Ṭhāṭa name is merely a convenient way of keeping a particular scale in memory, it matters little if the name of a mixed Rāga is adopted for this purpose instead that of a pure Rāga. Likewise, the present author is strongly in favour of naming Āsāvarī Ṭhāṭa as

Jaunapurī since there is no controversy at all about the notes used in Rāga Jaunapurī. However, for the last few decades there have been controversies regarding the use of R in Āsāvarī. Most of the traditional musicians of upper India, corroborated by the old Śāstras, are of the opinion that Āsāvarī takes flattened R while Paṇḍit Bhatakhaṇḍe had emphatically recommended natural R. The main point in the present context is why the Ṭhāṭa using natural R should be named after a controversial Rāga instead of a Rāga having a consensus about the notes to be used in it?

A Ṭhāṭa loses its character as soon as its notes are arranged to indicate a particular Rāga. After such an arrangement a Ṭhāṭa becomes an ascent of a Rāga. Even in case of the Rāga after which the Ṭhāṭa has been named, if any ascending arrangement of notes is made with a view to expressing the spirit of the Rāga, it is simply called Āroha and no longer a Ṭhāṭa; e.g., Bilāvala Ṭhāṭa is SRGMPDN but with the changed arrangement of SRGMRGPNDN it becomes an Āroha of a variety of Bilāvala.
(For the difference of a Ṭhāṭa and a Rāga, vide 'Rāga'). 'Ṭhāṭa' also means the frets of a stringed instrument (vide 'Acala Ṭhāṭa').

302. Ṭhekā

Literal meaning of Ṭhekā is 'Support', 'Prop', or 'Shore'. In music, it is a composition for the percussion instruments showing a definite rhythm (Chanda), beats (Mātrās), and Tālas (beats which are sounded). This last i.e., sounded beats or Tālas help determining a rhythm and the nature of a Tāla (vide). The strokes representing the composition are called Bolas (vide). Songs, Tarānās or Gats for instruments are composed in Tālas and are accompanied by percussion instruments with Ṭhekā by way of supporting the Tāla and rhythm of the melody. Demonstration in the percussion instruments takes the nature of melodic music in the sense that Ṭhekās are repeated and extempore improvisations presented in between. Some authors call 'Ṭhekā' a 'Gat' also. The improvisation, either extempore or composed, employing stroke phrases of the Ṭhekā, is known as Kāyadā (Qāedā) or Vistāra. When a Ṭhekā is played twice within the normal time limit for one cycle of the Ṭhekā, it is also called Kāyadā (Qāedā).

303. Ṭhoka

Vide 'Ālāpa'.

304. Ṭhumrī

A short and graceful song. One of the four major forms of classical music viz., Dhrupada, K͟hayāl, Ṭhumrī and Ṭappā. It seems probable that Ṭhumrīs evolved out of K͟hayāls in the same way as K͟hayāls themselves evolved out of Dhrupadas that is, by making K͟hayāls shorter and adding more graceful ornamentations by way of combination of notes. It is also marked by the manner of exposition depending upon the subject matter of the song and mood of the songster. The earlier Ṭhumrīs were more of the nature of K͟hayāls in exposition, but later these have undergone various changes according to different schools or Gharānās. At present there are primarily three schools of Ṭhumrī: (1) the Lucknow School founded by Wāzid Alī Shāh, (2) the Banaras School – it is not definitely known who founded this School, but it was definitely popularised by the eminent Ṭhumrī Singer Muizuddin K͟hān in the last decade of the nineteenth century and the initial years of the present century, and (3) the Punjab School, founded by mixing the Lucknow School Ṭhumrī with the folk music of the Punjab. Of all these, the Banaras School is the most dignified and sober; the notes used in it are mostly without unnecessary ornamentation and are resplendent in their purity. They penetrate deep into the heart of the listeners and inspire the emotions of serenity. Banaras Ṭhumrīs rarely mix Rāgas. The Lucknow school is lighter in comparison both in the subject matter of the songs and in the use of notes. Each note often appears as a cluster of grace-notes, various Alaṁkāras are used in greater number and the tempo is also quicker than in the Banaras Ṭhumrīs. The Punjab School employs unusual and unexpected combination of notes on top of the Lucknow school. Another type of Ṭhumrī is known as Lācāva Ṭhumrī. The Hindi word 'Lācāva' means 'To bow' or 'To bend'. Lācāva Ṭhumrī expresses more of the self-sacrificing attitude of the heroine than anything else. Love songs are composed in the Ṭhumrī form in most cases. Some authors have mentioned Ṭhumrī as the name of a Rāga and Shaurī Miyān has been accredited with its creation. Mention has also been made of a Tāla named Ṭhumrī.

305. Tihāī

This Hindi word means 'One-third'. 'Tīn Tihāī' means 'Three thirds making one'. The word 'Tihāī' is derived from 'Tīn Tihāī'.

The ending of the last phrase of the three phrases of a Tihāī must always synchronise with the 'Sama'. Tihāī is a sort of Paraṇa (vide); its repetition creates a sense of suspense in the minds of the listeners and the expected satisfaction of this suspense is brought about as soon as the Sama beat is struck. The great and well-respected Pakhāvaj expert of Bengal, the late Murārīmohana Gupta, in his book 'Saṁgīta Praveśikā', has divided the Tihāīs into 4 classes viz., (a) Plutātiyugala, (b) Atiyugala, (c) Yugala, and (d) Ghāṭiyugala. The above divisions have been made in accordance with the use of two connecting Bolas between the three phrases of a Tihāī. These four classes of Tihāīs are as follows:

(a) *Plutātiyugala*:

Dheredhere Kat Dhā Katā Katā DhereDhere Kat Dhā

Katā Katā Dheredhere Kat Dhā. Here the phrases are 'Dheredhere Kat Dhā' and the connecting Bolas are 'Katā Katā'. This Tihāī belongs to Cautāla and has 13 Mātrās and starts from and ends in the Sama. In this, 'Katā Katā' Bolas represent the division Plutātiyugala.

(b) *Atiyugala:*

Dheredhere Kat Dhā Katā Dheredhere Kat Dhā Katā

Dheredhere Kat Dhā. Here only single 'Katā' between any two phrases indicates Atiyugala division. This is also a Cautāla Tihāī and has 11 Mātrās in all.

(c) *Yugala:*

Dheredhere Kat Dhā Dheredhere Kat Dhā Dheredhere Kat

Dhā. Here 'Katā', as a connecting Bola, has been eliminated and is known as Yugala division. It is also a Cautāla Tihāī having 9 Mātrās.

(d) *Ghāṭiyugala:*

Dheredhere Kat Dheredhere Kat Dheredhere Kat Dhā. Here even a portion of the Tihāī phrase, namely 'Dhā', the complete phrase being 'Dheredhere Kat Dhā', has been omitted in the first two phrases. This variety is known as Ghāṭiyugala. This is also a Cautāla Tihāī having 7 Mātrās.

The present author does not consider A, B and D to be Tihāīs according to strict gramatical rules. According to his understanding, each of the three phrases of a Tihāī should be identical and without any extraneous connecting Bolas in between. As per this, only the Tihāī marked C conforms to the rules. The same rule, according to the present author, holds equally good in case of Cakradāra Tihāīs (vide 'Cakradāra'). A Tihāī, if repeated more than three times, loses the character of a Tihāī and may be called a 'Cakradāra Ṭukḍā' only. There is a type of Tihāī named 'Bemāñjā' in which the 1st Dhā of the Tihāī falls on Phāṁk, the 2nd Dhā on Prathama Tāla (13th Mātrā) and the 3rd Dhā on the Sama, e.g:

| | | 0| | | | 1| | | | x|
-Kredhin Dhāge Dhā - Kredhin Dhāge Dhā - Kredhin Dhāge Dha

306. Ṭīp

The colloquial name for the upper gamut. In the Śāstras mention has been made of 'Ṭīpa' as being the act of blowing with only the finger-hole nearest to the blow-hole of a flute open, and it is from this hole that the higher S is produced. 'Ṭīp' is a direct derivative of 'Ṭīpa'.

307. Tīvra-Komala Svara

Svaras that are sharper than flat but flatter than natural i.e., in a position between flat and natural are called Tīvra-Komala Svaras. In the Śāstras, g and n, having two Śrutis, are known as Śuddha and present-day-Komala Svaras, also G and N having four Śrutis are called Antara and Kākalī respectively and in present day are called natural i.e., Śuddha or sometimes Tīvra, but G and N having three Śrutis are called Tīvra-Komala Svaras, and these are used in Rāgas such as Bhīmapalāśrī (vide 'Śruti').

308. Tīvra Svaras

Tīvra means sharp, hence sharp notes. The present day Hindustānī vogue is to call natural notes R G m D N as Tīvra, but in Bengal these are called Śuddha or natural Svaras and only sharp M i.e., Kaḍi or Tīvra M is called as such (vide 'Śruti').

309. Toḍā

When such melodic compositions known as Tānas use Bolas that also have a rhythmic compositional value, such Tānas are called Toḍās. In pure Tānas the Bolas are absolutely unimportant and do not draw any attention to themselves but in Toḍās the rhythmic composition of Bolas also draws a considerable attention besides the melodic composition. Toḍā is used in instrumental Gats and in percussion instrument Tablā, but never in vocal music. Originally, Toḍās used the very same Bola-composition as was in the particular Gat with which the Toḍās were to be played; the difference between the Gat and the Toḍās was maintained by the freelance melodic or Rāga composition in the Toḍā as against the pre-composed nature of a Gat. Now any Tāna with complex Bolas of a rhythmic nature is called a Toḍā. Both Tāna and Toḍā must have definite pattern of melodic composition, otherwise it would be known as Vistāra and would be without any compositional pattern. Three examples of Vistāra, Tāna and Toḍā would make the distinctions clear. We are giving Vistāra, Tāna and Toḍā in Rāga Yamana and each of these has been composed so as to have four divisions in one Mātrā, or, in other words, each note or a gap ' - ' having a quarter of a Mātrā. The Sama is on P.

(a) *Vistāra*:

ṆRGR ṆRṆS ḌṆRG mPGm PDND NṘĠṘ ṠNDP RGmG P
ḌāRāḌāRā ḌāRāḌāRā etc.

(b) *Tāna*:

NṘĠṘ DNṘN PDND mPDP GmPD NṠṘṠ NDPm GRGm P
ḌāRāḌāRā ḌāRāḌāRā etc.

(c) *Toḍā*:

GGR -G	RSṆS	ḌṆRG	RRS -Ṇ	
ḌreḌā-Rā	ḌāRāḌāRā	ḌāRāḌāRā	ḌreḌā-Rā	
RRG -m	PDND	PmGR	GmPm	P
ḌreḌā-Rā	ḌāRāḌāRā	ḌāRāḌāRā	ḌāRāḌāRā	Ḍā

In the above examples, the Vistāra will be seen to have no particular rhythmic pattern while in Tāna and in Toḍā this pattern will be obvious and Toḍā will be found to contain rhythmic Bola pattern as well.

310. Tripallī

A Ṭukḍā or Gat of a percussion instrument, having in its composition, three different varieties of rhythm, is called Tripallī.

311. Trivaṭa

A variety of song having any three of the four elements of a Caturaṅga (vide) is called Trivaṭa.

312. Tuk

Means stanzas, Kali, Aṁśa or Caraṇa, very much akin but not exactly the same, as movements in Western music. In Dhrupadas there are four and sometimes five Tuks, viz., Sthāyī, Antarā, Sañcārī, Ābhoga and sometimes Bhoga. This last, according to some, is another name for Sañcārī. In Khayāl and other forms of songs, there are, more often than not, only two Tuks viz., Sthāyī and Antarā. In instrumental music it is the same as Khayāl, but since 1940 or so, another Tuk called Māṁjā or Māṁjhā meaning 'One in the middle', between Sthāyī and Antarā, has been introduced and takes the nature of 'Sañcārī'. In all at present six Tuks are admitted viz., Sthāyī, Antarā, Sañcārī, Bhoga, Ābhoga and Māṁjhā in Indian music (vide 'Dhātu').

313. Ṭukḍā

A portion. A rhythmic or melodic phrase, composed as a portion of a Tāla or, in other words, composed within a number of Mātrās or beats. But it is short of a complete cycle of — say 16 Mātrās in the case of Tritāla. A Ṭukḍā in percussion as well as in stringed instruments should have simple Bolas and should end in an open or Khuli Bola. Some hold that a Ṭukḍā should have a Tīhāī in the end (vide 'Bolas').

314. Uccāṅga Saṁgīta

Vide 'Classical Saṁgīta'.

315. Udātta

High sound.

316. Upaja

The literal root meaning of this word is 'Side issue'. In music it should mean the ornamental variation in melody or in rhythm of a short portion of a composition. It can also be called Kāyadā (Qāedā). Some hold that Ṭukḍās (vide) are known as Upajas.

317. Uṭhān

A sort of prelude to the major performance in the pair of percussion instruments Tablā and Bāṁyā. Literally, Uṭhān is 'Starting' i.e., beginning or a prelude. Since this beginning is a separate playing item entirely unconnected with the main performance, it may be considered to be a sort of prelude or overture. It is a variety of Kāyadā (Qāedā) (vide). (Vide 'Salāmī Ṭukḍā').

318. Uttara Bhāratīya

North Indian.

319. Uttaramandrā

Vide 'Mūrcchanā'.

320. Uttarāṁga

Vide 'Aṁga'.

321. Uttarāyatā

Vide 'Mūrcchanā'.

322. Vādaka Guṇa

The good qualities of an instrumentalist. In the Śāstras a number of good and bad qualities of an instrumentalist have been mentioned. The following are the good qualities. He is a good instrumentalist who is–

(1) Thoroughly conversant with the manner and mode of using his hands, fingers and plectrums (Mizrāb or Javā).
(2) Experienced in playing the tune of a song.
(3) Experienced in Tāla, Laya and accents.
(4) Thoroughly conversant with the Bolas used in manual practice.
(5) Experienced in the good and bad manual qualities.
(6) Conversant with the intention of the audience while playing on an instrument.
(7) Conversant with the theory of sounds.
(8) Conversant with the 'Sama' etc.
(9) Thoroughly capable of covering the faults of dancing, vocal and instrumental music.

(10) Conversant with the Graha and Nyāsa notes.
(11) Conversant with the standard qualities of songs and dances.
(12) Conversant with the different sound qualities of different instruments.
(13) Having a beautiful and well formed body.
(14) Conversant in uttering or reciting the manual Bolas or Vāṇīs.
(15) A good judge in determining the difference of various instruments.
(16) Conversant with the inception, enhancement and obliteration of Nāda or Sound.

One who has all the above qualities is the best instrumentalist, or Uttama Vādaka and one who does not have most of the above is the worst player or Adhama Vādaka. These qualities are applicable to both percussion or string instrumentalists. The following are a few extra qualities required of string-instrumentalists:

(1) The capability of tuning an instrument to perfection.
(2) Freedom from unpleasant mannerism.
(3) Unperturbed and calm mind.
(4) Doing proper honour to the elders.
(5) Not to pretend to play faster than one's capacity.
(6) Not to be vainglorious.
(7) Cleanliness in playing on an instrument.
(8) Not to try to make the accompanist or companions look small before others.

323. Vādī

This word has produced endless arguments and misunderstandings among the musicians arising out of the misinterpretations according to one's own imagination instead of the real meaning as per the Śāstras. We are trying to determine the real meaning according to the Śāstras. In Saṁgītaratnākara, the Svarādhyāya or the capter on musical notes, deals entirely with Svaras, their inception, inter-relation etc. In this chapter it has been considered unnecessary to refer to Rāgas or melodies since there is a separate chapter 'Rāgādhyāya' for the purpose. In the Svarādhyāya, primarily the description of Śrutis, the placement or identification of notes on particular Śrutis and the inter-relation of each note to the others have been dealt with. In order to determine such relationships, each note has been considered separately and called

Vādī. Vādī being the chief or principal note of the gamut, other notes must either be Saṁvādī, Anuvādī, or Vivādī to the principal note i.e., Vādī. The relationship between the notes thus determined is unalterably fixed and is universally accepted. The Saṁvādī notes according to the Śāstras are on the 9th and 13th Śrutis from Vādī. In the Western theory of notes, these are the 4th and 5th notes from the principal note. Some of the Western scholars name the relationship as 'Sonant', 'Consonant', 'Assonant' and 'Disonant' respectively. It may be noted here that the whole system of the developments of harmony rests on these relationship. The difference from the Indian system lies in the inclusion of the octave in Western music so that it becomes a chief consonant besides the 4th and the 5th notes. The Indian system does not include the octave, so the question of its being Saṁvādī does not arise. In the Śāstras, there do not appear to be mentioned the rules regarding Vivādī or Anuvādī but from the tables given, it is evident that the two notes having 3 Śrutis each viz., R and D are Vivādī to all other notes. The notes having 2 Śrutis each viz., n and g are Vivādī to R and D only and Anuvādī to the rest. It appears that the notes having 4 Śrutis have Anuvādī relationship with notes having 2 Śrutis each but there are no Saṁvādī or Anuvādī relationship of the notes having 3 Śrutis each with any other notes.

In the Śāstras, the principal relationship has been recognised to be Vādī—Saṁvādī i.e., Sonant—Consonant relationship. There are two rules mentioned in the Śāstras to satisfy this relationship:

(1) The note that is placed on the 9th and the 13th Śrutis from the principal note i.e., Vādī.

(2) Notes having equal number of Śrutis are Vādī-Saṁvādī to one another.

According to the first rule, it will be seen that, if S is considered Vādī, then M and P become its Saṁvādī. The question may arise as to how both M and P are Saṁvādī to S? In answer, it may be interesting to note that M, which is on the 9th Śruti from S, is again on the 13th Śruti in the lower octave from S. Thus it can be deduced from this that the Saṁvādī note should be on the 13th Śruti either on the lower or on the higher side of Vādī. The rule that the Saṁvādī note is on the 9th Śruti may actually be a bye-law to transfer the lower Saṁvādī to its octave in the middle scale. Several authors have called this Vādī-Saṁvādī relationship as 'Ṣaḍja-Pañcama Bhāva' and it has been given great importance.

Taking the 9th Śruti as a difference between Vādī and Saṁvādī, it is obvious that M and n have Vādī-Saṁvādī relationship but they are not of equal Śrutis as M has 4 while n has two. Subsequently, the second rule viz., that the notes having equal number of Śrutis each would be in Vādī-Saṁvādī relationship, was introduced to nullify Saṁvādī relationship between M and n.

In short, it can be concluded that the notes which are placed on the 13th Śruti from each other either in the ascending or in the descending order, have Vādī-Saṁvādī relationship. Thus we can find M and P both being Saṁvādī to S.

In this connection it should be noted that the present Śuddha scale i.e., Bilāvala or Western diatonic major scale, gives us P and D both Saṁvādī to R. But this is a mistake because R, according to the Śāstras, has 3 Śrutis and P has 4 Śrutis; besides P is not placed on the 13th Śruti from R. On the other hand, D is placed on the 13th Śruti and has 3 Śrutis. So R and D are Vādī-Saṁvādī but R and P are not. In the Madhyama Grāma, P has three Śrutis and is placed on the 13th Śruti from R in the descending order or on the 9th Śruti in the ascending order and are thus Vādī-Saṁvādī. In both Ṣaḍja Grāma and Madhyama Grāma, D is on the 13th Śruti in the ascending order from R. As such, R and D are Vādī-Saṁvādī in both the Grāmas (q.v. 'Pramāṇa Śruti'). Continuous and long use of harmonium has completely shaken the basis of our scale according to the Śāstras. Any way, we are making a list of the Vādī and Saṁvādī notes in conformity with the present practice among the classical musicians. Apart from the Saṁvādī notes mentioned below against a Vādī note, there cannot be any other note as Saṁvādī to any Vādī. We are setting out in a tabular form all the Saṁvādī notes of each note:

Descending Region		**Middle Region**			**Ascending Region**	
Saṁvādī	**Anuvādī**	**Vivādī**	**Vādī**	**Vivādī**	**Anuvādī**	**Saṁvādī**
Ṃ	ḍ	Ṇ	S	r	G	P
ṃ	Ḍ	S	r	R	M	d
P̣	ṇ	r	R	g	m	D
ḍ	Ṇ	R	g	G	P	n
Ḍ	S	g	G	M	d	N
ṇ	r	G	M	m	D	Ṡ
Ṇ	R	M	m	P	n	ṙ
S	g	m	P	d	N	Ṙ

r	G	P	d	D	Ṡ	ġ
R	M	d	D	n	ṙ	Ġ
g	m	D	n	N	Ṙ	Ṁ
G	P	n	N	Ṡ	ġ	ṁ
M	d	N	Ṡ	ṙ	Ġ	Ṗ

The above list, although not strictly according to the Śāstras, is a practical and workable one.

There are no other Saṁvādī notes apart from those mentioned above. Some hold r and P or G and n as Vādī-Saṁvādī, but that is definitely wrong. It has become a formal and universal practice to refer to Vādī, Saṁvādī, Vivādī and Anuvādī notes while mentioning Rāgas but this usage runs counter to the intents of the original Śāstras, where, in connection with the Rāgas, only such words as Aṁśa, Nyāsa, Apanyāsa etc. have been used. The words Vādī, Saṁvādī etc. are of course, used in the Rāgas not as such, but in a different way. These words are used in order to determine the Graha, Aṁśa, Nyāsa etc. In a particular Rāga this interrelationship of notes Vādī Saṁvādī etc. may be taken into account, but it should be remembered that the Rāgas themselves have no Vādī, Saṁvādī etc., instead they have Aṁśa Svara i.e., the principal note and then, taking this Aṁśa Svara as the Vādī, other lesser important notes are determined to be used in the Rāga in the form of Graha, Nyāsa, Apanyāsa etc. Such as a consonant note of the Aṁśa note can be used either as Graha, Nyāsa or Apanyāsa, but a dissonant note to the Aṁśa Svara, although present in the Rāga, can never be used as Graha, Nyāsa etc. This is the implication of the rule of the Śāstras that "Vivādī is a note to be avoided in the Rāga". Otherwise, no Sampūrṇa Rāga can have Vivādī notes, a Ṣāḍava Rāga has one Vivādī note while an Auḍuva Rāga has two Vivādī notes—absurd and ludicrous. In some Rāgas, there may be found mentioned R and P as Vādī-Saṁvādī and in some other Rāgas S and P are mentioned as Vādī-Saṁvādī. The present writer suggests that those Rāgas where R-P Vādī-Saṁvādī relationship is mentioned, can be considered as Rāgas belonging to the Madhyama Grāma and where S-P Vādī-Saṁvādī is mentioned, belonging to the Ṣadja Grāma (vide 'Pramāṇa Śruti').

324. Vādya

In the Śāstras, musical instruments have been classified into four groups:

(a) *Tanta* or *Strings* – The instruments employing either gut or steel strings, e.g., Vīṇā, Sitār, Piano etc.

(b) *Śuṣira* or *Winds* – Instruments played by the wind e.g., Flutes, Conchshell, Harmonium etc.

(c) *Ānaddha* or *Vitata* – In other words percussion instruments covered with hide, e.g., Tablā, Dhāka etc.

(d) *Ghana* or *Metals* – These are struck with something e.g., Gong, Ghantā, Jalataraṅga, Kharatāla, Cymbals, etc.

We are describing in brief the various musical instruments used in India. Some Western instruments, which have long gained prevalence in India, have also been included in this list.

(1) *Ānanda Laharī* (Tanta or String) – Indian folk instrument. A small Dhola or elongated gourd having one end covered with hide and the other open; one end of a string of gut is attached to a piece of small wood and the other end is passed through a small hole at the centre of the leather cover of the Dhola and brought out of the other open end and is tied to a piece of wood with a good grip. This instrument is held by the left upper arm pressing on to the sides while the left palm holds the wooden grip for making the gut taut. This gut is struck by a plectrum made of coconut shell or wood held between the right forefinger and thumb. By making the gut taut or loose alternately with the left grip, and at the same time striking the gut with the plectrum, the sound of this instrument, which is mainly rhythmic, can be varied high or low in pitch. Bāulas and beggars mostly use this instrument in accompaniment to their songs. Some name it 'Gubgubī'.

(2) *Bagpipe* (Śuṣira or Wind) – Although this instrument could be traced in England only from the middle ages, it was invented long before. It was in Scotland that the bagpipe thrived most and is as indispensable there as conchshell is in India. This instrument uses three drone pipes from which are sounded the key note, its octave and its major third. Besides these drone pipes, two other pipes are used. One is a blow pipe which inflates the bag constantly from which all the pipes come out from different places, and the other is the pitch pipe on which the melodies are played and which has finger holes like an ordinary flute and this pipe is called chaunter. The bagpipe is much prevalent in Eire also.

Probably the Highlanders introduced the bagpipe in India and usually Indian pipers wore Highland dress. The sound of a bagpipe is shrill, but in a band its individuality is remarkable. The common man has some curiosity about this instrument for its extraordinary shape. At present Indian pipers play Rāgas and cinema-tunes also.

(3) *Bāṁśī, Baṁśī or Bāṁsurī* (Śuṣira or Wind) – The most common Indian flute. Formerly, it was made from a section of bamboo (Bāṁs). So it was called Bāṁsī. Now-a-days these are made either of wood, bamboo, brass or even earth – yet the original name has been retained. There are different varieties of Bāṁśī:

(a) *Plain Bāṁśī* – The commonest of all flutes having the blow-hole similar to whistles. It is comparatively easier to blow this variety.

(b) *Āḍ Bāṁśī or Muralī* - It is played while held sidewise. The side having a simple blow hole has the end blocked by a piece of wood. The blowing technique is similar to the blowing of an empty bottle.

(c) *Veṇu* – Just like a flute of (a) variety – the pipe is plain open at both ends but having finger holes. This flute is held not absolutely straight downwards nor sidewise but at an angle between these two positions. The blowing technique is a bit difficult than the other varieties. This is now a days known as Ṭipārā-flute.

(4) *Bāṁyā* (Ānaddha or Percussion) – Earthen or copper drum to be played by the left hand together with Tablā. Tablā and Bāṁyā form an inseparable pair and it is played as an accompaniment for all forms of Indian classical music excepting Dhrupada and Ālāpa. The covering hide has a Gāba applied rather eccentrically than in the centre. The hide is stretched with leather thongs usually for earthen variety or with cotton cords for copper variety having rings passed through the cords to adjust the sound by stretching the hide. The earthen Bāṁyā has richer sound (q.v. 'Tablā').

(5) *Banjo* (Taṁta or Pluck string) – The difference between a guitar and a banjo is that the guitar uses wooden sound board whereas the banjo employs hide stretched over a wooden or metal ring on one side, the underside has nothing whatsoever, it is

similar to Ḍapha (q.v.). The stretched hide carries the bridge. In Calcutta, the banjo obtained popularity about 1940, but it is rarely found now-a-days (vide 'Guitar').

(6) *Bassoon* (Śuṣira or Wind) – Belongs to the class of oboe (q.v.). Its sound is lower in pitch than that of oboe and there is some difference in shape too.

(7) *Behalā* – *(Violin)* (Tanta or Bow string) – There are different opinions as to the origin of Behalā or Violin. Some hold that Pinākī Vīṇā invented by Rāvaṇa, the mythological King of Ceylon, is the actual predecessor of violin and that it is from India that the instrument had been introduced in different parts of the world. Some call it Bāhulin. There is, however, consensus throughout India that the Violin or Behalā as commonly found today is, by no stretch of imagination, of Indian origin. In Europe, the violin came into wide use from the sixteenth century but towards the end of the seventeenth century Stradivarious made various innovations and from the eighteenth century violin became the foremost among all other string instruments in an orchestra. Violin uses four strings. Formerly they were all of guts, but later steel or silver and silk chord coiled over by German silver wire came into use. Usually a violin uses three octaves of notes. Although its use in India has been prevalent for a long time, the sound production is far inferior to that of Western players and the playing technique is also quite different.

(8) *Bherī* (Ānaddha) – Another name for Mahā Nākāḍā (q.v. 'Nākāḍā'). Śuṣira or Wind. It is made of brass telescopic tubes which, when drawn out, make it long enough. The blowing technique is like that of a bugle or conchshell. Earlier, it was a military instrument but at present is used on ceremonial occasions.

(9) *Bugle* (Śuṣira or Brass or copper wind) – This is an European instrument of the variety of trumpet, without the keys, shorter and sturdier. According to the technique of blowing, one can produce five or six notes of different pitch from this instrument. It has neither finger holes nor valves. However, lately, valves have been added. The blowing process is like that of a conchshell. Sometimes cornets replace bugles. The bugle is a military instrument and is

employed to send out codes by different arrangements of different notes. Almost throughout the world, the bugle is used as military instrument.

(10) *Clarinet* (Śuṣira or Wind) – A variety of European wind instruments. It is made of ebony and the finger holes are covered with sprung nickel or silver keys. Clarinet uses a single reed in the mouth piece unlike the double reeds of an oboe - this is the chief difference between these two instruments. Although European, it has long been in use in India and in almost all of Indian concerts or orchestra performances, the clarinet is used. It is used as an accompanying instrument in vocal music as well as a solo-instrument.

(11) *Cornet* (Śuṣira or Wind) – An European instrument of the brass wind variety. The blowing technique employed is like that of an Indian conchshell. The pipe is drawn in such a way that from the blowing end the diameter is increased gradually and in order to shorten its length to make the pipe handy it is rounded two or three times. The keys of this instrument, three in number, are called the valves. By pressing these valves singly or jointly in various combinations, various notes are produced. Generally, cornets are used in a military massed band.

(12) *Damāmā* (Ānaddha – Percussion) – Resembles earthen Ṭikārā (q.v.) but much wider at the hide-end. In older days it used to be played along with the Ṭikārā in the warfield. At present, it is sometimes used on ceremonial occasions.

(13) *Ḍamarū* or *Ḍugḍugī* (Ānaddha or Percussion) – Indian folk instrument, known to be a favourite of Lord Śiva. If two wooden cups are covered with hide on the open ends and are joined together on the other ends, it would look like a Ḍamarū - it looks similar to an hourglass. Two lead pellets are attached to two free ends of a string which, in turn, is wound round the middle portion of the Ḍamarū in such a way as to let both ends of the string bearing lead pellets play freely upon both the ends of the Ḍamarū. The middle portion of Ḍamarū is held in the right hand and is shaken to and fro so that the lead pellets strike the drums of the instrument - different rhythmic sounds are produced by the expert

shaking of the Ḍamarū. This is now a days used by snake-charmers, itinerant-magicians etc.

(14) *Ḍapha* or *Ḍampha* (Ānaddha or Percussion) – A thin piece of wood about two or more inches in width is bent into a circular shape of a large diameter. On the one side, it is covered with a piece of hide - similar to a tabaret. It resembles 'Ḍaff' of the Arabs, 'Ṭoff' of the Jews, 'Tambourine' of the Egyptians and 'Tabaret' of the English. Indian gypsies even now use 'Ḍapha'. Some use this in Indian concerts also. This seems to be a very old instrument and is mentioned in the old Dhrupada songs.

(15) *Ḍhāka* or *Ḍaṁkā* (Ānaddha or Percussion) – Very old and the largest of Indian percussion instruments. Yet the largest among the class is known as 'Jayaḍhāka' - which is often made of sheet-iron. Usually Ḍhāka is made of wood and covered with hide on both the sides. Mostly it is played on one side with two sticks at a time. It is decorated with plumes of birds. Its accompanying instrument is Kāṁsara (q.v.). It is indispensable in ceremonial and religious functions.

(16) *Ḍhola* (Ānaddha or Percussion) – Smaller than Ḍhāka (q.v.) covered on both the sides with hide. On the left side, the central portion of the hide and the inside are covered with an indigenous paste containing boiled rice and other things, two or three inches or larger in diameter, and is of dark brown or black colour. The paste when dries up, becomes a permanent fixture and adds to the timbre of the sound produced by the left hand. This dried-up paste is called Kharali or Gāba. It is to be noted that some instruments take the Gāba on the outer side and some in the inner side. The hide on the right hand side is without Gāba. Ḍhola is played with a stick on the right hand and by the palm on the left. It is used in ceremonial and religious functions.

(17) *Ḍholaka* (Ānaddha or Percussion) – Smaller than but other-wise similar to the Ḍhola, excepting that the hides are stretched with a cotton string which passes through holes in the hide on each side in such a way that the string follows a zig-zag course along the wooden body of the instrument and both ends are finished in a knot. To tighten the hide to adjust the sound, small brass rings are passed between two legs of the zig-zag so that each

ring, when drawn towards the broader end of the zig-zag, tightens up the covering hides on both the sides. The left hand side uses Gāba on the hide in the inner side. It is played with both the palms and not with a stick as in the Ḍhola. It is indispensable in the Indian concerts accompanying a dramatic performance, on the board or in the open air.

(18) *Dilrubā* (Tanta or Bowstring) – A larger variety of Esrāja is called Dilrubā having much lower scale than Esrāja and is generally fit for Ālāpa only. The difference between the shapes of Esrāja and Dilrubā lies in the shape of the sound-drum which, in Dilrubā, resembles that of a Sāraṅgī while the sound-drum of an Esrāja resembles that of a Sārindā and is rounded in the end.

(19) *Dotārā* (Tanta or Pluck string) – There are several varieties of this instrument.

(a) A bamboo pole is fixed to a gourd at the open end of which a hide is stretched carrying the bridge. From two pegs fixed on the upper end of pole run two strings, the other ends of which are fixed on the body of the gourd passing over the bridge. This is called 'Ṭhanṭhanā' in Tanjore. Usually, these strings run side by side but some instruments, having two strings, one above the other, can also be found in Madras. In this case the bridge is provided with two holes placed one above the other. Both the strings are tuned at the same pitch. These instruments are mostly about five feet in length.

(b) There is another variety which resembles the Sarod to some extent. It has two or more strings but does not carry the steel finger plate so commonly found on the finger-board of Sarod. The instrument is carved out of a single piece of wood. It would not be improper to classify this instrument in the group of Rabāb. Although some instruments carry more than two strings, they are nonetheless called Dotārā which literally means 'Having two strings'. It is a folk instrument most prevalent in Bengal villages. It is an accompanying instrument to folk songs but is also often used as a solo instrument and is plucked with a Javā (plectrum). It is also known as Svarāja or Surasaṁgraha.

(20) *Dundubhī* (Ānaddha or Percussion) – Śāstrīya name for Nākādā (q.v.).

(21) *Ektārā* (Tanta or String) – A gourd is covered with hide and a section of a bamboo is fixed on to the gourd. A peg is fixed at the end of the bamboo for the steel or brass string passing over the bridge which stands on the hide. Ektārā looks like a small Tamburā. The player holds the bamboo in right hand and plays upon the string with the help of a plectrum (Mizrāb) worn on the forefinger of the same hand. Bāulas, Bairāgīs and beggars, while singing for alms, play this instrument as an accompaniment to their songs. In the Śāstras, this has been mentioned as Ekatantrī (one-stringed) Vīṇā. It is regarded as the principal Vīṇā, being the fountain head of all other Vīṇās invented subsequently. Since only one note can be sounded in this instrument, it is not possible to play any melody on it.

(22) *Esrāra* or *Esrāja* (Tanta or Bowstring) – This instrument is a combination of the long wooden portion of a Sitār carrying the frets and the wooden sound-drum of a Sārindā. Unlike the gourd sound-drum, a block of rounded wood is scooped out to form the wooden sound-drum. This wooden sound-drum is covered with a piece of hide and the strings are stretched along a bridge placed on the hide. The Esrāra is played with a bow. All the playing techniques of a Sitār for the left hand excepting Mīḍ can be used in this instrument. The vibrating strings and all other strings, excepting the main first string, which is a steel wire, are made of brass. The tuning of the strings is like that of a Sitār. Hitherto Esrāra had been an accompanying instrument of songs but it is also being used as a solo instrument for a number of years.

(23) *Flageolet* (Śuṣira or Brass or wood wind) – European wood or brass flute similar to the common flute made either of brass, wood or bamboo as found in India. The chief difference between the Indian flute and the flageolet is that the latter has two thumb holes on the underside of the main finger-holes while the former has one. This instrument is blown through the flue hole as in case of a whistle and is held straight downwards from the mouth. The blowing of the flageolet is easy.

(24) *Flute* (Śuṣira or Wind) – Made either of gold, silver, brass or wood. There are roughly three types of flutes.

(a) A straight pipe open at both ends and having only the usual finger holes just like the Indian Veṇu. This is blown through one end; the blowing is similar to children's blowing of an empty bottle.
(b) In this variety it is almost similar to flageolet.
(c) The third variety is held sidewise and blown in the same way as (a). This variety is mostly in use now a days. The (b) and (c) types of flutes have finger holes covered by silver-sprung keys. Flutes made for the highest pitch are known as Piccolos. Boehm flutes are made of gold or silver. Gold flutes have the sweetest timbre.

(25) *Ghaḍī* (Ghana or Struckmetal) – A round and flat piece of platter made of bell-metal or bronze, the diameter of which is anything between two feet and nine inches and the thickness varies between 3/8 inch and 1/4 inch. The platter has two holes side by side near the edge to attach the string or wire for hanging. It is struck with a wooden mallet. Formerly when there was no watch or clock to indicate the hours, this platter was struck to announce and broadcast the hours as indicated in the sundial, every three hours - and was called Ghaḍī (clock). At present, it is used in religious ceremonies as well as in the schools, colleges and workshops to announce the periods.

(26) *Ghaṇṭā* (Ghana or Struckmetal) – Made of bell-metal, bronze, or cast iron. There are various shapes and uses of Ghaṇṭā. In India, those used in worship have a metal handle attached, to be held and shaken by the left hand. Those hung by a heavy iron chain at the gates of temples or palaces are rung by shaking the striker fixed inside to announce the arrival of an outsider who wants an audience.

(27) *Gopīyantra* (Tanta or String) – A variety of folk instruments. The gourd of Ānandalaharī (q.v.) has two flat pieces of bamboo attached at the sides and the free ends of these pieces, about three feet long, are joined together and carry a peg for one end of a brass string, the other end of which is passed through the hide portion of the gourd and attached to a piece of small cross-peg

to hold it tight. The player holds the instrument by one piece of the bamboo in right grip and plucks the string with the forefinger of the same hand wearing a Mizrāb i.e., the plectrum used for Sitār or Vīṇā. This instrument being one stringed, the sound produced is in one pitch. Sometimes, to break the monotony, the two flat bamboo pieces are pressed together by the fingers of the left hand and the pitch become higher. A pleasant and rhythmic variation with two tones (lower and higher) breaks the monotony. This instrument is used by Bāulas, Ascetics and the begging-community.

(28) *Guitar* (Tanta or String) – It is held by some that the Moors took this instrument to Spain from the eastern countries. In his book, 'Yantra Kośa', Rājā Sir S.M. Ṭhākura writes that Kacchapī Vīṇā was taken to Persia and there, after undergoing some changes in shape, assumed the name of guitar. Guitar, Ayasor, Sitārā etc. are the names in circulation. At present there are two types of guitars prevalent in India, viz., the Spanish guitar and the Hawaiian guitar. These are almost similar excepting in the tuning methods. The Spanish guitar is played on the frets with fingers of the left hand while the Hawaiian guitar is played by sliding a piece of short and round metal rod over and along the strings ignoring the frets underneath. This small rod is held between the base of the thumb and first two fingers of the left hand. Three plectrums are worn on the thumb, the forefinger and the middle finger of the right hand to pluck the strings. At present the Hawaiian guitar is being used as an accompanying instrument in modern non-classical songs as well as a solo instrument. A variety of the Spanish guitar is called a Sitārā. The famous violin maker Stradivarious made two guitars also.

(29) *Harp* (Tanta or Pluck string) – A very old instrument. Some authors hold it to be the first of all instruments. This was used in Egypt even in the thirteenth century B.C. Usually three pieces of wood are joined together in a triangle and two of them carry the steel strings parallel to one another and made taut by pegs. On one of these two sides of the harp, a sound box of the same length as that side, is fitted for resonance.

The player, sitting on a stool, takes the harp between his knees and plucks the strings with fingers of both the hands. The full range of lower and higher notes are produced by the different gauges of the thickness of the strings used. There are different shapes of the harp in different regions. Indian Kātyāyana Vīṇā or Kānana is also a variety of the harp.

(30) *Hawaiian Guitar* (Tanta or Pluck string) – vide 'Guitar'.

(31) *Horn* (Śuṣira or Brasswind) – It is a brass wind instrument of European origin. It came down from the folk horn made of an actual animal horn. Trumpet, trombone etc. fall under the category of horn; besides a variety of trumpet is also called horn. It is a coiled pipe with three valves - the blowing technique is like that of a trumpet or a conchshell.

(32) *Jagajhampa* (Vitata or Percussion) – Much larger variety of Kāḍā (q.v.) made of earth and of similar use.

(33) *Jalataraṅga* (Ghana) – It falls under the category of struckmetal. A number of porcelain cups are filled with water and are fixed upon a semi-circular plank, the player strikes the cups with a pair of sticks each held in one hand to play a melody. The variation of the pitch of sound is effected by increasing or reducing the amount of water in each cup. It is like tuning a stringed instrument. The musical notes emanating from this instrument are very sweet and melodious. It is used as one of the instruments forming a concert. At present, the use of this instrument is rather small.

(34) *Jhāṁjha* or *Jhāṁjhara* (Ghana or Struckmetal) – There are two varieties of Jhāṁjha - one is medium sized and is played in pairs, one in each hand, striking each other. The other is large sized, played singly, and is hung by a string and struck with a stick. This larger variety is prevalent throughout the world and in some countries it is called a Gong. Jhāṁjha looks like a Karatāla (q.v.) i.e., if a brass platter without the sides is dented into a bulge in the centre it would look like a Jhāṁjha. In the central bulge there is a hole through which a string is passed.

(35) *Kāḍā* (Ānaddha or percussion) – Made of earth or wood and shaped hemispherical like a kettle-drum, the open end being covered with hide. It is played with a couple of sticks while hung from the neck. The covering hide is kept taut by being stretched by leather strings. It is used on auspicious or military occasions.

(36) *Kāṁsara or Kāṁsī* (Ghana or struckmetal) – This instrument is made of bronze, shaped like a platter with rather high sides something like a tambourine without cymbals and made of bronze all through. It is struck with a wooden stick and is chiefly used on auspicious and religious occasions. Rhythmic variations can be and are shown well in this instrument. Among the Hindus, conchshell, bells and Kāṁsī or gong are the indispensable instruments of religious functions and worship. Similar instruments in other countries are called 'Gongs'.

(37) *Kānana* (Tanta or String) – A very old instrument. Opinions vary as to its place of origin - whether Arabic, Egyptian or Indian. Some hold that this is the very same hundred-stringed Vīṇā as mentioned in the Śāstras and call it 'Kātyāyanī Vīṇā'. Formerly, Kānana used 40 or 42 strings, but now more strings have been added and iron pegs like those of pianos have been used to tighten the strings. Ends on the one side of the strings are fixed to the body of the instrument stretched over a bridge, the other ends are fixed to the iron pegs. The body resembles a wooden box and the strings are struck either with fingers or with a couple of sticks. It is played on the open strings like those of harps and pianos. It is sometimes called 'Svaramaṇḍala' also.

(38) *Karatāla* (Ghana) – The smaller variety of Jhāṁjha (q.v.) made of brass or bronze, chiefly used as an accompanying instrument of Khola (q.v.). It is one of the principal instruments accompanying Kīrtana (q.v.).

(39) *Khañjanī* or *Khañjarī* or *Mandirā* (Ānaddha or Percussion) – A small Ḍapha-like instrument with much wider (deeper) wooden ring, in which the hide is stretched on one side. It is held in the left hand and played with the right palm. Mostly used by itinerant bear and monkey dancers.

(40) *Kharatāla* (Ghana or Struckmetal) A pair of iron rods in square section and tapered to a point at each end about 9 inches long and 1/2 inch square. These two are closely gripped in the right fist and are struck together to produce "Click" sounds. These are chiefly used in Indian concerts as well as in Bhajana (q.v.) songs as solo instruments. Some use two pairs of Kharatālas, one pair in each fist.

(41) *Mādala or Muraja* (Ānaddha or Percussion) – Common name for Mardala, a Śāstrīya word. The body is made of wood covered throughout by leather thongs and both the ends are covered with hide stretched with leather thong. Both the ends are equal in diameter. This instrument is very much in vogue among the Sāṁotālas. In Bengal villages also it is used on auspicious occasions. In the Śāstras, it is known as Mardala, Mṛdaṅga - though made of wood, and Muraja and the application of Gāba on the left hand side has been recommended.

(42) *Mandoline* (Tanta or String) – European instrument of the class of guitar. This has four pairs of strings i.e., each pair lying closely is tuned to the same pitch. It has frets like a guitar and is played with a plectrum. Generally the back of the sound drum is egg-shapped. Mandoline is similar to lute which has long since fallen into disuse, and European authors have admitted the lute to be of eastern origin.

(43) *Mañjīrā* (Ghana or Struckmetal) – Made of bell-metal or bronze with hole in each for tying the grip-strings. The two are struck together to keep rhythm. The Mañjīrā is used as an accompanying instrument to Ḍhola (q.v.) on auspicious occasions.

(44) *Mṛdaṅga* or *Khola* (Ānaddha or Percussion) – This is a very old Indian instrument. The body is made of earth (Mṛd–earth, Aṅga - body) tapered on both sides and the right hand side is smaller in diameter than the left. The middle portion of the body is the largest in circumference. It is covered throughout with a leather thong like a Mādala, and hide on both the ends is stretched by leather thongs. It is commonly known as Khola and is played as an accompanying instrument to Kīrtana in Bengal. It is also played with Manipurī Dance. Although it is the only instrument made of earth that can be properly called Mṛdaṅga, the Śāstras use this word for wooden instruments like Mādala as well. The Pakhāvaj, though made of wood, is also known as Mṛdaṅga.

(45) *Nākāḍā* or *Nagāḍā* (Ānaddha or Percussion) – Śāstriya name Dundubhī. It is a hemispherical instrument made of earth and stretched by hide. It is usually hung round the neck and is struck with one or two sticks. It is decorated with plumes. Earlier, it was

a military instrument but is now used on ceremonial occasions. The largest variety is called Mahā Nākāḍā which is rather conical in shape than hemispherical and is placed on the ground and played with two sticks. The Ṭikārā is used as an accompanying instrument.

(46) *Oboe* (Śuṣira or Wind) – European wind instrument. It resembles the clarinet to some extent, but the principal difference between oboe and clarinet is, the former uses double reed placed together one above the other and the latter uses a single reed. Oboe is made of ebony and uses nickel or silver keys sprung to open or to close. In an orchestra, oboe has some place of prominence.

(47) *Organ* (Wind or Śuṣira) – Generally, organs are used in churches for episcopal music. It is the largest instrument for a soloist. Many hold that this instrument came into vogue about 2000 years ago and has been used with episcopal music since the 5th century A.D. It is sounded by wind passed through metal tubes; such tubes are of two kinds, one is a flue tube, the other is a reed tube. Flue tubes are like flutes with an ordinary hole for blowing, while reed tubes have reeds similar to those of a harmonium. These tubes vary in shape from long and large in diameter for bass notes to small and short for higher notes. Originally, manual blowers were used to sound these tubes; lately it is done through electrical means. In fact the mechanism of the sound production in an organ is just like that of a flute. Organs have undergone various changes and smaller instruments for household use have long been made. These household organs use reeds in place of flue pipes for the sake of compactness. Household organs generally have five octaves and can be called a bigger variety of the harmonium (q.v.). Organs are sounded by pressing the keys, whites for pure notes and blacks for chromatic notes. In this country, at the beginning of the century, organs were used almost in every musical household. Lately, the usage has largely dwindled.

(48) *Pakhāvaj* (Ānaddha or Percussion) – It is made of wood. Formerly it used to be made of earth, so the name was Mṛdaṅga (Mṛd - earth, Aṅga - body). Though made of wood, the old name

has been retained. The name Pakhāvaj has come to us from Persia (Pak͟hāvāj - from which deep sound comes out). The shape of Pakhāvaj is like Ḍholaka (q.v.) but the end on the right hand side is smaller than that on the left. On the right hand side Gāba (q.v. Ḍhola) is applied while on the left hand side, which is larger in diameter, dough is applied immediately before playing. The hides on both the sides are stretched by leather thong passing over eight wooden pegs which are adjusted to tune the instrument. It is played as an accompanying instrument in Dhrupada and Tāraparaṇa. Although the old name, Mṛdaṅga, has been retained, especially in Bengal there is an earthen instrument slightly different in shape of the same name and is used with Kīrtana songs.

(49) *Piano* (Tanta or String) – The main keyed instrument in Western music - resembles harpsichord but is a later invention. Harpsichord was invented probably before the sixteenth century A.D. and has since then been used indispensably in Western music. When Cristofari of Florence invented the piano in the eighteenth century, the harpsichord gradually fell into disuse. Spinet, virginal, clavichord etc. were named after the various shapes and designs of harpsichord. Both harpsichord and piano are played by the keys as used in organ. The strings of both are spread parallel to one another on a steel frame like those of European harp or the Indian Kānana - upto this both piano and harpsichord are similar. Their difference lies in the fact that in the piano, the strings are struck with a padded hammer brought to work by pressing a key for each note, while in harpsichord a device to pluck the strings upward is brought into action by pressing the key. This device is called a jack. Various improvements have been done in piano. Earlier, pianos used only five octaves but now a days seven octaves are used. A damper had been added to deaden quickly the prolonged sound emanating from the open string after being struck; conversely another device had been added to prolong such sound beyond the natural period of vibration. Now a days, each note has a pair of strings and sometimes three strings and has a hammer and a key for each note. In timbre, the piano somewhat resembles the Indian Sarod and Jalataraṅga. It requires more painstaking practice to play it well than any other European instrument. Also, it is considered to be the foremost instrument in importance. Actually, the name

is pianoforte but is commonly known as piano. In India, the use of piano has increased considerably.

(50) *Piccolo* (Śuṣira or Wood wind) – European instrument, a smaller variety of the flute playing the notes of the highest pitch (q.v. 'Flute').

(51) *Rabāb* (Tanta or String) – According to Rājā Sir Saurīndramohana Ṭhākura, as mentioned in his 'Yantrakoṣa' or 'The dictionary of Instruments', the Rabāb was invented about a thousand years ago by 'Abdu'l-lāh belonging to the village of Basud in Arabia. He called it Rubeb which later came to be known as Rabāb. The Westerners hold Tānsen to be its inventor but Rājā Ṭhākura's version seems to be correct. The instrument called Rudra-Vīṇā in India is Rabāb. In Saṁgītaratnākara, there is no mention of Rudra-Vīṇā; perhaps some later authors called the Rabāb a Rudra-Vīṇā as Sarod has been called by some as Śāradīya-Vīṇā. In the Śāstras, all the string-instruments have been called Vīṇās, so, Rabāb is also a variety of Vīṇā.

This instrument is entirely carved out of one piece of wood, including the sound drum, which is covered with a hide pasted round the circumference. This hide is called Khāl (leather) and carries the bridge made either of wood or ivory. The Rabāb uses six gut-strings but has no Cikārī strings. The vibration in gut-strings dies out quickly. So, it is not possible to play a very slow Ālāpa on this instrument. Necessarily, therefore, the Ālāpa (q.v.) composed for this instrument is somewhat different from the one composed for the Mahatī Vīṇā. Mainly the Joḍ (q.v.) and Tāraparaṇa (q.v.) are played upon this instrument. In playing the Tāraparaṇa, some Bolas are produced by thumping upon the hide with the right hand and some on the pole of the instrument with the left hand; this latter thumping is known as Capaka, which has lately been introduced in the Sarod. Very few instrumentalists of India play Rabāb now a days. It is played with a plectrum held between the forefinger and the thumb of the right hand. It was mainly played by the generation of Tānsen's son Bilās K͟hān.

(52) *Rāmaśiṁgā* (Śuṣira or Wind) – Very old Indian instrument. It is made either of brass or copper and in the shape of rather elongated "S". In olden times, it was a military instrument but at

present it is used on ceremonial and religious occasions. Both in shape and in timbre, it is different from all other Indian wind instruments. The blowing technique is like that of a conchshell or bugle.

(53) *Śahnāī* (Śuṣira or Woodwind) – It is carved out of a piece of wood, employs double reeds like bassoon and oboe and tapering in shape ending in a brass bell. The Śahnāī is never played alone; it is accompanied by a drone Śahnāī sounding usually the key-note or the Ṣaḍja, and a small Ṭikārā (q.v.) is played as percussion accompaniment. This group of three musicians is called 'Rośan Caukī'. Lately, this Rośan Caukī has found a worthy place in the classical musical soirees; earlier its use was limited to religious and ceremonial occasions. Rośan Caukī is also known as Nahabat or Naubat and on the gate-ways of palaces and shrines, Nahabatkhānā can be found even today. Here Nahabat was required to be played every three hours. Even now some of the temples of Mathura, Vṛndāvana, Vārāṇasī etc. maintain Rośan Caukī to play, every three hours, round the clock the Rāgas according to time. It is found in Persia also.

(54) *Śaṁkha* or *Conchshell* (Śuṣira or Wind) – It is most familiar among the Hindus who use this in religious and other ceremonies and also for a general call to indicate codes. The tip of the conch-shell is cut off and it is blown through this hole. A gold or silver short-tube, fixed at the hole with wax, has been recommended in the Śāstras but in practice it is not done. The peculiarity in blowing through the conchshell is to blow it with both the lips pressed hard together - as in blowing a bugle.

(55) *Sāraṅgī* (Tanta or Bowstring) – Some scholars hold that it is a form of Piṇākī Vīṇā (q.v.) since it is a bow instrument. But it is doubtful if it can be called a variety of Piṇākī Vīṇā only on this ground. Some say that it was invented by Rāvaṇa, the mythological king of Ceylon. Some people call it Sāraṅga Vīṇā. Anyway, it is undoubtedly a very old instrument.

It is carved out of a single piece of wood and a portion, which serves as the sound drum, is covered with hide. Generally it uses four main strings made of guts and eleven brass vibrating strings. It was originally a folk-instrument but for the last five hundred years or so it has become a chief accompanying instrument in Indian chamber music. Since the earlier part of this century it has established itself as a solo instrument in classical musical soirees. Earlier some Sāraṅgī players used fiftysix strings in this instrument and practised the Ālāpa form of music as played on the Surabahār (q.v.).

(56) *Sārindā* (Tanta or Bow string) – This is a bow instrument having rather a large sound drum and no frets. The sound drum has a rather peculiar shape. As seen from the front, the hide stretched on the wooden sound drum looks like a pointed oval, from which a semi-circular portion on each side has been cut off. A modern Esrāra has a similar sound drum. Sārindā employs three gut or horse hair strings and is played with a bow. It is a very old instrument although the country of its origin could not be traced.

(57) *Sarod* (Tanta or String) – It looks very much like the Rabāb in shape, the chief differences are that it uses the Cikārī (q.v.) and the Tarapha (q.v.) strings, the finger board is completely covered with steel plate and there are no frets. Earlier, when the Sarod used gut strings, the finger board was free from the steel plate. Towards the end of the nineteenth century, the steel wires replaced gut strings and the steel plate was found necessary. With the introduction of the steel wires, persistence of vibration increased. As such, very slow tempo music such as Ālāpa (q.v.) etc. became possible to be played on the Sarod. In addition, most of the techniques of Rabāb can be used in it although it is an instrument chiefly for the Gat (q.v.). On the Rabāb, which is mainly an instrument for the Ālāpa form, Gats cannot be played. Lately, on Sarod, Tāraparaṇas are being produced by thumping upon the hide-covering of the drum as on Rabāb (q.v.).

(58) *Saxophone* (Śuṣira or Brasswind) – It is a brass-wind instrument of European origin. One Adolphe Sax designed this instrument in 1840. Its shape is approximately like the letter 'S' and has six finger holes for both the hands and an additional twenty holes covered by sprung stops. Wood wind instruments of the West are sweeter while the brass winds are harsher. The saxophone combines both; so, being a brasswind instrument, it has a wood-wind sweetness, since it uses the mouth piece of a clarinet with single reed and the blowing technique is like that of a clarinet. Usually

the brass-wind instruments are blown in a manner like that of a bugle or the conchshell. So the sound acquires some harshness which is absent in woodwind. Saxophone has a soft yet loud tone.

(59) *Śiṁgā* (Śuṣira or Wind) – Originally made from the buffalo horn but now made of metals. So, horn-made ones have become rare, though men who live in the jungles use them even now. Its blowing technique is like that of a conchshell and is chiefly used to signify informations by codes.

(60) *Sitār* (Tanta or Pluckstring) – Sitār is a Persian word meaning 'Three strings'. In the Śāstras there has been mention of Tritantrī-Vīṇā or Kachapī-Vīṇā (q.v.). Some scholars hold that the present Kachuā-Sitār has taken its name from Kachapī-Vīṇā (the sound drum with the gourd looks like a tortoise which is 'Kachapa' in Sanskrit, hence the name). The use of Tritantrī-Vīṇā was wide in India and in the period between the last decade of thirteenth century and the first decade of the fourteenth, Amīr Khusro called it Sitār and put this name into circulation. Amīr Khusro was never an inventor of the Sitār as has been said by many an author. As a popular instrument, it has been developed and renovated over many centuries. At first, two further strings were added perhaps by Masīd Khān in the generation of Miyān Tānsen. Masīd Khān also invented Masīdkhānī Gat - a typical form of Gat for the Sitār. This system of playing sequence is known as 'Masīdkhānī Bāj' and was confined to his own generation alone. Masīd Khān also created another form of Gat and named it after one of his pupils Gholām Rezā and it became known as Rezākhānī Bāj although the present author holds that Gholām Rezā himself evolved this type of 'Bāj'. Later it became known as Pūrvī (eastern) Bāj also. There is an apparent likeness between the Rezākhānī Bāj and the Tarānā form of vocal music as Masīdkhānī Bāj has with slow Khayāl form of vocal music (vide Masīdkhānī and Rezākhānī). Towards the beginning of the twentieth century, Imdād Khān, the reputed Sitār player, created a new system of playing sequence of Masīdkhānī Gat which is known as 'Imdādkhānī Bāj'. Some refer to Imdādkhānī Bāj as 'Modern Masīdkhānī Bāj' (vide 'Imdādkhānī'). Miyān Tānsen's descendants through his son Sūrat Sen adopted the Masīdkhānī Bāj. Tānsen's generations who went to Jaipur and settled there, known as the 'Seniyās', also adopted the same Bāj, which is also known as Pachāvī or Pachāha Bāj, that is the Bāj of

the west. It may be noted that Jaipur is to the west of Delhi and Patna, the home of G͟holām Rezā is to the east of Delhi, hence the foregoing two styles of playing became known as Pachāha (western) Bāj and Pūrvī (eastern) Bāj respectively.

Even till about 1930 the Sitār of Jaipur did not have the Cikārī (q.v.) strings. These two strings were added later copying them from the Surabahār, an instrument of the shape of Sitār but much larger, for the lower scale, suitable for the Ālāpa form of music. This latter instrument was said to have been invented by one G͟holām Mohammad K͟hān, a pupil of Omrāo K͟hān and Pyār K͟hān, in about 1840. He added Cikārī (q.v.) strings to his Surabahār and also strings for sympathetic vibrations (Tarapha - q.v.). Thereafter the Cikārīs were added to the Sitār, yet the Seniyās of Jaipur continued without these. Though G͟holām Mohammad's son Sajjād Mohammad K͟hān became famous in Calcutta chiefly as a Surabahār player, he used to play the Sitār also. Imdād K͟hān, while in Calcutta, had an opportunity to listen to Sajjād Mohammad's Surabahār and Sitār for many years. At present a Sitār without Tarapha can rarely be found in the classical musical soirees although neophytes sometimes use them privately. The Sitār is chiefly an instrument for Gat and elementary Ālāpa, but since 1945 or so, a bass string has been added and regular Ālāpa is being played on it. However, the Jhālā (q.v.), so important a stage in Gat and also in Ālāpa, can hardly be satisfactory in a Sitār having the newly added bass string.

The pole of the instrument or in other words the finger-board carrying frets is called the Patarī, and the piece of wood covering the gourd and which carries the bridge is called Tablī. At present there are seven main strings and eleven and sometimes thirteen vibrating strings on a Sitār. A Sacala Ṭhāṭa (q.v.) Sitār carries seventeen frets, whereas an Acala Ṭhāṭa (q.v.) Sitār carries twentythree. However, this Sitār is seldom found. Usually the Acala Ṭhāṭa Sitār, which one mostly finds, carries nineteen frets. Since 1925 or so, a large Sitār carries another smaller gourd up behind the pole or finger board partly for decoration and partly for resonance. Curiously enough, in Jaipur, a Sitār without Cikārī used to carry another gourd just behind the main gourd or the sound drum; it was smaller than the main gourd and was fixed behind that portion of the finger board where a Sitār player puts his right thumb in playing it. Those Sitārs also had the smaller gourd up the pole as mentioned above. The three-gourd Sitār has become obsolete now a days.

(61) *Surabahār* (Tanta or Pluck string) – This instrument is said to have been created by G̱holām Mohammad Ḵhān a pupil of Piyār Ḵhān and Omrāo Ḵhān, both belonging to the generation of Miyān Tānsen. It is similar to the Sitār but larger, suitable for Ālāpa form of music. The differences between a Sitār and a Surabahār are:

- (a) The Surabahār is larger than the Sitār.
- (b) The Surabahār used seven strings when the Sitār had only five - the two added strings were Cikārī (q.v.).
- (c) Usually the Sitār had no Tarapha (q.v.) while the Surabahār had.
- (d) The lower notes could not be played in the Sitār whereas the Surabahār had full scope in the lower scales - so important in the Ālāpa form of music.

(62) *Suracain* (Tanta or Pluck string) – It is generally like a Surabahār, suitable for Ālāpa and without Tarapha (q.v.). The difference between a Surabahār and a Suracain is that its sound drum is carved out of a piece of wood instead of using the usual gourd. Perhaps it is a predecessor to Surabahār; it could not be traced who invented this instrument. Another instrument, a curious mixture of the Sarod in shape but carrying frets, is also called Suracain. This last can be played either with a Mizrāb (vide 'Vīṇā') or with a Javā (vide 'Dotārā').

(63) *Suramañjarī, Suramaṇḍala* or *Svaramaṇḍala* (Tanta or Pluckstring) – Other names for Kānana.

(64) *Surarabāb* (Tanta or Pluckstring) – A Rabāb having steel strings and the finger board covered with a steel plate, yet retaining the sound drum covered with hide, is called a Surarabāb. It is almost similar to Suraśṛṅgāra (q.v.) excepting for the hide used. While playing Tāraparaṇas (q.v.), the thumping is done on the hide (vide 'Rabāb').

(65) *Surasaṁgraha* or *Svarāja* (Tanta or Pluck string) – Different names for Dotārā (q.v.).

(66) *Suraśṛṅgāra* (Tanta or Pluck string) – It is a product of renovations done to Rabāb by an artisan of Banaras under the supervision of one Zafar Khān of the generation of Miyān Tānsen. The wooden sound drum of the Rabāb was replaced by gourd sound drum covered by a wooden bridge board instead of hide as in Rabāb. The wooden finger board of the Rabāb was covered by a steel plate and steel strings replaced the gut ones and thus Suraśṛṅgāra came into existence. In later years, two Cikārīs were added. This instrument was devised by Zafar Khān to increase the duration of vibrations and to make the sound more melodious, so that the slow tempo Ālāpa could be played on it. The sound of this instrument is very sonorous, sweet and the vibration is of increased duration. There are a few Suraśṛṅgāra players in India today.

(67) *Tablā* (Ānaddha or Percussion) – The commonest of all the Hindustāni percussion instruments to indicate Tāla and Mātrā (q.v.), used in accompaniment to all classical forms excepting the Ālāpa and Dhrupada. It is said that a Pakhāvaj (q.v.) had been cut into two halves to form Tablā for the right hand and Bāṁyā for the left. The Tablā and Bāṁyā are played simultaneously one by each hand. Although chiefly an accompanying instrument, the pair has long been accepted as a solo instrument in the classical musical soirees where harmonium or Sāraṅgī serves as the accompanying instrument to Tablā-Bāṁyā. Tablā takes the Gāba on the upper side of the hide stretched on a wooden body with a piece of leather string passing over a number of wooden pegs used for stretching the hide further to tune the sound. The wooden body is formed by hollowing out a round piece of wooden block leaving the bottom and about more or less an inch of thickness all along the sides (vide 'Bāṁyā').

(68) *Tamburā* (Tanta or String) – It is called Tamburū Vīṇā also. This instrument belongs to the class of Ektārā and only a few independent musical notes can be sounded on it. But a complete Rāga cannot be played on it. Usually, four strings are used and these are tuned in accordance with the Rāga to be sung, in other words, the 'Aṁśa' (q.v.) note of a Rāga and its Saṁvādī (q.v.) etc. Taking Ṣaḍja as the key note, the four strings are tuned. The Tamburā is always used as a backgroud instrument in vocal, and

lately, in instrumental performances. Vocalists and instrumentalists, while doing their daily practice, often use the Tamburā, droning along on a fixed pitch, so that the pitch of their voice or of the strings may remain unaltered. Further, the drone of the key note and its Saṁvādī etc., serves the purpose of a background of musical and harmonious notes for the Rāga practised. Some hold that the instrument took its name from the gourd which is called Tumbā in Hindi, while others hold that the name came after Tamburū – a Gandharva, who is reputed to have been its maker. The Tamburā is usually tuned thus - 1st or the steel string in M or P and the three brass strings in two middle S followed by one lower S.

(69) *Taūs* (Tanta or Bow string) – An Arabic word meaning - 'Peacock'. When the sound drum of an Esrāra is shaped to resemble the head of a peacock, it is called a Taūs, otherwise there is no difference between a Taūs and an Esrāra (q.v.). The legs and the claws of the peacock are carved out in such a way that the instrument can be stood vertically on the ground independently and it is played on thus. According to Rājā Sir S.M. Ṭhākura, Taūs was brought into existence towards the middle of the nineteenth century.

(70) *Ṭikārā* (Ānaddha or percussion) – This is made either of copper, brass, wood or earth. Shaped like a Kāḍā (q.v.), but much smaller, it is played with a pair of sticks as an accompanying instrument to Śahnāī.

(71) *Trombone* (Śuṣira or Brasswind) – An European instrument made of brass in the shape of an elongated 'S'. This shape apparently reduces its unwieldy length. It is made of two portions, one of which can be worked telescope like into the other so as to make variations of the pitch. It is used in European orchestra and the blowing of this instrument is like that of a bugle or a conchshell.

(72) *Trumpet* (Śuṣira or Brasswind) – European wind instrument. It is almost similar to a cornet but is more difficult to play upon. The sound of this instrument is more melodious or sweeter than that of a cornet. Originally, trumpets did not use valves but later three valves, like those of a cornet, have been introduced by way

of improvement. The sounding technique is like that of a bugle or a conchshell and it is a very important instrument in a European orchestra. Sometimes a muffler in the shape of a cup is fixed on the end of a trumpet to muffle the sound to a peculiar effect. Indian concerts mostly employ these muffled trumpets.

(73) *Tuṁbḍī* (Śvṣira or Woodwind) – A wind instrument made partly of an elongated gourd and partly of bamboo pipe. It is a folk instrument and is employed by snake-charmers. The gourd used is reared to take a special shape, that is, about two thirds of the gourd is shaped tubular and the rest of it round. To the end of this round portion are fixed two short parallel pieces of bamboo pipes, each having a reed. One of these two pipes is used as a drone and on the other is played the melody like on a flute. The speciality of this instrument lies in the fact that the wind contained in the round portion of the gourd continues to sound the pipe for a while during the inhalation of the air by the player. It resembles functionally somewhat to bagpipes especially in the use of a drone and the small amount of reserved air in the gourd. It requires a special training to blow this instrument. Anybody buying this flute would face a difficulty. Usually the snake-charmers selling it to outsiders, cut off the top of the elongated portion of the gourd in such a way that the blow hole becomes too large whereas the flutes used by themselves have a small blow hole so that it can be covered by the end of the tongue while inhaling air through nostrils, as a result the wind reserved in the round portion of the gourd slowly blows out the reeds of the pipe, being choked by the sealing of the blow hole by the tip of the tongue and the effect of the continuous sound is thus maintained, which can never be done if the blow hole is too large to be sealed by the tip of the tongue. This is a secret with the snake-charmers and seldom can one find anybody who is not a snake-charmer, playing this Tuṁbḍī. The present author made several experiments before he could find out this secret. It is also called Tiktirī (from bitter gourd) and Puṅgī. It is also called Vīṇ in Punjab and Uttar Pradesh.

(74) *Turī* (Śuṣira or Brasswind) – It somewhat resembles old European trumpet without any finger holes or valves. The blowing process is like that of a bugle or a conchshell. This is used on ceremonial occasions; earlier it was used in warfields. Unlike the

bugle, it does not produce more than one note, so it cannot give out any sound code bearing any meaning.

(75) *Tysokodo* (Tanta or String) – Imported into India from Japan. It seems to combine a Kānana and a guitar with symbols of notes printed on the keys similar to those of a typewriter machine. Four or more strings are used and the keys, when pressed, press the strings on frets and the strings are sounded with plectrums held by the thumb, the index and the middle fingers. For some time past, this instrument has put in an appearance in the classical music conferences and Gat-Toḍā and Tānas of classical music are being played on this instrument with ease. Indian players have called this as 'Bulbul-Taraṅga'. It is played with Javā – a triangular plectrum made either of steel wire, the portion to be held by fingers is covered with cotton string and covered with bees-wax or it can be made of a piece of coconut shell filed to a triangular shape.

(76) *Veṇu* (Śuṣira or Wind) – Vide 'Bāṁsī'.

(77) *Vīṇā* (Tanta or String) – In the Śāstras, all the string instruments have been called Vīṇās, so it seems that the name Vīṇā indicates string instruments in general. Kānana has been called Kātyāyanī-Vīṇā; Pinākī-Vīṇā is played with a bow; Sarod has been called Śāradīya-Vīṇā by some authors. A variety of Sitār is known as Kachapī-Vīṇā or Tritantrī-Vīṇā. There is a reference of Saptatantrī-Vīṇā, that is seven-stringed-Vīṇā, which can be compared to the present day Sitār having seven strings. Sāraṅgī has been referred to as Sāraṅga-Vīṇā by some. All these point to the fact that all string instruments are Vīṇās according to the Śāstras. In the Saṁgītaratnākara, the use of both guts and steel strings has been mentioned. The following are some of the different varieties of Vīṇā mentioned in both modern and ancient Śāstras:

1. Ālāpinī – Using guts of sheep intestines or cotton or silk strings
2. Bharata
3. Brahma
4. Citrā (Saptatantrī or seven-stringed)
5. Dakshiṇī
6. Ekatantrī

7. Ghoṣavatī
8. Hantikā
9. Jayā
10. Jyeṣṭhā
11. Kachapī
12. Kinnarī – (a) Bṛhatī, (b) Madhyamā, (c) Lāghavī
13. Kubjikā
14. Kūrmikā
15. Mahatī (The variety at present found in Upper India)
16. Mattakokilā (Ekaviṁśatitantrī or twentyone-stringed)
17. Nādesvara
18. Nakula (Dvitantrī or two-stringed)
19. Nakuloṣṭhi
20. Nāradīya
21. Niḥśaṅka
22. Parivādinī
23. Piṇākī (Dhanuyantra or bow-string)
24. Pona
25. Prasāriṇī
26. Rañjanī (having a pole carrying frets and a board covering the gourd and carrying the bridge like those in a Sitār)
27. Rāvaṇahantaka
28. Rudra (Rabāb)
29. Śāradīya (Sarod)
30. Sāraṅga (Sāraṅgī)
31. Śatatantrī (Probably Kānana)
32. Ṣaṭkarṇa
33. Śruti (Dvāviṁśatitantrī - twentytwo-stringed)
34. Sura (Suraśṛṅgāra)
35. Svara
36. Trisvarī
37. Tritantrī
38. Tumburū (Tamburā)
39. Udumbarī
40. Vallakī
41. Vipañcī (Navatantrī or nine-stringed)

The Vīṇā that is to be found at present in Upper India is considered by the author to be the Mahatī as mentioned in the Śāstras. There are mainly two basic differences between Mahatī-

Vīṇā and other string instruments prevalent in Upper India at present such as Sitār, Surabahār, Sarod, Esrāra, Rabāb, Suraśṛṅgāra etc:

1. All other instruments use a sound-drum (Khola) and a bridge-board which is known as Tablī. Tablī is either a wooden board or a hide stretched over and covering the sound-drum and carrying the bridge of the instrument. This board is joined to the pole or Ḍāṇḍī of the instruments carrying the frets or steel plate (in case of Sarod or Suraśṛṅgāra). Vīṇā, on the other hand, uses no sound-drum nor bridge-board or Tablī.
2. When seen facing all other instruments, the main string is to be found on the extreme right whereas that of the Vīṇā will be seen on the extreme left. This alone makes a basic difference in the playing technique of the Vīṇā and all other instruments.

Earlier, the pole of Vīṇā used to be made from a section of bamboo but nowadays, it is carved out of wood owing chiefly to the non-availability of long enough section of a bamboo. This is an instrument employing Acala Ṭhāṭa i.e., immovable frets. These frets are set to the pole (q.v.) or Ḍāṇḍī of Vīṇā with wax and other things. Usually there are placed three bridges. The main bridge carries four strings. Two other bridges are placed sidewise on the pole, the one on the left carrying two Cikārī (q.v.) strings and the one on the right carrying another open string to be sounded by the left thumb whenever necessary. The Cikārī strings are sounded by Mizrāb (wire plectrum) worn on the little finger of the right hand while other main strings are sounded by two Mizrābs each worn on the forefinger and the middle finger of the same hand. For playing on the Vīṇā the Mizrābs are worn in a different way from the way Mizrābs are worn to play Sitār or Surabahār. Miyān Tānsen's daughter's generations are said to have been the chief promoters of this instrument.

(78) *Xylophone* (Ghana) – Falls under the category of struck metal. Several pieces of glass or wood of the shape of a flat rectangle and sufficiently thick to bear light hammering are fixed on two lengths of cut-gut or thread which are fixed on a piece of wooden frame. These flat pieces of glass or wood are struck with a pair of sticks held in each hand to produce musical notes for a melody. The variation of pitch of sound depends on the size of the glass or

wood pieces. This is a very old instrument, and was much in use in Russia, Poland, Africa, China, Burma etc.

325. Vajan (Vazan)

Literally means weight, with reference to musical notes, it means measurement. The Indian theory of obtaining the notes from various animals and birds has not yet been scientifically established. The initial notes S of Indian scale has no fixed measurement. Any note can be considered as S in relation to which the other notes like R, G, M etc. come into existence. The Western theory of sound fixes a definite measurement for each note and it is in terms of number of vibrations per second. Taking the measurement of S to be 240 vibrations per second, we get:

S	- 240	P	- 360
R	- 270	D	- 400
G	- 300	N	- 450
M	- 320	Ṡ	- 480

The measurement based on number of vibrations per second (V.P.S.) for the initial note S or C (Western) also differs as follows:

The number of vibrations given is for the upper S or C (Western).

Scientific circles	-	512.0
England	-	517.3
Philharmonic Society	-	522.5
Neo Philharmonic Society	-	528.0
Russia	-	535.0
Military practice	-	540.0

In India, the Gramophone Companies and orchestras usually follow the military practice i.e., 540 V.P.S. as the measurement or Vazan for upper S.

326. Vakra

The opposite of straight or Śuddha, or in natural sequence. A Kūṭa Tāna is called Vakra, e.g., SGMP is a straight or Śuddha Tāna while SMGP is Vakra or Kūṭa Tāna; here the natural sequence is broken. Those Rāgas where the notes are used in sequences other than the straight or natural, are called Vakra Rāgas. It may be noted that in straight Rāgas, sometimes Vakra Tānas are used, but in the introductory phrases i.e., by which a Rāga can be easily recognised, the use of notes would only be in their natural sequence. Similarly, the Vakra Rāgas are those which use notes in a Vakra manner. Yamana is a straight Rāga, the introduction of which requires notes in their natural sequence, e.g., ṆRGmP. In this Rāga, Vakra Tānas are also used e.g., GmNDP. On the other hand, in a Vakra Rāga, notes in their natural sequence in introductory phrases would not reveal its character. For example 'SMRP' is a short phrase indicating Rāga Kāmoda. Here SMRP is not in the natural sequence (which would be 'SRMP'), but the natural sequence of these 4 notes would point to Rāga Sāraṅga and never to Kāmoda. In short, if the Pakaḍa (q.v.) of a Rāga contains notes in a Vakra sequence, that Rāga is known to be Vakra.

Some phrases of notes are called 'Vakra notes', but it is better to call the phrase not Vakra, but 'Belonging to Sañcārī Varṇa'. This is so because in case of Rāgas, the use of notes can either be in Ārohī sequence, or in Avarohī sequence or in Sañcārī sequence. This last sequence contains both Āroha and Avaroha. SRGM is in Ārohī sequence, MGRS is in Avarohī sequence, in GMRS, GM is in Ārohī and RS is in Avarohī. So the whole phrase GMRS is a mixed phrase containing both Āroha and Avaroha, so it is called Sañcārī phrase. Here, which particular note can be called Vakra? Usually, in this particular phrase, G is called Vakra note, but in the phrase 'NDPMGMRS' G and M both can be called Vakra notes, so it is needless to call a particular note Vakra, rather the whole phrase of notes should be called Vakra or Sañcārī phrase.

327. Vāṇī

Vide 'Ālāpa'.

328. Varṇa

In the musical Śāstras, only two out of innumerable meanings of this word have been taken into account. Firstly, in the meaning of the letters of the alphabet, and secondly, in the meaning of class or group. As in literature, music also has its alphabet in the symbols of SRGMPDN. In language, the alphabet has letters; these are the written symbols of the sounds uttered. So also in music, we use Varṇas to indicate the written or uttered symbols for the musical sounds we produce vocally or instrumentally. The symbols by which musical sounds are uttered or expressed and expanded into melodic compositions are called Varṇas. Here Varṇa means a musical note. As in literature, letters form a word, e.g., 'PEN' i.e., arrangement of letters in a particular sequence forms a word to mean a writing implement, so also a particular arrangement of musical notes or Varṇas would form a musical Rāga-phrase, e.g., ṆRG, which is a short phrase mainly belonging to Rāga Yamana. As in literature, a haphazard arrangement of letters does not form a meaningful word, so also a haphazard arrangement of Varṇas (here musical notes) would not indicate any Rāga such as SNMD - this is not a musical phrase indicating any Rāga (q.v. - 'Pada').

In the Śāstras, the words Sthāyī Varṇa, Ārohī Varṇa, Avarohī Varṇa and Sañcārī Varṇa are mentioned. Sthāyī Varṇa viz., SSS, Ārohī Varṇa viz., SRG Avarohī Varṇa viz., GRS, Sañcārī Varṇa viz., SGR. Many subsequent authors had misinterpreted the Śāstras and confused the above words with the stanzas (similar to movements in Western music) of a composition, since in the context of stanzas the words Sthāyī and Sañcārī have also been used but in a different meaning. Those authors have referred to the four stanzas viz., Sthāyī, Antarā, Sañcārī and Ābhoga as Varṇas. In fact, Varṇa should be used with reference to the Alaṁkāras only viz., Sthāyī, Ārohī, Avarohī and Sañcārī and not with reference to the stanzas of compositions.

329. Varṇālaṁkāra

Alaṁkāras composed of short phrases (musical words) of musical notes or Varṇas. For example, SGR is a phrase composed of Sañcārī Varṇa. Alaṁkāra composed of such phrases of Sañcārī Varṇa is called Sañcārī-Varṇālaṁkāra or Sañcārī-varṇagata Alaṁkāra: 'gata' here means 'Belonging to Sañcārī Varṇa, viz., 'SGR, RMG, GPM, MDP, PND'. This is a complete Sañcārī Varṇālaṁkāra and the name of this Alaṁkāra is 'Mandrādi', which literally means 'Mandra-Ādi' i.e., 'Lower-note in the beginning' or 'Prefixed by a lower note' (q.v. 'Alaṁkāra').

330. Vegasvarā or Besarā Gīti

Vide 'Gīti'.

331. Viḍhāra, Viḍāra or Vidāra

Probably the word Viḍhāra has come out of Vidāra meaning 'Dividing', 'Disintegrating', 'Destroying' etc. In music, Viḍhāra has come to mean 'To destroy the natural sequence'. In a Vistāra (q.v.), the use of an unexpected or unnatural sequence of notes or combination of notes, in conformity with the rules of a Rāga, is called the Viḍhāra style. Although sometimes a Rāga cannot be fully recognised for some time, yet it does not produce the perception of any other Rāgas in the minds of the listeners. It is a particular quality of cleverness for a worthy musician. A Vistāra in Viḍhāra style can be done in Yamana Rāga thus: GmN, mND, RG, ṃḌṆ, Dm, GRS. In the Madh portion of Ālāpa (q.v.) Viḍhāra can be used. There are Saragams (q.v.) and Gats composed in the Viḍhāra style.

332. Vikṛta Svara

Literally altered notes. At present S and P do not lend themselves to be altered whereas R,G,D and N can be altered by flattening and M by sharpening. In the Śāstras G flat used to be known as unaltered note but at present it is known as Komala G or G flat. The sharp M is an altered M, so it is a Vikṛta Svara. In a word, when a note is shifted from its natural Śruti to any other Śruti, it is called a Vikṛta Svara or altered note (vide 'Śruti').

333. Vilambita Laya

Slow tempo. It is a relative term and by Vilambita is meant half of medium Laya (vide 'Laya').

334. Viloma

Descending. It is the converse of ascending or the natural sequence of notes e.g., SRGMPDN; its Viloma is NDPMGRS. It is also called Avaroha (q.v.).

335. Vinyāsa

Vide 'Bidārī'.

336. Viṣama

Vide 'Tāla'.

337. Vistāra

Literally, Vistāra and Tāna are the same but in practice they are different. The exposition of a Rāga through an a-rhythmic composition, slow or fast, short or long, may be called Vistāra, whereas a Tāna is rhythmic and is embelished with various Alaṁkāras. Thus the difference between Vistāra and Tāna can be shown in a fair way. Prastāra (q.v.) is also a kind of Vistāra but the former is done according to particular rules whereas the latter is free from any such rules and is extempore (vide 'Tāna').

338. Vivādī

It has been mentioned in the Śāstras that two notes having only one Śruti (q.v.) between them are Vivādī to each other. For example, in the diatonic major scale G and M are Vivādī or dissonant to each other. A list of Vivādī notes is given in the table below:

Vivādī Note	Vādī Note	Vivādī Note
Ṇ	S	r
S	r	R
r	R	g
R	g	G
g	G	M
G	M	m
M	m	P
m	P	d
P	d	D
d	D	n
D	n	N
n	N	Ṡ

In some Rāgas, sometimes the application of Vivādī notes becomes interesting and pleasing. For example, in Bihāga Rāga G is the Aṁśa Śvara and M its Vivādī, but the phrase GMG is indispensable in this Rāga. It is to be noted here that one cannot remain on M for long and if M is used as a Bidārī (q.v.), the spirit of the Rāga Bihāga will certainly be destroyed to some extent, yet modern musicians constantly delve upon M as an experiment. It should never be used as an ending note of a Pada or Phrase in Rāga Bihāga either as Nyāsa, Apanyāsa, Sanyāsa or Vinyāsa. The real implication of the Rāga rule is that the Vivādī note is to be always shunned in a Rāga, and not that the Vivādī note should be kept outside the scale or Ṭhāṭa (q.v.) of a particular Rāga. If at all M is used longer in Bihāga, it should be kept oscillating between G and P e.g., MG, MG, MG, or PM, PM, PM.

339. Yati

Dallying upon a particular note a little more than on others to make such a note more prominent. Yati is as equally important in music as in poetics. (Also vide 'Layakārī').

340. Zamzamā

Meaning of this Urdu word is 'Adding of notes'. Musically, it indicates the small melodic phrase marked by repetition of notes e.g., SRSR or Gm Gm Gm Gm. This is a Śabdālaṁkāra.

341. Zarab

In music it means the stroke that sounds the stringed instruments. It is also called 'Bola'.